Prof. Paul F. Cunningham
Rivier College, Psychology
420 Main St.
Nashua, NH 03060-5086

D1370697

Undergraduate Education in Psychology

UNDERGRADUATE EDUCATION IN PSYCHOLOGY

A Blueprint for the
Future of the Discipline

Edited by Diane F. Halpern

American Psychological Association • *Washington, DC*

Published by
American Psychological Association
750 First Street, NE
Washington, DC 20002
www.apa.org

To order
APA Order Department
P.O. Box 92984
Washington, DC 20090-2984
Tel: (800) 374-2721; Direct: (202) 336-5510
Fax: (202) 336-5502; TDD/TTY: (202) 336-6123
Online: www.apa.org/books/
E-mail: order@apa.org

In the U.K., Europe, Africa, and the Middle East, copies may be ordered from
American Psychological Association
3 Henrietta Street
Covent Garden, London
WC2E 8LU England

Typeset in Goudy by Stephen McDougal, Mechanicsville, MD

Printer: Data Reproductions, Auburn Hills, MI
Cover Designer: Naylor Design, Washington, DC
Technical/Production Editor: Emily Welsh

The opinions and statements published are the responsibility of the authors, and such opinions and statements do not necessarily represent the policies of the American Psychological Association.

Library of Congress Cataloging-in-Publication Data

Undergraduate education in psychology : a blueprint for the future of the discipline / edited by Diane F. Halpern.
    p. cm.
  Includes bibliographical references and index.
  ISBN-13: 978-1-4338-0545-5
  ISBN-10: 1-4338-0545-6
  1. Psychology—Study and teaching (Higher) I. Halpern, Diane F. II. American Psychological Association.

  BF77.U53 2009
  150.71'1—dc22   2009012012

British Library Cataloguing-in-Publication Data
A CIP record is available from the British Library.

Printed in the United States of America
First Edition

This book is dedicated to good teachers. They change the world for the better, one student at a time.

CONTENTS

CONTRIBUTORS

William Addison, PhD, Eastern Illinois University, Charleston

Cindy Altman, MSEd, Duquesne University, Pittsburgh, PA

Jeffrey Andre, PhD, James Madison University, Harrisonburg, PA

Barry Anton, PhD, University of Puget Sound, Tacoma, WA

Suzanne Baker, PhD, James Madison University, Harrisonburg, PA

Robin M. Bartlett, PhD, Northern Kentucky University, Highland Heights

Bernard C. Beins, PhD, Ithaca College, Ithaca, NY

Daniel J. Bernstein, PhD, University of Kansas, Lawrence

Mukul Bhalla, PhD, Argosy University, Washington, DC

Charles T. Blair-Broeker, MAT, Cedar Falls High School, Cedar Falls, IA

Judith E. Owen Blakemore, PhD, Indiana University–Purdue University, Indianapolis

Karen Brakke, PhD, Spelman College, Atlanta, GA

Charles L. Brewer, PhD, Furman University, Greenville, SC

Deborah S. Briihl, PhD, Valdosta State University, Valdosta, GA

William Buskist, PhD, Auburn University, Auburn, AL

Bettina J. Casad, PhD, California Polytechnic Institute, Pomona

Robin L. Cautin, PhD, Manhattanville College, Purchase, NY

Stephen L. Chew, PhD, Samford University, Birmingham, AL

Fred Connington, MS, Liberty High School, Liberty, SC

Laurie Corey, PhD, Westchester Community College, Valhalla, NY

Jacquelyn Cranney, PhD, University of New South Wales, Sydney, Australia

Rita M. Curl-Langager, PhD, Minot State University, Minot, ND

David B. Daniel, PhD, James Madison University, Harrisonburg, PA

Jessica Henderson Daniel, PhD, Children's Hospital, Boston, MA

Wallace E. Dixon Jr., PhD, East Tennessee State University, Johnson City

James E. Dobbins, PhD, Wright State University, Dayton, OH

Dana S. Dunn, PhD, Moravian College, Bethlehem, PA

Ann T. Ewing, PhD, Mesa Community College, Mesa, AZ

Amy C. Fineburg, MA, Spain Park High School, Hoover, AL

Susan M. Frantz, MA, Highline Community College, Des Moines, IA

Dennis B. Galvan, PhD, Gallaudet University, Washington, DC

Regan A. R. Gurung, PhD, University of Wisconsin—Green Bay

Robin Hailstorks, PhD, American Psychological Association, Washington, DC

Diane F. Halpern, PhD, Claremont McKenna College, Claremont, CA

Elizabeth Yost Hammer, PhD, Xavier University of Louisiana

Yolanda Y. Harper, PhD, University of Memphis, Memphis, TN

Robert W. Hendersen, PhD, Grand Valley State University, Allendale, MI

Jennifer J. Higa, PhD, University of Hawaii—Honolulu Community College

Debra Hollister, EdD, Valencia Community College, Orlando, FL

Jeffrey D. Holmes, PhD, Ithaca College, Ithaca, NY

Wei-Chen Hung, PhD, Northern Illinois University, DeKalb

Kenneth D. Keith, PhD, University of San Diego, San Diego, CA

Mary E. Kite, PhD, Ball State University, Muncie, IN

Art Kohn, PhD, Portland State University, Portland, OR

Meera Komarraju, PhD, Southern Illinois University, Carbondale

Janet E. Kuebli, PhD, Saint Louis University, Saint Louis, MO

R. Eric Landrum, PhD, Boise State University, Boise, IA

Linh Nguyen Littleford, PhD, Ball State University, Muncie, IN

Trudy Frey Loop, MA, The Altamont School, Birmingham, AL

Salvador Macias III, PhD, University of South Carolina, Sumter

Maureen A. McCarthy, PhD, Kennesaw State University, Kennesaw, GA

Mark McDaniel, PhD, Washington University, St. Louis, MO

Thomas V. McGovern, PhD, Arizona State University West, Glendale

Loretta N. McGregor, PhD, Arkansas State University, Jonesboro

Julie Guay McIntyre, PhD, The Sage Colleges, Troy, NY

Wayne S. Messer, PhD, Berea College, Berea, KY

Harold L. Miller Jr., PhD, Brigham Young University, Provo, UT

Keith Millis, PhD, Northern Illinois University, DeKalb

Steve A. Nida, PhD, The Citadel, Charleston, SC

Melanie C. Page, PhD, Oklahoma State University, Stillwater

Loreto Prieto, PhD, Iowa State University, Ames

Vincent Prohaska, PhD, Lehman College, the City University of New York, Bronx

Patricia Puccio, EdD, College of DuPage, Glen Ellyn, IL

Antonio E. Puente, PhD, University of North Carolina, Wilmington
Thomas P. Pusateri, PhD, Kennesaw State University, Kennesaw, GA
Kristin A. Ritchey, PhD, Ball State University, Muncie, IN
Courtney A. Rocheleau, PhD, Appalachian State University, Boone, NC
Karen C. Rose, PhD, Widener University, Chester, PA
Cecilia Shore, PhD, Miami University, Miami, FL
Randolph A. Smith, PhD, Lamar University, Beaumont, TX
Jeffrey Stowell, PhD, Eastern Illinois University, Charleston
Jaye Jang Van Kirk, MA, San Diego Mesa College, San Diego, CA
Mary Jean Voigt, MS, Boylan Catholic High School, Rockford, IL
Sheila J. Walker, PhD, Scripps College, Claremont, CA
Kenneth A. Weaver, PhD, Emporia State University, Emporia, KS
Frank C. Worrell, PhD, University of California, Berkeley
Martha S. Zlokovich, PhD, Psi Chi, the National Honor Society in
    Psychology

ACKNOWLEDGMENTS

This book is the product of a great collaboration among a virtual Who's Who in undergraduate education in psychology. Teams of authors worked together in person at a week-long retreat and then via a variety of communication technologies to provide a blueprint for the future of education in psychology. At every step of the way, we had superb support from the staff in the Education Directorate of the American Psychological Association (APA). Cynthia Belar, executive director of the Education Directorate, has been a steadfast leader in improving education at all levels. Her enthusiastic support for and participation in the conference was sincerely appreciated. Our primary leader in the Education Directorate is Robin Hailstorks: Robin provided us with support and guidance as we moved through the many stages of conference planning and into conference follow-up. Her breadth and depth of knowledge about issues in undergraduate and high school education was invaluable. Martha Boenau, long-time staff member in the Education Directorate, has been the heart of this project. These three extraordinary staff members are an incredible support group.

How does a group of 80 people work cooperatively together? Of course, having great people in the group is the key, but an important, and innovative, element of our group work over many months is the wiki that Sam Blanchard set up for us at Anderson University.

We deeply appreciate the financial support for the conference provided by a number of organizations, including the University of Puget Sound; APA; the National Science Foundation[1]; the American Psychological Foundation; Psi Chi; the New England Psychological Association; the Southwestern Psy-

[1]The National Science Foundation supported the working conference through Grant No. 0813816. Any opinions, findings, and conclusions or recommendations expressed in this book are those of the authors and do not necessarily reflect the views of the National Science Foundation.

chological Association; APA Division 2 (Society for the Teaching of Psychology); APA Division 10 (Society for the Psychology of Aesthetics, Creativity, and the Arts); APA Division 17 (Society of Counseling Psychology); APA Division 18 (Psychologists in Public Service); APA Division 20 (Adult Development and Aging); APA Division 35 (Society for the Psychology of Women); APA Division 53 (Society of Clinical Child and Adolescent Psychology); and the Assembly of Scientist–Practitioner Psychologists.

Undergraduate Education in Psychology

INTRODUCTION: A CALL TO ACTION

DIANE F. HALPERN

This book presents the findings and recommendations of the 2008 National Conference on Undergraduate Education in Psychology. For this conference, 80 psychologists and other academics charged with the task of designing the best possible future for undergraduate education in psychology spent a week at the University of Puget Sound during the summer of 2008. We met in working groups and plenary sessions in which ideas were debated and visions of quality programs in psychology were created. We envisioned a future for higher education in which change could be brought about in a sound, scientific way that would yield long-lasting positive benefits for all of the stakeholders. Conference participants were selected for their commitment to excellence in education in psychology, especially at the undergraduate level. We represented the full range of diversity in psychology, including participants from all levels of education, ranging from high school teachers to those who taught only graduate students. We were a racially diverse mix of early- and late-career psychologists from large and small institutions, including professional schools; from different areas of expertise within psychology; and including people with disabilities and knowledge about disabilities.

The National Conference on Undergraduate Education in Psychology was designed to update the findings and recommendations from a conference that was held 17 years earlier. The American Psychological Association's first national conference on undergraduate education in psychology took place in 1991 at St. Mary's College of Maryland. Topics at the first conference included curriculum, advising, active learning, assessment, and linkages of psychology teachers across educational settings. The St. Mary's Conference had profound effects on undergraduate education in psychology. Most notable were a recommended standard curriculum for the psychology major, suggested ways to assess student learning, and the encouragement of active learning. These recommendations were disseminated through several new books, journal articles, and teaching conferences. The growth of teaching and learning communities among psychology faculty at the secondary school, community college, 4-year college, and university levels was stimulated by this conference. The St. Mary's Conference resulted in demonstrated impact, but significant changes in technology, student enrollments, demands for accountability, psychologists' understanding of how people learn, and other issues raised important questions about topics that were not addressed at the earlier conference and others that needed to be revisited.

The popularity of the psychology major continues to increase. On the basis of the most recent data, approximately 88,000 students graduate from American colleges or universities with baccalaureate degrees in psychology each year (Snyder, Dillow, & Hoffman, 2008). We have no worldwide data to add to this figure, but many countries are experiencing a huge gain in the number of students taking courses in psychology. For example, Zhang Kan (2008), director of the Institute of Psychology and president of the Chinese Psychological Society, reported that when psychology resumed as an academic department in the late 1970s, there were only four departments of psychology in all Chinese universities. Now there are 200 to 250 psychology departments, and the number continues to grow. Available data from other regions of the world support the conclusion that the growth in psychology education is occurring at a rapid rate in many places around the globe. For example, Hayes (1996) reported that "in recent years the UK, in common with many other countries, has seen a sizable growth in the number of psychology students" (p. 130). As another example, similar growth was reported in Yemen. Alzubaidi and Ghamen (1997) reported that

> the numbers of students taking psychology programmes are increasing every new academic year. For example, the number of students enrolled at the Department of Psychology has doubled from 327 to 667, making this department one of the most popular in Sana'a University. (p. 364)

Although a global review of the growth in the number of psychology students is beyond the scope of this book, our experiences at international psychology conferences and the available data make us confident that most of the world is experiencing large increases.

Our slogan for the National Conference on Undergraduate Education in Psychology was "to affect 1 million." But when we considered that over 1 million students take at least one psychology class every year in the United States, and with the large numbers of students taking psychology classes around the world, our goal seemed far too modest. Through the important dialogue that took place at the Puget Sound Conference, we plan to have a long-lasting effect on higher education for many years and perhaps a decade or more. We tried various extrapolations under different assumptions to decide how many people we realistically could affect, but we realized it would be difficult to defend our assumptions, so our goal remains to affect 1 million. We ask all readers to help us attain that goal by discussing our recommendations on college campuses and with accrediting agencies, parent and alumni groups, public policy makers, and prospective employers. We hope that the discussions will lead to actions that improve higher education in general and in psychology in particular.

In addition to growth in psychology at the postsecondary level, in 2008 more than 113,000 high school students took the Advanced Placement Examination in Psychology (College Board, 2008), which did not exist at the time of the St. Mary's Conference. The number of students who take the Advanced Placement Examination is a small fraction of those who take high school level courses in psychology, which represents a major change in where students are learning psychology, and by every estimate, the number is growing rapidly. On the basis of these data, we infer that students who enter college are much more knowledgeable about psychology than their counterparts a decade ago. Furthermore, as of January 2008, nearly 50% of all college students have had their initial exposure to psychology in community colleges (American Association of Community Colleges, n.d.). College enrollments overall continue to increase at a faster rate than faculty hires, meaning that more and more undergraduates receive instruction from graduate students and adjunct faculty, who typically do not play the myriad roles in advising and research training that are more likely from tenure-track faculty. These are a few of the major factors that are changing the landscape of undergraduate education in psychology.

Changes in education, the workplace, health care, and everyday life point to an increase in psychology's importance as a core academic discipline and as a service discipline for other majors in the 21st century. Most of the problems facing Americans and people in other countries are behavioral problems that require behavioral solutions. Heart disease, cancer, and stroke are the principal causes of death in the Western world, due, in large part, to lifestyle variables such as overeating, lack of exercise, smoking, and stress. Drug addictions, racism and sexism, environmental pollution, violence and terrorism, child abuse, and parental separation and divorce are among the many maladies plaguing our society; their causes can be found in behavior. An aging population and an explosion in information technologies are also among the many changes that create behavioral problems in American society. Of paramount importance is a changing job market in which a college degree is a requirement for 90% of the fastest growing jobs. Crucial to many of these jobs is skill in critical thinking, an ability that is solidly nested in the undergraduate psychology curriculum.

As a discipline, psychology is often the bridge between the humanities and physical sciences. Psychology's dual emphases on the scientific method and understanding the human condition create natural links among disciplines. We believe that psychology is the ideal major for students who desire multidisciplinary perspectives on critical topics as well as the best place for applying the latest advances in learning technologies. However, the undergraduate landscape is changing as rapidly as the world around us, and new challenges require a new look at every aspect of the undergraduate experience. In the following chapters, we examine recent changes in our students and faculty; in our knowledge about how people learn; and in our beliefs about what our students need to know to be informed citizens of the world, caring family members, and productive workers who can meet the challenges of the coming decades.

The organization of this book follows that of the conference. Chapters 1 through 9 present the findings and recommendations of Working Groups 1 through 9, respectively. Each working group was charged with examining one specific question about education in psychology:

- Working Group 1: Why do we need to rethink how we educate students in psychology?
- Working Group 2: Who is teaching psychology, and what is the quality of instruction?
- Working Group 3: What is being taught and learned in psychology courses, including the impact of fragmentation of psychology toward specialized disciplinary societies and new interdisciplinary specialties (e.g., neuroscience) on the psychology major?
- Working Group 4: Who are the students in undergraduate psychology, and how do we challenge the traditional one-size-fits-all curricular approach to meeting the needs of a diverse student population?
- Working Group 5: When and where are students taking psychology courses?
- Working Group 6: What are the modes of teaching for different content, contexts, and students?
- Working Group 7: How can we promote learning with new technologies that include interactive learning agents and online programs that teach collaborative peer evaluation, game-based models of learning, and virtual learning environments among others?
- Working Group 8: How are we using knowledge gained over the last decade about effective teaching and learning?

- Working Group 9: What are the desired outcomes of an under-graduate education in psychology?

Chapter 10 represents a culmination of the findings, listing a set of guiding principles for quality undergraduate education in psychology. These guiding principles were developed by members of the conference steering committee. Finally, chapter 11 presents a brief conclusion.

With the exception of the concluding chapter, each chapter provides recommendations for all of the major stakeholders in higher education—students, faculty, psychology departments, academic administrators, public policy makers, and the general public. Our emphasis on recommendations reflects our hope that readers will be moved to action, and just in case some readers are not sure how to begin, we provide data-based directions that will move psychologists toward improvements in psychology education and the entire undergraduate course of study. These recommendations reflect the value we place on providing students with the knowledge and skills they will need to succeed as psychologically literate citizens of this century. Psychologically literate citizens have basic knowledge of the critical subject matter of psychology and can and will apply their knowledge of psychology to a broad range of situations. We develop the idea of psychological literacy in more detail in several chapters throughout this book.

We invite readers to respond to our call for action and to join with us in the redesign of undergraduate education in ways that can have positive and long-lasting effects on the millions of students worldwide who enroll in undergraduate psychology courses.

1

PSYCHOLOGICALLY LITERATE CITIZENS

THOMAS V. McGOVERN, LAURIE COREY, JACQUELYN CRANNEY,
WALLACE E. DIXON JR., JEFFREY D. HOLMES, JANET E. KUEBLI,
KRISTIN A. RITCHEY, RANDOLPH A. SMITH, AND SHEILA J. WALKER

We, the authors of this chapter, who made up Working Group 1, were given a broad conceptual question by the conference steering committee: Why should we rethink how we educate undergraduate students?

We answered the question in two ways. First, we adopted the term *psychological literacy* to synthesize all the scholarly and programmatic work on the teaching of psychology produced since the last American Psychological Association (APA) National Conference in 1991 and now being implemented by faculty in American, Australian, and European postsecondary institutions. Second, we created the concept of *psychologically literate citizens* to integrate global, discipline-based efforts to advance an undergraduate paradigm with a broader, transdisciplinary narrative being written in higher education about ethical and social responsibility.

In our readings to prepare for this conference, we discovered that academic psychologists in Australia and Europe, for example, have learning outcomes statements for their majors, comparable to the APA *Guidelines for the*

Undergraduate Psychology Major (APA, 2007a). Their definitions grew out of national contexts that emphasize accountability, similar to the quality benchmarks approach described in the *American Psychologist* by Dunn, McCarthy, Baker, Halonen, and Hill (2007). In contrast to Dunn et al.'s goal of accomplishing liberal learning outcomes in diverse American settings, the multinational and multicultural texts we examined were closer to undergraduate accreditation models as the necessary platforms for advanced professional training, quality control, and geographical mobility for employment. We believe that psychological literacy may now be a global, common denominator outcome among psychology faculty. In addition, it is a readily accessible metaphor to engage wider audiences and important stakeholders whose image of the psychologist derives more from pop-culture stereotypes than from psychologists' long heritage of scientifically based and reflective pedagogy.

We wanted to push beyond creating a synthesis blueprint of best practices from paradigms of discipline-based undergraduate psychology. There is a broader 21st century narrative taking shape in higher education. It is transdisciplinary, multicultural, pluralistic, and based on information-age demands and student populations that are incredibly diverse, multigenerational, and made up of digital natives. Undergraduate psychology has a rich story to tell and deserves to be a wellspring for this unfolding narrative. Psychologists have the opportunity to challenge an ever increasing number of students to be critical scientific thinkers and ethical and socially responsible participants in their communities. Beyond psychological literacy as a synthesis metaphor, the integrative outcome and aspiration of psychology programs should be about graduating psychologically literate citizens for a global 21st century, starting from the very first course in undergraduate psychology.

In this lead chapter, we synthesize important findings and recommendations from task force reports, spotlighting what must be basic reading for departmental program efforts in support of psychological literacy. Our goal is to broaden faculty horizons by describing exciting efforts on behalf of undergraduate psychology education. Finally, we evaluate the transdisciplinary and global conversations taking place in higher education in support of developing psychologically literate citizens.

We organized the chapter as a progression of ideas from defining psychological literacy and its historical antecedents in American undergraduate education to the global disciplinary convergences around this concept to our interpretations of an emerging transdisciplinary narrative and creating the concept of a psychologically literate citizen—someone who responds to the call for ethical commitment and social responsibility as a hallmark of his or her lifelong liberal learning. To illuminate these two concepts, we created case study stories about students and faculty drawn from our collective experiences.

DEFINITION OF PSYCHOLOGICAL LITERACY

Psychological literacy is a complex term. We chose it, consistent with how the word *literate* was first used (circa 1550), to mean "a liberally educated or learned person" (*Shorter Oxford English Dictionary*, 2002, B1). We construe its connotative value in a similar way as higher education's emphases on across-the-curriculum outcomes such as writing, ethics, numeracy, information literacy, scientific literacy, and critical thinking. Ideally, it can be the defining quality for the 88,134 baccalaureates in psychology now awarded every year because psychology continues to be one of the most popular disciplines in all the humanities, social sciences, and sciences (Snyder, Dillow, & Hoffman, 2008).

Our description is consistent with *The APA Guidelines for the Undergraduate Major* (APA, 2007a). That text was endorsed as APA policy to be read as a "living document" (p. 7) to stimulate continuing faculty engagement for program development, evaluation, and renewal. The guidelines describe five learning goals consistent with the science and application of the discipline and five learning goals consistent with liberal arts education that are further developed through the discipline. For each goal, there are suggested learning outcomes around which a curriculum may be developed and assessed effectively. The guidelines have university faculty members and administrators as their primary audience. Our goal is to broaden that audience and its understanding of psychology by using a powerful and accessible unifying concept.

Psychological literacy means

- having a well-defined vocabulary and basic knowledge of the critical subject matter of psychology;
- valuing the intellectual challenges required to use scientific thinking and the disciplined analysis of information to evaluate alternative courses of action;
- taking a creative and amiable skeptic approach to problem solving;
- applying psychological principles to personal, social, and organizational issues in work, relationships, and the broader community;
- acting ethically;
- being competent in using and evaluating information and technology;
- communicating effectively in different modes and with many different audiences;
- recognizing, understanding, and fostering respect for diversity; and
- being insightful and reflective about one's own and others' behavior and mental processes.

Consider the following two collective experience case studies (and the vivid anecdotes used in chap. 4, this volume) and how they illustrate psychological literacy as an important learning outcome with lifelong benefits.

Case Study 1: The Psychology Major Parent

A father learns from his son's teacher that the boy has been bullying other students. The teacher recommends that the father place his son in a program to improve social skills and offers the name of another parent who could attest to the program's effectiveness. The father wonders whether the problem is severe enough to warrant such intervention and talks it over with his wife, who was a psychology major.

Remembering her many discussions with a faculty mentor and her peers, the wife was uncomfortable basing their family's decision on personal testimonial. She suggested they research the techniques used in the local school program and the qualifications of those who designed it. She insisted on knowing whether the program had been evaluated for its effectiveness.

During college, after taking several thematic courses, she served as an undergraduate research assistant for a biological psychologist who conducted studies on psychoneuroimmunological aspects of aging women's health. Her faculty mentor was a stickler for data-based versus common-wisdom conclusions about diagnoses and treatment interventions.

Whatever their decision, this mother, her spouse, their son, and potentially other teachers and students reaped the benefits of the psychological literacy learned during her undergraduate career.

Case Study 2: General Psychology's Vital Legacy and Civic Discourse

A local newspaper broke the story of a planned group home for the developmentally disabled in an affluent suburban community. Although the town residents were mostly college educated and upper middle class and supported the concept in the abstract, they suffered from the not-in-my-backyard syndrome. Their contention was that it would not be good for their children to see and be exposed to the behavior of young adults at the group home. They also worried that property values would decline. Vehement opposition was the norm. Town meetings were held to defuse the situation.

One resident had taken a general psychology course in college and learned about similar communities where group homes had successfully been integrated into the community. His instructor's theme for the whole course was on challenging common stereotypes about human behavior through critical thinking and effective arguments.

The resident spoke eloquently at a town meeting, emphasizing the humanity of the young people who would be served and reflecting on his professor's discussion of the many variations of human behavior. This general psychology student alumnus suggested the townspeople look for data instead of relying only on their assump-

tions. He asked them, too, to consider whether their perceptions would be different if they had a sister or brother or child with the needs of this population. As empathy began to develop, the attendees became more open to considering the proposal and thinking beyond their surface reactions to a perceived problem.

Despite having taken only one course in psychology, this student eloquently articulated the scientific approach to problem solving and understood the group dynamics of stereotyping and prejudice in the community situation. He demonstrated the core concepts of psychological literacy that can become even more sophisticated beyond the first course in the discipline.

As illustrated in the two case studies, a basic psychological literacy is a reasonable expected outcome, even after just one course. Introduction to Psychology is now a centerpiece of general education requirements in the American curriculum; it is the second (behind Basic English Composition) most frequently taken course by college graduates (National Center for Education Statistics, 2008). This literacy becomes more sophisticated in the nursing or education or business administration major who is required to take general psychology and 2 to 3 other cognate courses (e.g., abnormal and health psychology, adolescent psychology and tests and measurement, group dynamics and organizational and industrial psychology). We expect that psychology majors, having taken 10 to 12 courses organized around established goals (APA, 2007a), are very sophisticated in their understanding and application. Achieving these outcomes is a developmental process mapped by Halonen et al.'s (2003) rubric for scientific thinking. It is a cognitive and affective process that intersects with other liberal learning outcomes and the increasing emphasis on critical thinking being required in humanities, social sciences, and ethnic and gender studies undergraduate courses, for example. At the program level, Dunn et al.'s (2007) quality benchmarks are an effective guide. In Exhibit 1.1, we adapted these authors' schema in the domains of curriculum, student learning outcomes, and faculty characteristics that best promote the achievement of psychological literacy.

HISTORICAL ANTECEDENTS

Arriving at a convergence about learning and assessing outcomes and a disciplinary paradigm for undergraduate education did not happen overnight (see McGovern, 2004; McGovern & Brewer, 2003, 2005; Puente, Matthews, & Brewer, 1992, for historical reviews). APA sponsored multiple national conferences and surveys of undergraduate education (Lloyd & Brewer, 1992), beginning after World War II and continuing with the 80 psychologists who gathered at the University of Puget Sound in 2008. The St. Mary's Conference in 1991 was an energizing catalyst that continued with the Psychology Partnerships Project (Andreoli-Mathie & Ernst, 1999) for the production of a cornucopia of materials listed as follows in chronological order:

EXHIBIT 1.1
Quality Benchmarks for Psychological Literacy and Becoming Psychologically Literate Citizens

Curriculum

- Executes curricula so students demonstrate psychological literacy;
- Sequences curricula to reflect developing student cognition;
- Provides balanced curricula so students are able to evaluate and integrate elements of a multifaceted discipline, and can articulate the outcomes of transdisciplinary learning;
- Integrates multiple perspectives in a critical, complementary manner;
- Infuses ethics training at appropriate levels of the curriculum;
- Integrates diversity and global issues at multiple levels of the curriculum; and
- Systematically plans for community activity (e.g., service learning) to help students integrate their learning and become psychologically literate citizens.

Student learning outcomes: Skills of psychologically literate citizens

- Writing—implements systematic developmental plan for required writing;
- Speaking—requires developmental oral performances that may culminate in presentations in professional contexts;
- Research—requires scholarship as a performance obligation that integrates content and skill;
- Collaboration—embeds multiple collaborative activities requiring preparation and feedback so that students learn how to listen with empathy and understand the group dynamics of teamwork, conflict resolution, and social engagement; and
- Information literacy and technology—refines use of both sets of skills through systematic learning.

Faculty characteristics

- Models the qualities of psychologically literate citizens as members of diverse academic communities;
- Engages students through effective and creative pedagogical strategies;
- Pursues developmentally appropriate research agenda;
- Develops successful strategies to secure resources that enhance autonomy;
- Pursues enhanced opportunities for community service that can benefit from faculty expertise;
- Enacts the values of the discipline through service and leadership roles in organizations;
- Demonstrates accessibility with appropriate boundaries and actively mentors;
- Models ethical behavior and facilitates its promotion by others; and
- Initiates professional development and renewal activities for teaching and learning.

Adapted from "Quality Benchmarks in Undergraduate Psychology Programs," by D. S. Dunn, M. A. McCarthy, S. Baker, J. S. Halonen, and G. W. Hill, 2007, *American Psychologist, 62,* 650–670. Copyright 2007 by the American Psychological Association.

- *The Teaching of Psychology: Essays in Honor of Wilbert J. McKeachie and Charles L. Brewer* (S. F. Davis & Buskist, 2002);
- *Guidelines on Multicultural Education, Training, Research, Practice, and Organizational Change for Psychologists* (APA, 2003);
- *A Rubric for Learning, Teaching, and Assessing Scientific Inquiry in Psychology* (Halonen et al., 2003);

- *Toward an Inclusive Psychology: Infusing the Introductory Psychology Textbook With Diversity Content* (Trimble, Stevenson, & Worrell, 2003);
- *Measuring Up: Educational Assessment Challenges and Practices for Psychology* (Dunn, Mehrotra, & Halonen, 2004);
- *Best Practices for Teaching Introduction to Psychology* (Dunn & Chew, 2005);
- *Internationalizing the Undergraduate Curriculum* (Lutsky et al., 2005);
- *National Standards for High School Psychology Curricula* (APA, 2005);
- *Standards and Outcomes: Encouraging Best Practices in Teaching Introductory Psychology* (R. A. Smith & Fineburg, 2005);
- *Handbook of the Teaching of Psychology* (Buskist & Davis, 2006);
- *APA Guidelines for the Undergraduate Psychology Major* (APA, 2007a);
- *Quality Benchmarks in Undergraduate Psychology Programs* (Dunn et al., 2007); and
- *Teaching, Learning, and Assessing in a Developmentally Coherent Curriculum* (Appleby et al., 2008).

Like our chapter 3 colleagues who wrote about curriculum and our chapter 9 colleagues who wrote about desired outcomes, our readings and analyses of all these resources led us to the conclusion that there now is a consensus in undergraduate psychology education that includes

- defined and measurable student learning outcomes,
- multiple measures and methods to assess these outcomes,
- a sophisticated pedagogy for diverse student populations who are now citizens of a global community, and
- quality benchmarks required for academic reviews and program development.

These are the means to achieve what we label as *psychological literacy* as we try also to capture the imagination of broader audiences and constituencies. As we describe in the next section, our judgment about this consensus was reinforced by discovering similar outcome statements from psychology faculty groups around the world.

PSYCHOLOGICAL LITERACY IN A GLOBAL CONTEXT

Many of us were ignorant about the outcomes and processes of global psychological education before we met to consider this question: Why should we rethink how we educate undergraduate students? The more we learned, the more we found psychological literacy as a global concept even more compelling.

Ministers of education and university leaders from 29 European countries met in Bologna in 1999 to create a European Higher Education Area (EHEA). By 2007, participating countries numbered 46. They meet biennially to arrive at consensus objectives that will not homogenize national educational systems but provide tools to connect them. By 2010, the EHEA hopes to define comparable degrees completed in a three-cycle structure (bachelor's, master's, doctoral degrees) with generic descriptors for each cycle based on transparent learning outcomes, competencies, and credits for qualifications within the first and second cycles. The operational goal is to shift from a degree structure based on years of study to a European Credit and Transfer System that is student centered and outcomes based. All participants are committed to actively promote graduates' mobility, quality assurance in programs, and emphasize lifelong learning that will make the EHEA globally competitive for faculty and students.

From another two continents, 27 ministers and senior officials from across the Asia-Pacific region issued The Brisbane Communique in 2006 with comparable statements about higher education quality assurance principles. They also committed to meet biennially to integrate their work with the European Bologna Process.

The Association of Universities and Colleges of Canada issued their statement about the Bologna Process in 2008 with their intention to engage with their European partners in this now-global renewal process in higher education. The disciplinary product of the Bologna Process that captured our attention was the EuroPsy, a European certificate in psychology.

It is beyond the scope of this chapter to describe the sociopolitical-economic assumptions and operational details of global activities on undergraduate education in general and in disciplinary psychology in particular. We offer only a sampling to introduce the reader to a larger vision about psychological literacy that we see emerging outside of American higher educational institutions. Interested faculty members will find practical information at the home Web site of the Association for International Educators (http://www.nafsa.org), and more conceptual and political essays at the home Web site of the Institute for Higher Education Policy, which tracks postsecondary education issues around the world (http://www.ihep.org).

Europe

In the Bologna Process, faculty from every academic and professional area of study meet regularly to define their outcomes and assessment strategies. The European Federation of Psychologists' Associations agreed on standards for the first phase or cycle (bachelor's degree). Programs must provide a broad introduction to the knowledge and skills of psychology as a scientific discipline. Second-phase or second-cycle (master's degree) programs must prepare students for autonomous practice in a chosen field of applied psychology. J. E. Hall and Lunt (2005), Lunt (2002, 2005), and Peiro and Lunt (2002) have provided excellent introductions, summarized aptly in this way: "The nature, extent, and implications of this process are still unclear, in particular whether it is part of a 'harmonization' or 'convergence' project or rather more of a comparability and equivalence initiative" (Lunt, 2005, p. 86).

The *EuroPsy: The European Certificate in Psychology* (2006) promotes quality assured psychological services for consumers and mobility for practitioners across Europe. The first phase or cycle must include an orientation to psychology (e.g., methods, history, specialty fields), explanatory theories (e.g., cognitive, psychobiology, developmental, social, clinical and health, work and organizational psychology, psychopathology), technological theories (e.g., psychometrics), skills (e.g., assessment, interviewing, test construction, group interventions), methodology (e.g., experimental, qualitative and quantitative methods, statistics, data acquisition and analyses), academic skills (e.g., bibliographic skills, reading and writing, ethics), and an understanding of nonpsychological theories (e.g., epistemology, philosophy, sociology, anthropology). The second phase or cycle must prepare students to be specialized practitioners after completing a master's degree or may lead to advanced study at the doctoral level.

The Bologna Process and the EHEA also promote country-by-country translation statements for specific majors. For example, the United Kingdom's (UK's) Quality Assurance Agency for Higher Education (2007), on the recommendations of the British Psychological Society, the Association of Heads of Psychology Departments, and the Higher Education Academy Psychology Network, published benchmarks, recognizing that "psychology is one of the most popular subjects in HE [higher education] in the UK. It is the largest scientific discipline and the second largest discipline overall" (p. 1).

The defining principles for UK undergraduate psychology programs include scientific understanding, multiple perspectives, real-life applications of theory to experience and behavior, role of empirical evidence for theory and data collection, research skills, and developing increasingly sophisticated levels of knowledge for appreciation and a critical evaluation of the human experience. The UK statement defines measurable learning outcomes in subject knowledge and in subject-specific and generic skills. Our analyses suggest that these outcomes are very similar to the American psychology goals and learning outcomes (APA, 2007a). The sections in the UK statement on teaching, learning, assessment, and benchmark standards also matched with the best practices in assessment described in the APA handbook *Measuring Up: Educational Assessment Challenges and Practices for Psychology* (Dunn et al., 2004) and the quality benchmarks statement in Dunn et al. (2007).

Australia

In Australia, undergraduate psychology programs provide their students with broad foundational knowledge as well as research methods skills, data analysis, and report writing in a 3-year course of study, followed by an honors year prior to graduate professional training (Australian Psychology Accreditation Council, 2008). In a comprehensive national study, Lipp et al. (2006) evaluated the methods used in teaching psychology in 33 Australian universities and recommended that the next steps should be to delineate graduate attributes (i.e., outcomes) for development and assessment in undergraduate psychology (see Cranney & Turnbull, 2008, for how the delineated outcomes overlap with APA, UK, and Bologna student learning outcomes). Lipp et al. also recommended that the quality assurance methods implemented by most universities should be consistent with best practices for continuing renewal (e.g., employer surveys, senior capstone surveys). Undergraduate programs must intentionally integrate internationalization, indigenous issues and cultural competence training, and also promote increasing indigenous participation at all levels of psychology training. Moreover, Lipp et al. argued that it was essential for faculty to articulate their goals and learning outcomes to students beginning with the very first course in psychology.

The Australian Learning and Teaching Council that sponsored the Lipp et al. (2006) study group funded another study group by Cranney et al. (2008) to articulate a vision statement titled "Psychology Leading Australia Toward Better Health and Wellbeing." These authors asserted that in a global world psychologists must educate many public audiences, that ours is both a discipline and a profession, and that both scientific and practitioner activities contribute to individuals' and societies' well-being.

Summary of Emerging Perspectives on Psychological Literacy

It is beyond the scope of this chapter to complete a fine-grained evaluation of all that is emerging in each individual country's discussions about undergraduate psychology in Africa, Asia, the Americas, and Europe, although we have much to learn from their individual contexts and developing responses by their psychological associations and higher education groups. In this chapter, we focused on Europe and Australia because their texts illuminated pluralistic possibilities that synergized sociocultural, political, economic, and geographical differences. The value we have placed on pluralism when considering the diversity within American postsecondary institutions and their missions is even more important when trying to expand our horizons for global undergraduate education. Comparing many discipline-based groups' recommendations for enhancing quality, we concluded that in undergraduate psychology there is now a sophisticated emphasis on student learning outcomes that should be judged as deeply responsive to many publics' demands for accountability. The unifying concept of psychological literacy has great potential to capture the imagination of diverse global stakeholders invested in transforming higher education. With common understandings and rigorously defined standards, there still remains a healthy diversity in undergraduate programs. This was a commonly espoused principle in all that we read, with a bright spotlight shining on the universal demands for citizens' well-being and quality health care, and a need for greater commitment to all populations who have still-limited participation in the fruits of economic growth. Psychologists need to be leaders in problem solving in these areas, especially because we can contribute integrated scientific and practitioner strengths.

This conference's question—Why should we rethink how we educate undergraduate students?—could be truly transformative if psychologists probe even deeper: Why and how should undergraduate psychology education enhance the postbaccalaureate global alternatives for psychology's students by promoting psychological literacy? As psychologists understand and challenge their students' assumptions and stereotypes, teaching an ever-increasing diversity of students who take psychology courses and who major in this field, they can now heighten their expectations. Why and how should psychologists achieve the goal of educating sophisticated, psychologically literate citizens—future leaders— committed to acting in socially responsible ways in local, national, and global contexts. Psychologists' collective and sustainable futures depend on achieving this outcome, so they must rethink now. Consider the following case study as a preview of what we consider possible; its themes are consistent with the principles espoused in chapter 2 of this volume.

Case Study 3: Professing Literacy and Citizenship

Each semester, Dr. Cantrell teaches research methodology, analyzing and resolving a problem identified by a community partner. She models how to engage in active strategies for addressing problems encountered daily among the poor, probing her students' assumptions and biases about rural versus urban populations, the differing experiences of racial and ethnic groups, and how new-to-America immigrant families add yet another dimension to their developing sensitivities.

After meeting with the principal of the local elementary school, Dr. Cantrell discovered that very few students were making appointments with the new guidance counselor. The principal was considering terminating the guidance counselor so that monies could be better spent on other staff.

Dr. Cantrell posed this problem to her class: Why weren't the school children meeting with the guidance counselor? She guided her class to generate hypotheses about the problem and its causes and to seek out empirical studies that addressed related issues. They designed a survey instrument and collected their data, discovering that the children had little understanding of the role of a guidance counselor. They learned that no school counselor programming was undertaken by either the principal or the counselor.

Dr. Cantrell took an extra step so that her students fully understood the scientific and practical implications of this field research experience. They reflected on what knowledge and skills they had gained as a result of the project. They examined how they used theories and methods from their psychology courses and coursework in other disciplines. They evaluated whether their efforts were worthwhile and if they would be confident to undertake such a project by themselves in the future. Dr. Cantrell asked her students what other educational inputs they needed to increase their confidence. The students summarized their reflections in their capstone portfolios.

Dr. Cantrell's project and her methods are not the only means to achieve these ends. The chapters that follow offer myriad approaches, such as service learning internship placements, community partnerships, interdisciplinary collaborations, and problem-based learning. Dr. Cantrell modeled the qualities of psychological literacy and taught her students about its powerful effects. Their real-world experience generated benefits during the semester and will motivate lifelong learning to be sophisticated psychologically literate citizens.

PSYCHOLOGICALLY LITERATE CITIZENS

There is a rich narrative being composed in global higher education about psychologists' social responsibilities and commitments. This story is transdisciplinary, multicultural, multigenerational, and replete with 21st century themes and characters. Psychologists need to build on an already sturdy disciplinary platform for undergraduate psychology and to connect to this larger narrative about liberal learning. We propose the concept of the psychologically literate citizen to connect psychology faculty and students to this narrative, and we offer the following conceptualization to jumpstart discussion among our colleagues and other readers.

Psychologically literate citizens intentionally build on their psychological literacy, integrating it with the interdisciplinary and extracurricular lessons learned during their undergraduate experiences. They try to grow more sophisticated as ethical and socially responsible problem solvers. It is an achievable outcome when faculty provide students with opportunities to use their psychological literacy outside formal learning environments, and they begin to do so of their own initiative to accomplish goals that are important to them, their families, their colleagues, their communities, and to the larger society, state, nation, or world.

The term communicates a palette of possibilities, a more ambitious but absolutely necessary outcome for our graduates and an agenda for faculty as scientist–educators. The term reflects contemporary understandings of liberal learning by building on psychological literacy but pushes that expectation to ask: How will future leaders solve problems in a transdisciplinary, global, and information age? Psychologically literate citizenship describes a way of being, a type of problem solving, and a sustained ethical and socially responsive stance towards others. (In chap. 4, this volume, the authors use vivid anecdotes and develop systematic proposals for fully engaging the many different students whom psychologists now encounter in their classes.)

A Transdisciplinary Narrative

Since the publication of "Liberal Education, Study in Depth, and the Arts and Sciences Major—Psychology" (McGovern, Furumoto, Halpern, Kimble, & McKeachie, 1991), the Association of American Colleges and Universities (AAC&U) and the APA have synergized efforts on behalf of undergraduate education. The AAC&U's reports enriched psychologists' understandings of psychologically literate citizens who become committed to the principles of lifelong learning and problem solving on behalf of a diverse society and social justice.

In *Greater Expectations: A New Vision for Learning as a Nation Goes to College* (AAC&U, 2002), a blue-ribbon panel proposed that faculty educate students to become "intentional learners" (p. 21) empowered by intellectual and practical skills, informed by knowledge and different ways of knowing, and ethically responsible for their personal actions and civic contributions. "A liberal education *is* a practical education because it develops just those capacities needed by every thinking adult" (p. 26). In a follow-up report, Huber and Hutchings (2004) concluded that "intentional learning" becomes "integrative learning" when the campus, college, or department creates opportunities and spaces for "connecting skills and knowledge from multiple sources and experiences; applying theory to practice in various settings; utilizing diverse and even contradictory points of view; and, understanding issues and positions contextually"; the major fields and professions "serve as the foundations, but integrative learning goes beyond academic boundaries" (p. 13). Humphreys and Davenport (2005) found that when students were asked about the outcomes of their liberal learning during college, they were not very explicit. Their responses stayed at the level of general attitudes and intellectual dispositions (e.g., personal maturity, self-management, teamwork skills) rather than more reflective comments about values or ways to transfer and apply that learning outside the classroom.

Three formative themes are central in the AAC&U's efforts to renew liberal learning: across-the-curriculum emphases on intellectual inquiry, expanded opportunities for social responsibility and civic engagement, and integrative learning (Schneider, 2003). In *College Learning for the New Global Century: A Report From The National Leadership Council for Liberal Education*

TABLE 1.1
Comparison of Ranked Public Expectations for a College Education With Those Identified by Transdisciplinary Faculty and Psychologists

Public expectations	AAC&U	APA
1. Career preparation		Career development
2. Sense of maturity	Foundation and skills for lifelong learning	Personal development
3. Civic responsibility	Civic involvement and engagement	Sociocultural and international awareness; applications
4. Leadership skills	Teamwork and problem solving; synthesis and integrative learning	Applications of psychology
5. Postgraduate preparation	Knowledge of human cultures, physical and natural world; quantitative literacy	Knowledge base of psychology; research methods
6. Values, morals, and ethics	Ethical reasoning and action	Values in psychology
7. Tolerance and cultural respect	Intercultural knowledge and competence	Sociocultural and international awareness
8. Problem solving and analysis	Inquiry and analysis; critical and creative thinking	Critical thinking skills
9. Communication skills	Written and oral communication	Critical thinking skills
10. Computer skills	Information literacy	Information and technical literacy

Note. Data from "Summary of Existing Research on Attitudes Toward Liberal Education Outcome for the Association of American Colleges and Universities," by Hart Research Associates, retrieved April 28, 2008, from http://www.aacu.org; "College Learning for the New Global Century: A Report from the National Leadership Council for Liberal Education and America's Promise," by the Association of American Colleges and Universities, retrieved April 28, 2008, from http://www.aacu.org/publications; and "APA Guidelines for the Undergraduate Psychology Major," by the American Psychological Association, retrieved November 11, 2008, from http://www.apa.org/ed/psymajor_guideline.pdf

& *America's Promise* (AAC&U, 2007), the authors identified four outcomes that should commence in secondary schools and continue at successively higher levels in college: knowledge of human cultures and the physical and natural world, intellectual and practical skills, personal and social responsibility, and integrative learning.

As scientists, we asked the question whether the AAC&U outcomes had external validity. Hart Research Associates (2004) summarized recent survey research on many stakeholders' perceptions of desired outcomes for a college education. In *Should Colleges Focus More on Personal and Social Responsibility*, Dey and Associates (2008) continued to build an empirically based case for the AAC&U student learning outcomes. In Table 1.1, we compare and contrast data from the public perceptions with the blue-ribbon task force statements made by AAC&U (2007) and the APA *Guidelines for the Undergraduate Psychology Major* (APA, 2007a).

A core theme in the transdisciplinary narrative is a demand for public accountability reported in Hart Research Associates' (2008) *How Should Col-*

TABLE 1.2
Employers' Report Card on Graduates' Preparedness in 12 Key Areas and Needed Improved Assessments

Area	Mean rating (Range = 1–10)	% well prepared (Ratings of 8–10)	% not well prepared (Ratings of 1–5)
Teamwork	7.0	39	17
Ethical judgment	6.9	38	19
Intercultural skills	6.9	38	19
Social responsibility	6.7	35	21
Quantitative reasoning	6.7	32	23
Oral communication	6.6	32	23
Self-knowledge	6.5	28	26
Adaptability	6.3	24	30
Critical thinking	6.3	22	31
Writing skills	6.1	26	37
Self-direction	5.9	23	42
Global knowledge	5.7	18	46

Assessment practices needing to be enhanced	Employers' recommendations (%)
1. Faculty-evaluated internships or community-based learning experiences	50
2. Essay tests for problem-solving, writing, analytical-thinking skills	35
3. Electronic portfolios of students' work with examples in key skill areas and faculty assessments of them	32
4. Faculty-evaluated senior projects demonstrating depth of skill in major and advanced problem solving writing, and analytical reasoning skills	31
5. Normed tests that compare students on critical thinking	8
6. Multiple-choice tests of general content knowledge	5

Note. Adapted from "Summary of Existing Research on Attitudes Toward Liberal Education Outcome for the Association of American Colleges and Universities," by Hart Research Associates. Retrieved April 28, 2008, from http://www.aacu.org. Reprinted with permission of the Association of American Colleges and Universities.

leges Assess and Improve Student Learning: Employers' Views on the Accountability Challenge. In Table 1.2, we summarize the employers' report card on graduates' preparedness and their recommendations for improved assessment practices. Once again, there is an excellent match between the employers' perceptions and the efforts already being made by psychologists for authentic assessments of what we call psychological literacy; even a cursory review of the table of contents in APA's sponsored book *Measuring Up: Educational Assessment Challenges and Practices for Psychology* (Dunn et al., 2004) attests to this match.

We found additional support for our proposal of educating psychologically literate citizens in the cross-disciplinary higher education research literature. After analyzing the results from 2,600 evaluation research studies published from 1990 to 2002, Pascarella and Terenzini (2005) drew conclusions about the main effects of college. Faculty can be confident of the following student changes (in order of greatest magnitude): epistemological sophistication or maturity, reflective judgment, liberal arts competencies, declines in authoritarianism and dogmatism, principled moral reasoning, and critical thinking skills (pp. 572–578). Integrating these cross-disciplinary effects with psychological literacy outcomes will require whole-department discussions as well as making explicit connections through curricular requirements and team-teaching efforts with faculty across the campus.

Psychology educators recognize that creating psychologically literate students is a developmental process. Beginning psychology students come to the classroom with strong beliefs and attitudes about the nature of human behavior, some of which are supported by psychological science and some of which are not. They assert an unsophisticated common sense psychology, using sound-bite statements that mimic popular culture and unscientific attitudes and stances. Unlearning such attitudes and beliefs takes a substantial amount of cognitive effort and courage on the part of both educators and students. As faculty, psychologists likely have heaved sighs of relief at simply disabusing students' erroneous preconceptions. Their teaching efforts plant the seeds for lifelong learning effects, as we tried to illustrate in the two student case studies at the beginning of this chapter. Although psychological literacy remains an admirable goal, focusing only on the literacy aspect is shortchanging its powerful effects. Having gained a reasonable amount of psychological literacy does not ensure full-fledged psychologically literate citizens. Cognitive and affective insight must go hand-in-hand with behavioral changes, as we tried to illustrate in Case Study 3.

Why do we propose expecting psychologically literate students to focus on more than themselves, to value applying their knowledge, and to develop the shared virtues of globally oriented values? Citizenship is one of the character strengths of the virtue of justice (C. Peterson & Seligman, 2004). It is a characteristic woven into the fabric of healthy community life and celebrated in historical, multicultural, sacred, and secular texts (Dahlsgaard, Peterson, & Seligman, 2005). Psychologically literate citizens learn to lead by intentionally and courageously using their psychological literacy for sustained community benefit. They do so in large and small efforts at making a difference. We offer the following food for thought about how psychologists sometimes provide their expertise to solve problems, and teach their students to do so in appropriate ways, as well:

- A new parent sees an advertisement for a set of DVDs designed to make children smarter and wonders whether to purchase them;
- a new dog owner wants to teach her dog to be vigilant about strangers but not to bark incessantly;
- a person suffering from depression must decide whether to ask for medication from the family physician or look for a therapist;

- a salesperson struggles to remember the names of his many diverse customers;
- a business manager desires to use effective human resource strategies to increase employee productivity; and
- a Red Cross official wants to educate leader-spokespersons to deliver culturally sensitive and effective endorsements of an inoculation program in another country.

Undergraduate psychology—whether in one course, several, or a full major—offers the very best potential of liberal learning. It is at the juncture of the humanities and the sciences where students gain the human-focused values and the scientific tools necessary to see and to care about the human condition and to improve it. The 21st-century world has shrunk. Global problems intersect with local problems. Human behavior has both constructive and exciting and destructive and depressing consequences and possibilities. Psychologically literate citizens must learn to patiently and persistently work through the still-existing divisions among peoples and to challenge their prejudices and lack of full understanding about the differences of age and generational cohorts, class, disabling conditions, ethnicity, gender, race, religion, and sexual orientation. Psychologists must educate students who can act as stewards to help ensure the survival of the planet and to actively contribute to the betterment of all peoples.

Recall the opening question for this chapter: Why should we rethink how we educate undergraduate students? The more we read from the transdisciplinary narrative, the more new questions emerged for us. How can faculty and students learn to teach and to learn sustainably? How can psychologists motivate their students, colleagues, families and neighbors, and thus themselves to think ethically about individuals and systems? Educating others about the science and practices of psychology has consequences for the health of local, national, and global communities. Psychologists have built effective programs to achieve and measure the literacy outcomes. Is it now time to make the commitment to educate themselves and their students as psychologically literate citizens and to engage in new scholarship on teaching and learning to discover how best to achieve this outcome?

In our final case study, we illuminate the potential in making such a commitment. (In chapter 4 of this volume, readers meet Clarice, another undergraduate exemplar with a similar story.)

Case Study 4: From Online General Psychology to a Lifelong Commitment

Maxine Cooke-Mendoza lives in a southern rural county and represents a congressional district with African American, Asian, Latino, and Anglo populations. Despite their many, many differences, her community has worked through several economic and social catastrophes and has tried to demonstrate traditional values whereby neighbors speak to each other, volunteer their time to help others, and generally care about those who are less fortunate.

After high school, as the oldest sibling in her family, she went to work full time but took several online courses through her local community colleges. She discovered psychology and became an asynchronous learner and active participant in the introductory course designed by an enthusiastic and highly interactive instructor. She recalls how he constantly addressed students' real world questions with empathy and with many "minihomilies" about the importance of critical thinking and scientific analyses of problems.

After three semesters, without the financial resources to attend college, she enlisted in the military so that she could later reap the educational benefits afforded to veterans. Little did she know that she would need both the medical and the educational benefits. In a wartime combat environment, she was wounded severely and lost both her legs. Three years of rehabilitation followed. Dealing with both depression and dread about the future while hospitalized, she recalled often the lessons learned from her introductory psychology instructor and called him. He got her involved in an online program to finish her associate's degree, and after being discharged, she enrolled full time in the local public university with psychology as her major.

Maxine always felt challenged to participate in developing her own academic program. There were great interactions among students and professors, allowing real dialogue to grow and flourish. Her courses were intellectually challenging, but she thrived most on the feedback from regular assessments of what and how she was learning. Hands-on experiences beginning with her experimental methods lab, followed by community data gathering projects in social psychology, and a service learning capstone internship consolidated her personal confidence and inspired her emerging commitments. It took 4 more years for her to complete her baccalaureate, and through an unexpected set of circumstances, Maxine was nominated for local political office and won. Three years later, she was elected to her current statewide legislative position.

She thinks it important to ask and does, often: How did an undergraduate degree in psychology prepare someone first for the military, then for devastating medical problems, then for success as an online student, then for full-time undergraduate work and off-campus civic engagements, then for getting elected, and now for surviving the rigors of political office? Although Maxine would not be familiar with the term psychological literacy, its critical ingredients underlie the answers to all the above questions. It helped her to think more clearly about complex problems; understand the dynamics of multiethnic team work and conflict resolution; probe her assumptions about health and wellness; and critically evaluate alternative decisions about her educational, medical, and career options.

After graduation, she wanted to "give back" in gratitude to all those who had helped her. This lifelong motivation and how she lives is what psychologists envision for alumni who become psychologically literate citizens.

RECOMMENDATIONS AND CONCLUSION

We celebrate the continuing disciplined work, reflection, and creative energy of the many psychologists who built a well-defined paradigm for undergraduate education. Psychologists' students can be justifiably proud of their choice to study psychology. What they learn will be of lifelong benefit.

Psychologists must narrate this story to university administrators, employers, legislators, and the American public. Outcome stories, like our case studies, inspire, and motivate.

Our story's theme is psychological literacy. Its main characters are psychologically literate citizens in American and global psychology settings who contribute to the creation of a transdisciplinary narrative.

After evaluating the importance of psychological literacy for future undergraduate education outcomes, we have only one recommendation: Read the next chapters to discover many innovative means for achieving psychological literacy and for increasing the numbers of alumni we can truly call psychologically literate citizens.

These are ideas whose time has come and just begun.

2

TOWARD A SCIENTIST–EDUCATOR MODEL OF TEACHING PSYCHOLOGY

DANIEL J. BERNSTEIN, WILLIAM ADDISON, CINDY ALTMAN,
DEBRA HOLLISTER, MEERA KOMARRAJU, LORETO PRIETO,
COURTNEY A. ROCHELEAU, AND CECILIA SHORE

At some point in the distant past, teaching undergraduate psychology was straightforward. A college professor with a doctorate in psychology gave lectures to a group of young people whose main occupation was being a student. Today, psychologists' vision of what it means to be a quality instructor of psychology has expanded as the contexts in which psychology is taught have become more varied and complex (see chaps. 4 and 5, this volume). The instructor's level of expertise in the discipline, knowledge of and preparation for effective teaching, past experience in teaching roles, personal and cultural identity, and institutional context all combine to complicate the picture. Instructors face different challenges, have different strengths and weaknesses, have access to different resources, and require different forms of support to perform well in their role.

Graduate programs in psychology will serve their students well by preparing them for this complex educational environment with an academic background in teaching per se and professionally supervised teaching experiences. There is much more to being a successful teacher than knowing more psychology than the students and being able to organize a coherent, clear, and engaging lecture. High-quality outcomes result from an interaction of teacher, student, and contextual variables. No one teaching style or method is the best way to teach for all instructors, students, and situations; we affirm the St. Mary's conference (McGovern, 1993) recognition of individual differences among faculty, their perspectives on teaching, and their teaching methods. To serve our communities properly, preparation for teaching psychology needs to keep pace with the expanding vision of psychology's teaching mission and domain.

To meet the challenges associated with accepting responsibility for learning rather than just providing access to resources and coherent presentation of material, we suggest that psychology learn from its own successful scientist–practitioner model of preparation for clinical, counseling, and school psychology. Similar to a scientist–practitioner, a scientist–educator treats professional work as an inquiry into the effectiveness of practice. A scientist–educator adopts the same framework in preparing, designing, and carrying out a course or other learning activity (e.g., research mentoring, advising, supervising). It is critical to be familiar with evidence-based practice in the teaching of psychology, identifying those methods that are appropriate to one's own teaching. In chapter 6, the authors also suggest that teachers be aware of successful teaching methods and select from them as appropriate. Central to this enterprise is the systematic collection of evidence regarding the effectiveness of teaching and use of these data to guide the development and refinement of both the conceptual understanding of teaching and its practice in an iterative, recursive fashion. The scientist–educator does not necessarily engage in formal educational research but does more than merely use others' teaching techniques without evaluation of their effectiveness.

Figure 2.1 provides one possible framework to conceptualize the processes that would be undertaken by a scientist–educator to incorporate evidence-based inquiry, evaluation, and public discussion into his or her teaching endeavors. This instructor's work is informed by the practice of others, is carried out systematically, and is evaluated by its impact on learners. The scientist–educator reflects on the results of the instruction, makes that work visible to peers, and redesigns course conception, measures, and activities accordingly. Our framework for the work of the scientist–educator has features in common with the TACOMA (Teaching As a Contextual Outcome of Multiple Agents) model described in chapter 6 of this volume and the model of teaching and learning depicted in Figure 8.1 of chapter 8. All three models involve alignment of goals, methods, and assessment; all emphasize evidence-based practice, reflection on student success, and public sharing; all recognize multiple approaches to teaching because learning is context dependent.

For example, teaching and learning are usually done within a community that has a set of shared goals for its learners. Any instructor should clearly

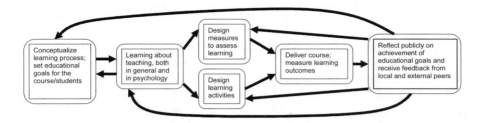

Figure 2.1. A scientist–educator's inquiry into learning.

identify goals for learning that arise from professional and institutional conversations and supplement these with any individual learning goals. Possibly the instructor may endorse the goal from chapter 1 to educate students toward psychological literacy and/or becoming psychologically literate citizens. He or she will then become informed about evidence-based examples of teaching related to these goals and maximize learning by implementing empirically validated techniques (such as those described in chaps. 6, 7, and 8, this volume) that are appropriate for the students and setting. In chapter 8 of this volume, there is a similar and complementary iterative model that emphasizes the interaction of teaching with principles of learning; in that model, teaching practices derive from learning principles so inquiry into teaching can in turn contribute to the development of learning principles. The feedback mechanism in the two models is the same, but the present model focuses instead on interaction between evidence of learning in particular courses and the practices used in those courses. Both approaches provide useful forms of iterative inquiry.

Public discussion of results is an essential feature of any scholarly endeavor, so a scientist–educator engages in continuous evaluation of how well students are achieving intellectual goals and periodically makes available a description of his or her practices and samples of learning for review and discussion among peers. This can occur in both formal outlets such as conferences or online sites and informal outlets on one's own campus. The process of inquiry is ultimately a dynamic one, characterized by an ongoing feedback loop with inputs from reading about teaching, observation of student intellectual work, and peer commentaries. Both chapters 6 and 8 also emphasize that this iterative reflective practice is central to successful, effective teaching.

In the following sections, we explore how the scientist–educator model is applicable to characteristics of the person who is teaching and the context for that work, is central to a developmental understanding of professional competence, and is characteristic of high-quality instruction. We believe that this approach is essential in preparing our current students to be excellent and effective teachers in any teaching context.

WHO IS TEACHING PSYCHOLOGY?

Preparation in one's discipline, in pedagogy, and in evaluation is essential to the success of educators, regardless of setting and appointment type; effective teaching can be found across many institutional contexts. For example, Leslie and Gappa (2002) reported that part-time faculty are comparable to full-time faculty in terms of meeting student learning outcomes, achieving student retention, and earning high student evaluations. To determine how best to prepare and support scientist–educators of all kinds, it is first necessary to identify who is currently teaching psychology, including their academic preparation and demographic characteristics.

Teacher Position and Preparation in Different Contexts

Approximately 30,000 psychology faculty members are distributed among baccalaureate colleges (48%), 2-year colleges (37%), and combined undergraduate and graduate departments (15%; Kyle & Williams, 2000). In addition, there are an estimated 12,000 psychology teachers in high schools (Ernst & Petrossian, 1996). The level and type of institution tend to dictate both the nature of faculty appointments and the preparation that educators have for their role in the classroom. For instance, whereas the percentage of full-time faculty is 66% in 4-year schools, it is only 38% in 2-year schools. The preparation that psychology educators bring to their role also differs by setting. In some contexts (predominantly 4-year institutions), nearly all full-time faculty hold a doctoral degree in their disciplines, whereas in 2-year institutions, master's degree recipients make up 51% of full-time faculty and 74% of part-time faculty (Johnson & Rudmann, 2004; Kyle & Williams, 2000). Quality Principle 4 presented in chapter 10 recommends that administrators not ask faculty members to teach subjects in which they have little background. Although some faculty members in 2-year institutions may have more modest preparation in their discipline, their institutions tend to provide excellent support for their teaching (Wallin, 2007).

Faculty members at 4-year institutions, however, generally have limited study in pedagogy. Early career psychologists endorsed the statement, "My graduate department provided teaching training to graduate students" with an average 2.5 on a 1–4 scale (American Psychological Association [APA], n.d.). Meyers and Prieto (2000) reported that 94% of psychology graduate departments use teaching assistants (TAs) and 57% give TAs full course responsibility, but only about 10% of TAs receive both formal pedagogical preparation and supervision of their teaching duties. The majority of TAs receive either an average of about 20 hours of preparation or some supervision once per week, and many others receive little, if any, formal training. Undergraduate students may also serve as TAs; they are often senior-level psychology majors and top performers in their programs. These students typically serve in apprenticeship roles and rarely have formal academic preparation as teachers (McKeegan, 1998).

At the high school level, Weaver (2005) reported that only one quarter of high school psychology teachers are certified in psychology; instead, they possess certification in broader domain areas such as social studies or social sciences. In contrast, these educators generally have a high degree of preparation in pedagogy and evaluation of effectiveness through reflective practice.

Teacher Demographic Characteristics

Demographic diversity promotes psychology as representative of the range of human experience, both in terms of its content and its practitioners. Although psychology has prioritized the recruitment and retention of diverse students and faculty, psychologists have not reached parity with the students they teach (see chap. 4, this volume) or the society they represent and serve.

The demographic characteristics of faculty also tend to vary according to academic setting and appointment type. Gender inequities in the psychology professoriate remain, despite improvement in recent years (Kite et al., 2001). In 4-year institutions and in full-time positions, men typically outnumber women, whereas the reverse is true in 2-year institutions and in part-time positions. However, the gender balance in psychology is likely to shift in the near future as female graduates in psychology significantly outnumber males (see chap. 4, this volume). The overwhelming majority (85%–90%) of psychology educators are European American and occupy a slightly larger percentage of full-time than part-time positions (Johnson & Rudmann, 2004; Kyle & Williams, 2000).

The APA's Committee on Lesbian and Gay Concerns (1993) indicated that 27% of psychology-related graduate programs reported having an openly gay or lesbian faculty member. Given the size of typical graduate departments and the estimated base rate of gay and lesbian faculty members, these data suggest that psychology has not yet succeeded in promoting workplaces that welcome and encourage full disclosure of gender and sexual identity.

Psychology Faculty of the Future

The psychology profession will be most effective when its population matches the diversity of its students and nation, and the optimal psychology educator will engage students from a wide range of backgrounds and cultures, filling the academic pipeline with a fully diverse stream of people. To meet these standards with faculty members representing the full range of human diversity, characteristics of quality graduate preparation and high-quality teaching must be identified.

PREPARATION AND DEVELOPMENT OF FACULTY MEMBERS

To achieve the scientist–educator ideal, psychology instructors must receive appropriate preparation and ongoing support throughout their careers. Given the wide range of appointments and institutions of those who teach psychology, we believe graduate programs should provide appropriate orientation and background for students intending to teach.

Professional Practice Orientation

For years academia has operated under the belief that knowing a subject's content is all that is necessary to teach it effectively. This assumption neglects many of the multidimensional professional competencies in teaching, such as pedagogy, assessment of student learning, evaluation of effectiveness, classroom management, ethical conduct, and inclusive teaching. Professional competence in teaching should be grounded in the theoretical and empirical bases for pedagogy drawn from psychology, as noted in chapter 8. A thoughtful and reflective attitude toward one's own teaching, as described in the scientist–educator model, is the foundation of scholarly teaching practice and should be honored by faculty reward systems.

Needs of Novice Teachers

All psychology teachers, regardless of their institutional mission, would benefit from formal preparation in both psychological content and teaching methods. High school teachers generally have good training in teaching methods but may be assigned to teach psychology without having ever completed any psychology coursework. Many high school teachers recognize the need for additional preparation in psychology, but such resources may not be readily accessible. Part-time and nontenure-track faculty members may begin teaching with modest preparation in both content and methods. As described earlier, graduate student TAs do not typically receive in-depth preparation for teaching, even when they teach independent courses, and new full-time tenure-track faculty members report receiving little systematic background or practice in teaching. This lack of preparation must be addressed to facilitate student engagement and retention (Dunn, McCarthy, Baker, Halonen, & Hill, 2007).

Preparing Instructors

Some outstanding preparation programs already exist. For example, the University of New Hampshire has integrated preparation for teaching into its psychology graduate curriculum (Benassi & Fernald, 1993). At the disciplinary level, the APA and the Society for the Teaching of Psychology (STP) continue to be leaders in faculty development efforts. The Teachers of Psychology in Secondary Schools has expanded its efforts; the Association for Psychological Science has begun providing teaching support; and subdisciplinary organizations such as the Society for Research in Child Development and the Society for Personality and Social Psychology have begun providing preconference workshops for continuing faculty development. Cross-disciplinary programs also exist. Preparing Future Faculty (PFF), a joint initiative by the American Association of Colleges and Universities and the Council of Graduate Schools, aims to improve the preparation of graduate students for faculty roles (Gaff, Pruit-Logan, & Weibl, 2000). In 2000, the APA expanded previous cross-disciplinary efforts by sponsoring the development of four model discipline-specific PFF programs at the Universities of New Hampshire, Colorado, Georgia, and Miami. There are now roughly a dozen APA-sponsored PFF programs.

Preparation programs can take a number of forms. Many programs focus on the development of qualities or behaviors that are typically displayed by master teachers to improve teaching competence (Keeley, Smith, & Buskist, 2006; Mowrer, Love, & Orem, 2004). These programs include expected features such as serving as apprentices and processing feedback with a supervisor (e.g., Heppner, 1994; Seijts, Taylor, & Latham, 1998) and observing others teach and being observed while teaching (e.g., Saville, 2004). There are more specialized skills developed as well, including interacting with students, assessment and examination techniques, awareness of ethical issues in teaching, and basic principles of learning and motivation (e.g., Buskist, Beins, & Hevern, 2004; Lewis, 2003; Mueller, Perlman, McCann, & McFadden, 1997).

In addition to providing general support for psychology instructors, preparation programs can also help to address the relative lack of diversity within the field. Many students from diverse backgrounds leave psychology before completing their studies. Retention of all students, including those of minority cultures, is enhanced when courses engage students' individual experiences and provide them with opportunities to interact with other learners in the development of their knowledge. Preparation programs can help teachers develop competencies that address the needs of diverse students by using a wide variety of teaching modalities, giving examples that are drawn from various cultural contexts, developing assignments that incorporate various learning and thinking styles, and creating an inclusive climate in the classroom. In chapter 4, the authors emphasize the need for explicit preparation for inclusive teaching, and as these strategies improve retention of all students, psychology teachers will begin to reflect the diversity of the larger population.

The scientist–educator model suggests that there is an additional component that should be included in preparation for teaching, namely using evidence of learning (both success and failure) to inform the ongoing development of instructional design and practice. Psychology graduate students are skilled in analyzing data and using evidence to evaluate the effects of an intervention; a scientist–educator uses that skill to ask how effective a course has been in helping students learn and uses evidence to guide future practice. As exemplified by the case of Professor Cantrell in chapter 1, this is more than merely applying teaching tips from an empirical literature; it is ongoing inquiry into how well those ideas actually function.

Consistent with the scientist–educator model, it is imperative that instructors also become knowledgeable about fulfilling their professional obligations in an ethical manner. Instructors should be familiar with the "Ethical Principles of Psychologists and Code of Conduct" (APA Ethics Code; APA, 2002a) as these standards apply to the teaching process and to the treatment of students in their classes. There are a number of standards in the APA Ethics Code that address the instructor–student relationship, but they can all be subsumed under this general principle: "Psychologists strive to benefit those with whom they work and take care to do no harm" (APA, 2002a, p. 3). In terms of the preparation and delivery of course material, educators' primary ethical obligation concerns accuracy in teaching (APA, 2002a, Standard 7.03). Orientations for novice instructors should review these ethical guidelines, and instructors should revisit the guidelines when a situation arises, consulting with a supervisor when they are uncertain about a course of action.

Continuing Faculty Development

The specific determinants of effective teaching are ever changing. The subject matter changes; the cohort of students changes; the contexts of instruction change; and instructors change through self-reflection on the effectiveness of their instruction. As a result of these rapid changes, instructors need continuing support and development that are tied to their unique context and individual needs. Perhaps there is need for national board certification for secondary and postsecondary psychology teachers comparable to that which is available for high school teachers in other disciplines. Such an optional certification would identify faculty members who undertake a rigorous process of teaching improvement, leading to recognition and reward. Maintaining certification would sustain the scientist–educator approach to teaching by encouraging teachers to continually gather data, assess their effectiveness, and implement modifications as appropriate.

Although there is a clear need for ongoing teaching development, it is less clear that quality programs are available for such career-long development. Recent data suggest that faculty development programs addressing issues such as student-centered learning; integrating technology into "traditional" teaching and learning settings; and active, inquiry-based, problem-based learning receive moderate support in the form of resources, recognition, and reassignment of faculty time (Sorcinelli, Austin, Eddy, &

Beach, 2006). Some institutions do provide support for ongoing teacher development; for example, Valencia Community College in Florida provides step pay increases to adjunct faculty who participate in the Associate Faculty Program of the school's Teaching/Learning Academy (Clarke & Bishop, 2006). The development of similar programs at other institutions would be possible with continuing support from their administrations, private foundations, and discipline associations such as the APA or the STP.

Benefits of Providing Preparation

There is good evidence that allocating resources to faculty development programs results in better teaching and learning outcomes. Graduate training in teaching and ongoing faculty development provide direct benefits for instructors (Chism & Szabo, 1997) and increase long-term motivation to pursue teaching and academic careers (Buskist, Benson, & Sikorski, 2005). These programs also have indirect effects on student learning through increased confidence in teaching as well as increased liking for teaching that encourages new teachers to create environments that foster higher levels of student learning (Gibbs & Coffey, 2004; Komarraju, 2008).

Even if graduate students do not intend to pursue a career with a primary emphasis on teaching, preparation to teach is valuable for two reasons. First, new faculty members who receive teaching preparation in graduate school can dedicate more time and energy to other areas of responsibility, such as research, enabling them to be more productive overall. Second, virtually all graduate students will someday serve in professional roles (including those outside of academia) that use many of the same skills that teachers do, including an ability to present information, organize teamwork, and evaluate others. Hence, we recommend that all psychology graduate students be required to complete coursework and supervised experiences in teaching.

Participation in faculty development sometimes meets with resistance from both faculty members and students. Faculty members concerned about receiving lower student evaluations may be hesitant to use innovative teaching methods that result in better learning but are difficult and sometimes disliked by students. A more well-rounded evaluation process that provides rewards for innovation, risk taking, and change would support a scientist–educator approach to teacher preparation.

DEFINING AND EVALUATING THE QUALITY OF INSTRUCTION

Evaluation of teaching presumes an understanding and articulation of the properties of excellent and effective instruction. Before elaborating on a framework of evaluation, it is first necessary to identify the dimensions of quality to be judged.

Defining the Quality of Instruction

Effective instructors have an understanding of the subjects they teach and use a variety of instructional methods while applying various assessment strategies to measure student success. Studies of teaching identify best practices (e.g., Chickering & Gamson, 1987) or measure a set of teaching activities that are associated with an indicator of good teaching (e.g., Keely et al., 2006). Increasingly, the conversation on the definition of effective teaching focuses on indicators of successful student learning, not just teacher behavior, and this strategy requires a contextual approach because faculty members and programs vary in the goals they have for their students and their institutions (see chap. 3, this volume). Although the APA Guidelines for the Undergraduate Psychology Major (APA, 2007a) give instructors a wide range of disciplinary and liberal learning goals, the scientist–educator model provides an analysis of quality that is independent of any particular set of goals. This analysis can be neutral on the question of the appropriateness of the goals while holding the instructor to the criterion of achieving the identified goals. This definition of quality is dynamic because it focuses on the interaction between the actions of the instructor and continuous evaluation of the effect of those actions.

From the perspective of a scientist–educator, teaching includes the forms of inquiry typical of any form of scholarship. Following Boyer's (1990) analysis of four domains of scholarship, Glassick, Huber, and Maeroff (1997) identified a sequence of activities that characterize the work of scholars. These include identifying clear goals, being informed about prior research and intellectual work in the field, using appropriate methods of inquiry, gathering evidence, reflecting on what is learned from analysis of the evidence, and making the results available for examination by others. A scientist–educator engages teaching within the same framework, and one possible version of the components is described in the left-hand column of Table 2.1. As stated in chapter 1, a successful inquiry into the learning generated by a course begins with goals (e.g., producing psychologically literate citizens), uses measures and methods from existing examples (perhaps across disciplines), analyzes the student work produced, and makes public the lessons learned (again, perhaps in a transdisciplinary forum).

The framework in Table 2.1 offers a starting point for a conversation on the development of skills in the components of inquiry found in the scientist–educator model. For each component of scholarly teaching, there is text describing increasing levels of skill or success, from entry level to advanced performance. This approach is typical of a cognitive apprenticeship model for students' learning (Collins, Brown, & Holum, 1991; Halonen et al., 2003), showing varying levels of skill that appear with experience and preparation. The particular framework shown for faculty accomplishment was adapted from a transdisciplinary rubric developed for scholarship of teaching and learn-

TABLE 2.1
Expertise Levels of a Scientist–Educator

Components	Entry into teaching	Basic skill	Professional	Advanced
Goals of the course or other learning activity	Course/activity goals are absent, unclear, or inappropriate.	Course/activity goals are well articulated and appropriate to the courses and to the curriculum.	Course/activity goals identify intellectually challenging and enduring targets and/or are especially well matched to students.	Course/activity goals identify levels of performance that represent excellence and are of interest to many stakeholders.
Preparation for the course or learning activity	Teacher is not adequately knowledgeable and/or has no background in teaching.	The teaching is based on prior scholarship in its area, including current content as well as pedagogical methods and conceptual frames.	The teacher's preparation includes broad synthesis of prior work in content as well as practice in pedagogical methods and conceptual frames.	The teacher acquires and integrates knowledge and skills drawn from the literature of multiple disciplines, both in content and pedagogy.
Methods used to conduct the teaching	No apparent rationale for teaching methods is used; there is no instructional design.	The work follows the conventions of teaching practices within its domain of discipline and institution.	The teaching takes full advantage of effective methods discussed within its discipline.	The work generates new practices that will enable others to improve or enhance their teaching.
Evidence gathered to demonstrate the impact of the teacher's work	There is no measure of student learning, or assessment methods do not match espoused goals.	There is evidence linking students' performances to espoused goals.	Student performances indicate that deep and/or broad learning is taking place.	The learning demonstrated is exemplary in either depth of learning and/or in breadth of students' success.
Reflection on the teaching and its impact on student learning	The teacher provides no indication of having reflected on or learned from prior teaching.	The teacher articulates lessons learned from reflecting on prior teaching.	The teacher has examined the impact on students' performance within a conceptual framework and adjusted practice based on reflection.	Enhanced achievement of learning goals results from reflection on evidence within a conceptual framework, or the teacher revises the conceptual framework based on student learning outcomes.
Communication of teaching results to others	The practices and results of teaching are kept private.	The teacher's work and students' performances are publicly accessible for others to use, to build on, and to review critically.	The teacher's reflective work has been read and adjustments in practice have arisen through the public discourse.	The teacher's work has had an impact on the practices and inquiry of many others and has contributed to related conceptual frameworks.

ing projects (Bernstein & Huber, 2006). Similar developmental models for quality benchmarks within psychology programs are presented by Dunn et al. (2007).

Evaluating Quality of Instruction

The evaluation of teaching quality typically occurs when institutions make decisions about continuing employment or salaries. The scientist–educator framework is useful in framing evidence from the instructor and peers, especially when there is a portfolio of work from the instructor's courses. A typical portfolio may include course syllabi, assignments, and samples of student work; reflections from the instructor on outcomes and teaching philosophy; summaries of student ratings; and reports of class observations (Hutchings, 1998; Seldin, 1997). These materials can be roughly categorized into three sources of evidence: the instructor, peers, and students. All three sources are essential to appropriate evaluation of teaching quality, with potential for confirmation through converging measures.

The Instructor's Voice

A critical part of delivering a course is the collection of evidence of the success of the enterprise; in teaching there are natural products of learning found in student work, including examinations, projects, and papers. A scientist–educator maintains a systematic archive of teaching materials and a sample of student work for continuous reflection on the success of all learning activities, initially as formative evaluation to inform continued teaching practice. Reflections are most useful if they are complete and candid, identifying strengths and areas for potential growth. The scientist–educator framework provides a useful outline for reflection, leading the instructor to comment on goals, methods, and results of teaching. It is especially useful as an occasion for the instructor to plan for future offerings of a course, informed by previous experience with the same course. A portfolio with a narrative and materials from several offerings of a single course is an excellent body of evidence for making teaching visible to colleagues, students, and other teaching communities.

Peers' Voices

Instructors sometimes experience formal peer observation of classroom performance, and they can receive beneficial feedback about many aspects of class interaction. External observers may laud the instructor for what was done well, offer valuable suggestions for development, and aid in the formulation of future goals and methods for achieving them. Multiple observations permit observers to note consistency and change in a colleague's teaching, and they are more useful than single visits. Bernstein (2008) reviewed research on peer observation, and the consensus of professional opinion (e.g.,

Cohen & McKeachie, 1980) favored using observations for development rather than evaluation.

The scientist–educator model suggests a framework for peer review of course content and materials. If the instructor makes available syllabi, assignments with graded student work, and a reflective narrative on the lessons learned across offerings, peers can address the quality of the teacher's scholarly inquiry into the success of the course over time. Peers identify the level of skill in each component of this inquiry into teaching, with perhaps the most weight placed on the depth of learning, the breadth of success among students, and how well the instructor adapts teaching over time on the basis of reflection on evidence from prior teaching.

Students' Voices

Student ratings of teaching (SRTs) are often a primary component of evaluations of instructional quality, although there remains considerable debate regarding their use. Thorough review of research on this topic is beyond the scope of this chapter, but a great deal of evidence indicates that appropriate rating instruments can provide valid and reliable measures of at least some aspects of teaching performance (e.g., Arreola, 2007). Some critics of SRTs contend that the modest correlation observed between student ratings and grades occurs because students tend to assign positive ratings in appreciation for good grades or that overreliance on SRTs in promotion and tenure decisions results in an increase in consumer-oriented teaching and a potential decrease in student learning (e.g., Greenwald & Gillmore, 1997).

The lengthy and exhaustive debate over the usefulness of SRTs suggests they are best used as one of several indicators of teaching quality rather than as a sole outcome measure. Quality Principle 4 (see chap. 10, this volume) recommends that teachers not be downgraded in annual review if students do not respond favorably to innovations. When faculty members experiment with new methods of teaching, it is essential to include a peer voice in evaluation to identify situations in which appropriate innovations may have affected student perceptions.

Students are in an ideal position as field observers of basic features of classroom performance and climate, especially for descriptions of actions rather than inference of higher order evaluation. SRT procedures should be completed in private and remain anonymous, and perhaps the most useful form of SRTs are formative ratings and comments collected during the semester. These low-stakes comments can be useful to a faculty member at a time when change can be implemented with the same students who made the observations.

Indicators of Excellent Teaching

Institutions can readily see that an instructor meets standard expectations for the number of assigned courses and student perceptions, but administrators should help instructors understand that high-quality education also includes evidence of student learning. Regardless of where instruction takes place, student learning outcomes should be the primary driving force in defining and evaluating quality teaching (see chap. 9, this volume, for more discussion of assessment of learning). Instructors interested in identifying appropriate learning outcomes can consult Halonen et al. (2003), APA (2007a), Dunn et al. (2007), and APA's assessment cyberguide (APA Task Force on Undergraduate Psychology Major Competencies, 2002a), for a comprehensive treatment of gathering evidence of learning for both course and broad programmatic goals.

To summarize, instructors need a vision of effective instruction to guide the design and implementation of their courses, and they should close the loop by assessing their students' achievement. Continuous improvement in learning is at least as important as the achievement of any particular goals that an instructor or program has for students. The scientist–educator will reflect on publicly observable evidence of effectiveness and identify the next steps to take in developing his or her teaching.

Incentives and Rewards for Quality Teaching

Incentives and rewards for effective teaching can take many forms, including local and national teaching awards, merit-based salary increases, access to development funds, or hiring decisions based on previous teaching success. Indirect recognition may include departmental support for innovative course offerings or teaching techniques or the development of forums in which faculty are encouraged to discuss pedagogical issues with colleagues. In addition, students who communicate their positive regard for the instruction they received enhance the future efforts made by their instructors.

It should be recognized that teaching complements and overlaps in meaningful ways with research and service, especially as seen in research mentorship, advising, and supervision of internships. These forms of teaching should be included in reward structures for faculty, along with empirical assessments of the effects of faculty development. Faculty members' professional efforts around teaching issues should be encouraged and rewarded in ways equal to other scholarly undertakings. We affirm the principle from the St. Mary's conference (McGovern, 1993) that teaching, research and scholarship, and service are complementary and integrative endeavors, and faculty should be rewarded for efforts in all domains. Although the relative emphasis placed on these three differs from institution to institution, all stakeholders' interests, including those of students, faculty, and administrators, are best met when faculty engage in quality work in all three areas.

The scientist–educator model suggests that excellence in the teaching portion of an academic position includes scientific inquiry into successful learning and that inquiry should be based on analysis of systematic evidence.

There will be some teachers who conduct that inquiry with sufficient rigor to yield generalizable results worthy of wide distribution through publication so others can build on their work. Like scientist–practitioners, however, most scientist–educators will use their scientific skills to determine how well their own teaching is working and to discover how to improve the effectiveness of their own courses. Both informed inquiry into learning and formal research on teaching methods (scholarly teaching and the scholarship of teaching, as discussed in chap. 8, this volume) require extensive formal preparation in graduate school, and both should be recognized and honored in academic personnel processes. Whether included in the category of teaching or scholarship, excellence is found in the reflective use of evidence to advance the practice of teaching and learning.

RECOMMENDATIONS AND CONCLUSION

All psychology educators need both content and pedagogical knowledge to be effective, along with skills in inquiry that allow them to engage in iterative evaluation of their effectiveness. Otherwise, they may serve their students in a suboptimal manner and exacerbate public misconceptions about the credibility of psychological science. Institutions find it difficult to provide adequate faculty development for all instructors within the constraints of time and resources available. Accordingly, members of the psychological community either need to reallocate existing time and resources or seek out and lobby for funding from government and private sources to assure high-quality teaching in the scientist–educator model.

Given our analysis of the human and institutional contexts of the teaching of psychology, as well as the optimal practices in pedagogy, we conclude our analysis with the following specific recommendations:

- Regardless of the emphasis placed on the teaching mission at a given institution, psychology departments should promote and adopt criteria for the evaluation of teaching that are consistent with a scientist–educator model, including the public distribution of instructional goals, methods, outcome data, and reflection on teaching informed by knowledge of scholarly literature on theory and practice of teaching and learning.
- All instructors, regardless of setting, should receive preparation for teaching, emphasizing content, pedagogy, and evaluation. Scientist–educators continually reflect on and develop their skill and effectiveness as teachers (as defined by student learning) over the full extent of their careers, as increasing skill development does not result simply from experience per se.
- Graduate education in psychology should include required preparation consistent with the scientist–educator model. Al-

though critical for students employed as teaching assistants, a foundation in the teaching of psychology should be part of the academic preparation graduates receive for any professional career. Coursework and supervised teaching experiences should be routinely evaluated as to effectiveness and impact on student learning.

- All psychology educators, including high school teachers, undergraduate and graduate student teaching assistants, lecturers, adjunct instructors, and tenure-track and tenured faculty members should have access to and participate in ongoing faculty development in teaching. This would include venues and communities for public sharing of intellectual work and growth concerning the teaching of psychology.
- Students from all cultural backgrounds should be educated and graduated in the discipline so that future generations of psychology teachers will better reflect the full spectrum of diversity in society. The development and widespread use of inclusive teaching methods that engage all learners, with inductive teaching connected to their personal experience, is essential to expanding the demographic base of psychology.
- Professional associations in psychology should create and value an optional, board-certified specialty in the teaching of psychology. Board certification in psychology should be available for high school teachers, comparable to that in other disciplines; there should also be a certification for postsecondary psychology instructors. Such board certification would serve as evidence of masterful performance in scholarly teaching in line with a scientist–educator approach.
- Professional associations and funding agencies should commit financial support to efforts aimed at the enrichment of psychology education and educators at high school, community college, 4-year, university, and commercial and private settings. Opportunities for training and enrichment should be delivered in line with APA guidelines for psychology education (e.g., high school and undergraduate learning outcomes). Financial support should also be apportioned for research on effective teaching methods as well as effective faculty training and preparation methods.
- The APA Ethics Committee should expand the section in the 2002 APA Ethics Code concerning ethical behavior as it pertains to teaching activities. All psychology instructors have an ethical responsibility to learn about and use the most effective forms of teaching available to them. Any future revisions to the APA Ethics Code should include explicit text declaring

adequate preparation and continuing education in pedagogy for psychology educators to be an ethical mandate.

If all of these recommendations are carried out, the effectiveness of teaching psychology would be greatly improved. Instructors would be better prepared to create good learning environments and to know what kind of learning was occurring. The scientist–educator will be informed about the substance of psychology and about the practice of reflective teaching. When evidence of successful learning is routinely a part of excellent teaching, it will also aid in evaluation of the people doing the teaching. Reflective teaching engages the inquiring voice of the instructor, who is learning from the performance of students and responding to feedback from peers. If these qualities are found among teachers of psychology from secondary school through graduate school, then students of psychology will benefit greatly.

3

THE UNDERGRADUATE PSYCHOLOGY CURRICULUM: CALL FOR A CORE

DANA S. DUNN, CHARLES L. BREWER, ROBIN L. CAUTIN,
REGAN A. R. GURUNG, KENNETH D. KEITH, LORETTA N. McGREGOR,
STEVE A. NIDA, PATRICIA PUCCIO, AND MARY JEAN VOIGT

What is being taught and learned in the undergraduate psychology curriculum? Debate regarding the undergraduate psychology curriculum is dynamic and longstanding (e.g., Brewer et al., 1993; Buxton et al., 1952; Kulik, Brown, Vestewig, & Wright, 1973; McKeachie & Milholland, 1961; Scheirer & Rogers, 1985; see also, McGovern, 1992). The most recent curricular review (Brewer et al., 1993) was part of the American Psychological Association's (APA's) National Conference on Enhancing the Quality of Undergraduate Education in Psychology, which convened at St. Mary's College of Maryland in 1991 and sought to integrate current scholarship on the teaching and learning of psychology (see McGovern, 1993). In a report on the curriculum, Brewer et al. (1993) reaffirmed the conception of psychology as a liberal arts discipline, noting the synergy existing between psychology

We are grateful to David Myers and Cynthia Belar for contributing to our curricular discussions during our meetings at the University of Puget Sound, June 2008.

courses and those in other liberal arts disciplines (see also McGovern, Furumoto, Halpern, Kimble, & McKeachie, 1991). Furthermore, the Brewer report proposed a framework for the psychology major identifying four groups of courses, preferably to be taken in the following order: the introductory course; methodology courses, including research methods, statistics, and psychometrics; content courses, including those that address natural and social science features of the discipline; and integrative experiences that include internships, research projects, or a capstone course. Although not a prescription for the psychology curriculum, the framework proposed by Brewer et al. (1993) was intended as a guiding structure to highlight the common features of all psychology programs as well as to maximize opportunities for students to acquire and develop the skills and abilities important for all psychology majors.

Subsequent data indicate that important components of Brewer et al.'s (1993) recommendations have not been widely implemented (Messer, Griggs, & Jackson, 1999; Perlman & McCann, 1999a, 1999b; Stoloff et al., 2008; Stoloff, Sanders, & McCarthy, n.d.). At the same time, there has been a proliferation of narrowly defined course offerings that reflect the growing specialization within the discipline. Although specialization reflects progress and confers many benefits on the field, fragmentation of the discipline may be problematic if unifying elements of the discipline are obscured. Moreover, developments have emerged outside of psychology that further blur the discipline's boundaries (McGovern & Brewer, 2003). Together, these forces provide great impetus for a reevaluation of the undergraduate psychology curriculum.

In this chapter, we discuss the need for curricular reform, advocate a curricular model that affirms basic past assumptions and integrates recent scholarship, and make concrete curricular recommendations for faculty and administrators of undergraduate psychology departments. We wish to make our intentions clear by defining our use of the term *core* at the outset of the chapter. The word *core* means the central or the most important part of the curriculum. Core courses are typically required of all students who major in psychology. In addition, we believe that psychology programs should structure their curricula to allow psychology majors to take elective courses that suit their own interests or career aspirations.

WHY CURRICULAR REFORM NOW?

Various factors within and outside the discipline create the need to reassess the undergraduate psychology curriculum. These factors raise concerns about the lack of coherence of the current curriculum and the integrity of the discipline's identity.

Contextual Factors Operating Within Psychology

The science of psychology has expanded both rapidly and broadly in recent years. This remarkable growth has been accompanied by educational pressures in the form of academic specialization and fragmentation, and rising interest in applied psychology.

Increasing Specialization and the Resulting Fragmentation

Remarkable developments within psychology have led to insights that would have been hard to imagine just a few years ago. They have led, for example, to the emergence of new and different areas of specialization (e.g., positive psychology) as well as separate, stand-alone departments (e.g., neuroscience) distinct from traditional psychology departments. This trend is evidenced in numerous other ways. During the last 2 decades there has been an increase in the number of specialty conferences focusing on research within narrowly defined domains (e.g., Society for Research in Child Development, Society for Neuroscience, Society for Personality and Social Psychology). In addition, there are now 54 distinct divisions within the APA; 7 new ones were added since 1990 (and a brief moratorium in the 1990s did little to stem the tide of division propagation). The present undergraduate curriculum reflects this proliferation of specialty areas. For example, Stoloff et al. (n.d.) identified 40 different undergraduate psychology courses being offered at colleges and universities. Typical major requirements range from 7 to 10 courses—or slightly less than one third of all courses students complete during their baccalaureate education (Stoloff et al., 2008). Such variety is not necessarily problematic. Increasing specialization reflects advancements in the field, promotes the expansion of knowledge within these narrowly defined areas, and often provides context for interdisciplinary activity. These are all important positive outcomes.

One risk associated with a proliferation of specialized areas, however, is fragmentation of the discipline. These specialized areas may become isolated entities that are not recognizable as domains of the same discipline or that cannot communicate meaningfully with one another. If psychology's undergraduate curriculum reflects this fragmentation, imparting to students a view of the discipline as a unified whole becomes more challenging (Solomon, Kavanaugh, Goethals, & Crider, 1982).

Indeed, the idea of a broad-based general perspective on the discipline seems to be waning in popularity. For example, organizations that focus on general psychology are struggling to remain viable. In recent years, the regional psychological associations have generally experienced a decline in attendance at their annual meetings (Packard, 2007). Consider, too, what has happened to the single APA division that does not serve a specialty area—APA Division 1 (General Psychology). In 1982, this division boasted a membership of 5,098; by 2006, that figure had dropped to 1,826 (APA, 2007b). This 64% decline contrasts with an increase of nearly 17% in APA's total membership during the same period (APA, 2007b). Of course, some of Division 1's membership decline may reflect shifts into new divisions as they have appeared; nevertheless, APA members may belong to more than one division, and the main message here is that it seems clear that psychologists are becoming less and less likely to identify themselves as generalists.

The undergraduate psychology curriculum also reflects this trend. A systematic review of 500 undergraduate psychology programs reveals that a substantial number do not require courses representing the disciplines' basic content domains: 40% require research methods, 21% physiological psychology, 19% developmental psychology, 17% social psychology, and 9% cognitive psychology (Perlman & McCann, 1999b). A more recent review of 374 programs (Stoloff et al., 2008) essentially duplicates these earlier findings. However, using a broader coding scheme for research-methods-type courses (i.e., research methods, statistics, integrated methods and statistics, experimental psychology, psychological testing, advanced statistics, and computer applications), Stoloff et al. found that 98% of the programs in their sample required such a course. More generally, these researchers observed that although

> virtually every student majoring in psychology is required to take an introductory course and one or more statistics and/or research methods courses . . . [f]ewer than half of the programs require a course in developmental, physiological, abnormal, or social psychology. Approximately one third of the programs require a course in personality, history and systems, or cognitive psychology. These courses represent the core content of the psychology major program. No other courses or content areas are required by more than a quarter of the institutions we sampled. (Stoloff et al., 2008, p. 22)

Stoloff et al. also noted a decline in a required capstone experience among their programs (from 63% of programs reported by Perlman & McCann, 1999b, to 40%). A broad-based perspective on the field depends on exposure to each of the core content areas mentioned previously, but fewer than half of programs require courses in these areas. We do not oppose course offerings in specialty topics (e.g., forensic psychology, human sexuality), but we stress that they should not replace students' exposure to the core content areas of the field.

Increasing Popularity of Applied Psychology

An analysis by the APA's Committee on Employment and Human Resources (Howard et al., 1986) revealed that beginning in the early 1970s the number of psychology PhDs granted in health service provider subfields (e.g., clinical, counseling, school psychology) dramatically outpaced those in traditional research and academic domains (e.g., experimental, physiological, developmental psychology). Moreover, traditional subfields experienced a decline in doctoral production. For example, between 1972 and 1984, the number of new PhDs in experimental, comparative, and physiological psychology decreased at an average of 5.1% per year. In contrast, during that same time period the number of new PhDs in clinical, counseling, and school psychology increased annually at an average of 5.5%. These data do not include the PsyD degree in psychology, whose inclusion would surely amplify these discrepancies. Furthermore, the emergence of the professional school movement attests to the enormous growth of professional psychology over the past 3 decades (Benjamin & Baker, 2004).

It seems reasonable to speculate that trends in doctoral production reflect and motivate changes in the undergraduate psychology curriculum. Although no current data regarding undergraduate psychology majors' interests exist, anecdotal evidence suggests that many students entering college aspire to become health service providers. Anecdotal evidence further suggests that students conceive of psychology as a helping profession rather than a laboratory science. Thus, students' narrow conception of the field may lead them to be disinclined to explore more traditional subfields within the discipline. It seems likely that student interest in applied areas increases the demand for relevant course offerings and that a preponderance of such courses may result in a diminishing interest in traditional experimental work. To be sure, we are not suggesting that burgeoning interest in applied psychology is a negative trend or that undergraduates' pursuit of courses in applied psychology is problematic. Rather, we emphasize that applied and traditional experimental subfields compose a unitary discipline and that, vocational aspirations notwithstanding, all psychology majors should be grounded in the essential components of the field.

Some Factors Outside the Discipline

The discipline of psychology has not evolved in isolation. A variety of socioeconomic, educational, and technological trends have influenced curricular decisions and directions.

The Rise of a Consumer-Driven Culture and Higher Education

Perhaps now more than ever, higher education is affected by economic concerns and motivations. Many students and parents view education in vocational rather than academic terms. They consider learning as a means to an end rather than an end in itself. Along with rising college costs, this consumer-driven orientation may help to explain some current trends in higher education.

It is not unusual for students to be simultaneously enrolled in more than one institution, a phenomenon referred to as "swirling" (Bordon, 2004).

It is also not uncommon for students to take courses at one institution while maintaining their primary enrollment status at another. In fact, 59% of students completing their bachelor's degree from 1999 to 2000 attended more than one institution (Peter & Forrest Cataldi, 2005; see also, chap. 5, this volume). These market-driven trends bear relevance to the undergraduate psychology curriculum because curricula differ across institutions in different ways. To be sure, we expect curricular differences owing to variations in faculty, resources, and student populations. These differences may become problematic, however, when they involve the essential components of our discipline. In this regard, swirling may render it more difficult for students to obtain a broad and integrated understanding of the field.

Another relevant trend relates to transfer students. Many of them take a large number of psychology courses at a 2-year institution before ultimately completing their baccalaureate in psychology at a 4-year college or university. At present, 46% of undergraduates in the United States are enrolled in 2-year colleges (American Association of Community Colleges [AACC], 2008a); half of all students who complete a baccalaureate degree attend a community college in the course of their studies (AACC, 2008b). Regardless of institution type, transferring psychology courses from one school to another can be complicated because psychology curricula differ markedly from one another. Indeed, not all courses are transferable, and students are often required to retake a course at their new institution. The phenomena of transferring and swirling may be rendered less problematic to the extent that all psychology curricula ensure students' broad-based exposure to the discipline's core.

The Accountability Movement in Higher Education

The issue of accountability is relevant, albeit indirectly, to curricular reform (e.g., P. L. Maki, 2001, 2004; O'Neil, 1992; Schneider & Schoenberg, 1998). The increasing cost of higher education has prompted various constituencies (e.g., regional accreditation bodies, state legislatures) to demand the empirical demonstration of quality education at all varieties of undergraduate institutions. Psychology has addressed these demands by assessing teaching and learning outcomes (e.g., APA Task Force on Undergraduate Psychology Major Competencies, 2002a; Dunn, Mehrotra, & Halonen, 2004; see also chap. 9, this volume). The accountability movement helps to ensure that undergraduate programs are relevant, coherent, and of high quality. In this vein, we recommend continued assessment of curricula, particularly as they relate to learning outcomes.

The Technological Revolution

The emergence of the Internet has irreversibly transformed higher education, largely through the unprecedented amount of information it makes available. Furthermore, this flood of information has the potential to shape students' conceptions of the field of psychology because it can amplify the historic discrepancy between psychology's public image and its true nature (Benjamin, 1986). New and emerging technologies are affecting the dynamics of the classroom and even impinging on the need for the traditional classroom (see chap. 7, this volume). These changes highlight the importance of making deliberate choices about the psychological content that is conveyed to students and the form this message will take (see chaps. 6 and 7, this volume, regarding the form).

Resolution: Curricular Reform Is Needed

Improving the psychology curriculum is an established tradition, as is reflecting on the broader educational experience students receive when they major in psychology (see chap. 1, this volume). A confluence of factors within and outside the discipline necessitates curricular reform. Accordingly, our recommendations in this chapter concern the appropriate scope and content of the undergraduate curriculum and the specific skills that psychology majors should acquire.

WHAT SHOULD BE TAUGHT AND LEARNED IN THE UNDERGRADUATE PSYCHOLOGY CURRICULUM?

Internal and external pressures on the discipline since the St. Mary's conference suggest a need for a common, coherent core curriculum for the undergraduate psychology major. At the same time, previous curricular work implies a lack of agreement among undergraduate psychology faculty concerning what constitutes a core curriculum for the major beyond courses in introductory psychology, scientific research methods, and statistics (Brewer et al., 1993). The need for a comprehensive core of content in psychology is clearly addressed, however, in two recent documents: an article advocating the use of quality benchmarks in undergraduate psychology programs (Dunn, McCarthy, Baker, Halonen, & Hill, 2007) and the APA *Guidelines for the Undergraduate Psychology Major* (APA, 2007a). Dunn et al. proposed quality benchmarks—criteria designed to assess performance in key domains (e.g., curriculum, student learning outcomes and development)—to advance academic program reviews by helping psychology departments define their missions and objectives and to document their effectiveness. Using benchmarks enables programs to identify their distinctive and successful qualities as well as areas in need of improvement or further development. As Dunn and colleagues noted, "when interpreted in light of an institution's mission and culture, [benchmarks] can assist program personnel in optimizing experiences for students" (p. 653).

In their discussion of benchmarks for the curricular domain in quality undergraduate programs, Dunn et al. (2007) called for a science-based curriculum (see also Halonen et al., 2003); a curricular structure specifying core requirements and course sequencing (see also APA, 2002a); a balanced, broad curriculum; and disciplinary breadth. Dunn et al. also recommended infusing training in ethics and cultural diversity at all levels in the curriculum, and they suggested community service learning as a vehicle for integration of student knowledge.

The *APA Guidelines for the Undergraduate Psychology Major* grew out of the work of the American Psychological Association Board of Educational Affairs (BEA) Task Force on Psychology Major Competencies (APA, 2007a). The BEA task force built on earlier undergraduate curricular work (e.g., Brewer et al., 1993; Buxton et al., 1952; Kulik et al., 1973; McKeachie & Milholland, 1961; Scheirer & Rogers, 1985) and also provided an extensive feedback and review process not seen in previous undergraduate curricular work. The final BEA task force report, the *Undergraduate Psychology Major Learning Goals and Outcomes* (APA Task Force on Undergraduate Psychology Major Competencies, 2002a, 2002b) was widely distributed to a variety of institutions and relevant organizations representing precollege, undergraduate, and graduate education in psychology as well as to representative professional organizations with an interest in the undergraduate psychology curriculum. This feedback was incorporated into the final version of the Learning Goals and Outcomes endorsed by the BEA in March 2002. In July 2002, the Learning Goals and Outcomes report was disseminated to APA governance groups and divisions in preparation for approval as an APA policy guideline. Later revisions were adopted as the *APA Guidelines for the Undergraduate Psychology Major* by the APA Board of Directors and the APA Council of Representatives in August 2006 (APA, 2007a).

The APA *Guidelines for the Undergraduate Psychology Major* establish 10 recommended outcome goals for the undergraduate psychology major (APA, 2007a). Specific learning outcomes are further identified for each of the 10 goals, delineating competencies expected of students with baccalaureate degrees in psychology (see also chap. 9, this volume). The guidelines do not cover or prescribe specific courses but highlight general outcomes for the major including the following: knowledge of the breath of psychology, research methods, critical thinking skills, applications, values, information literacy, communication skills, sociocultural awareness, personal development, and career planning. In addition to reaffirming the work that began at St. Mary's, which places scientific methodology at the center of the undergraduate psychology curriculum, the guidelines identify four general content domains in which the undergraduate psychology major should demonstrate knowledge and understanding. These major content areas represent the breadth and depth of the discipline and include biological bases of behavior and mental processes, learning and cognition, developmental changes across the life span, and sociocultural (identified in previous guidelines as individual differences). Knowledge of the history of psychology, "including the evolution of methods in psychology, its theoretical conflicts, and its sociocultural conflicts" is also identified as an outcome (APA, 2007a, p.12).

Our recommendations for the future teaching of psychology draw on the guidelines (APA, 2007a) and the work of Dunn et al. (2007) on quality benchmarks for undergraduate psychology programs. Both our recommendations and our perspective are consistent with the emphasis on psychological literacy and the global convergences in defining undergraduate learning outcomes described by the authors of chapter 1. In looking to the future of teaching and learning in the undergraduate psychology curriculum, we strongly affirm the continuing place of psychology as a science in the context of the liberal arts and sciences curriculum. In addition to its role as an important liberal arts discipline and as preparation for graduate study in the field, psychology will also continue to play an important role as a "hub" science (e.g., Cacioppo, 2007), serving students from related disciplines in education and the medical and social sciences. These recommendations illustrate the complementary relationship of the guidelines and the benchmarks in a quality undergraduate curriculum and in determining desired outcomes at the level of teaching and student behavior. In addition, we indicate typical areas of coursework that may help to achieve these outcomes.

Recommended Core Curriculum

The proposed curriculum emphasizes course content and learning outcomes rather than specific courses. It assumes that all students complete introductory psychology before taking other courses in the discipline. Figure 3.1, which relies on concentric circles for heuristic reasons, represents the proposed core curriculum. As depicted in its center, we recommend that all programs require psychology majors to take courses in *scientific* methods—research methods and statistics—because this material is central to the discipline. We further advise that methodology courses be taken soon after completing the introductory psychology course. The rationale for this recommendation is simple: Success in undergraduate psychology courses often requires competence in research design as well as data analysis and interpretation—the primary learning objectives of methodology courses. Moreover, without familiarity with the basics of scientific methodology, students' appreciation of all later course material in the major is seriously limited. Acquiring these skills early is beneficial to students, who are then prepared for more sophisticated work in the discipline.

As represented in Figure 3.1, further recommendations correspond to succeeding concentric circles, starting with the second one from the center. Note that outer circles depend on the knowledge and skills derived from the circles found within them. We emphasize that issues of *diversity* and *ethics* should be well integrated into the contents of all courses in each of these domains. Students should complete at least one course in each of four spe-

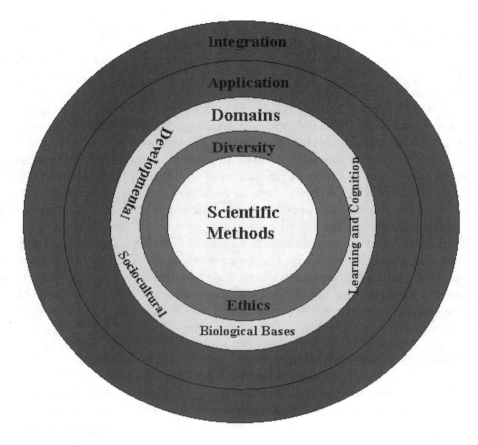

Figure 3.1. A core curriculum model for the undergraduate psychology curriculum.

cific domains: *biological bases, developmental, learning and cognition, and socio-cultural approaches*. Undergraduate programs should indicate specific learn-ing goals within each of these areas. Programs should ensure that students have opportunities for the *application* of acquired knowledge and skills. Such experiences enable students to appreciate the discipline's practical uses and may serve to expand their knowledge base and strengthen relevant skills. Students may also learn about the application of psychology through rel-evant courses. Finally, we recommend that all psychology majors participate in a *capstone* experience, in which they are encouraged to integrate disparate components represented in their knowledge base. Ideally, this culminating educational experience will involve a considerable amount of course content and a wide range of skills related to the discipline.

The following section presents recommended core curriculum content and outcomes for the psychology program and individual students as well as examples of typical courses or experiences that may help to produce the desired outcomes. As already noted, Figure 3.1 illustrates the relationships among these areas, beginning with scientific methods, issues of ethics and diversity, essential content domains, application, and an integrative capstone experience.

1. Scientific Methods

Students majoring in psychology should be well versed in scientific methodology, including descriptive and inferential statistics and research methods. Different approaches for covering these fundamental areas are possible. Both quantitative and qualitative research methods should be taught.

Program Goal. Teach the skills and behaviors of scientists.

Student Outcome. Identify and explain the scientific foundations of psychology, use and evaluate scientific evidence for psychological claims.

Typical Courses. Research methods, statistical methods, tests and measurements, psychological assessment; some courses with significant laboratory components may be appropriate here as well.

2. Diversity and Ethics

Psychologists must concern themselves with diversity, or the ways in which people differ from one another (Bucher, 2004; Matsumoto & Juang, 2008; see also APA, 2003), including ethnicity, gender, race, disability, sexual orientation, social class, culture, age, and religion. Culture is multifaceted, with connected components and influences touching on every aspect of daily life. Quality curricula need specialty courses and the infusion of culture into mainstream courses. Learning about diversity and culture should be a critical learning outcome for all students (see also chap. 4, this volume).

We believe ethics is fundamental to the study of psychology at every level. Faculty must ensure that students are familiar with the APA "Ethical Principles of Psychologists and Code of Conduct" (APA, 2002a). Faculty and students should conduct themselves in a manner consistent with the Ethics Code in all their coursework, research, and program-related activities.

Program Goal. Integrate diversity concerns across the curriculum.

Student Goal. Recognize existence of universal and culture-bound psychological principles; exhibit sensitivity, appreciation, and respect for all dimensions of human diversity.

Typical Courses. Introductory psychology, social psychology, cross-cultural psychology, clinical psychology, behavior disorders, life-span development. Although issues of diversity should be a concern in all courses, they are likely to be more salient in some than others.

Program Goal. Teach ethical awareness and skills across the curriculum.

Student Goal. Demonstrate ethical knowledge and skills appropriate to level of experience and education.

Typical Courses. Introductory psychology, research methods, clinical psychology, independent research, senior thesis.

3. Content Domains

In addition to introductory psychology and basic research methods, students should undertake coursework in four basic content domains of psychology. These domains are biological bases, learning and cognition, life-span developmental psychology, and sociocultural approaches.

Program Goal. Teach a balanced program incorporating core courses essential to the field.

Student Goal. Demonstrate knowledge of theory and research central to the major domains of the field.

Typical Courses. Learning, cognition, abnormal, personality, social psychology, biopsychology, animal behavior, life-span development, cross-cultural psychology, psychometrics.

4. Application

The application of knowledge gained during a student's program of study is important. Quality programs provide students with opportunities to use their knowledge in an applied setting, such as human service agencies, laboratories, or independent study opportunities. Thus, service learning can contribute to the application of psychological knowledge. Students may also gain an appreciation of the discipline's practical utility—how, for example, research findings can be used to improve employee well-being, manage business matters, or improve product design—through relevant coursework.

Program Goal. Teach a program with sufficient breadth to offer students exposure to a range of opportunities and applications in the field.

Student Goal. Demonstrate knowledge of theory and research associated with domains beyond the core subjects.

Typical Courses. Health psychology, psychology of adjustment, industrial and organizational psychology, human factors, counseling, careers in psychology, internship.

5. Integration

To encourage analysis, synthesis, and integration of students' knowledge and experience, we recommend a culminating experience for all senior psychology majors. This may include capstone courses, internships, and research projects in collaboration with a faculty mentor. We note, too, that the authors of chapter 1 recommend integrative experiences consistent with contemporary, transdisciplinary liberal learning outcomes, ideally to develop lifelong learning alumni who are psychologically literate citizens.

Program Goal. Teach a program that integrates multiple perspectives and themes.

Student Goal. Demonstrate knowledge of overarching themes, broad or enduring controversies, and major problems in psychology.

Typical Courses. History and systems of psychology, advanced theory courses (e.g., personality, social, motivation, learning, development), independent research, special topics or other capstone activities.

Content in the Introductory Psychology Course

The introductory psychology course is the foundation for the psychology major as well as one of the cornerstones of social science general education programs nationwide. Around 1.5 million students take introductory psychology classes every year (Griggs, Jackson, & Napolitano, 1994). For psychology majors, intermediate and upper level specialized courses expand on material covered in the introductory course. For nonmajors, introductory psychology may be the only psychology class they ever take. Given the ubiquitous relevance of psychology to other majors and fields, most jobs, and the world in general, as well as the many contributions an understanding of psychology can have to personal growth and development, all students need to receive a common core of content.

Although many institutions already standardize the textbooks adopted for the introductory course, few standardize the content of what is taught. Variability in the content of the introductory course is accentuated because few faculty are well versed in all areas of psychology. Such broad training is not generally a part of graduate programs in which students are typically required to gain breadth in one or two areas of psychology beyond their main focus of study. Naturally, too, there is also variability in how well this course is taught at the postsecondary level. Given that the introductory course serves as a foundation for the major and is sometimes the only exposure to the field for nonmajors, widely variable content and delivery do the field and the students a disservice. Parallel to our call for a common core to the psychology major, we suggest a common core for the introductory psychology course.

Our recommendation for core content for the postsecondary introductory psychology class builds on established APA policy and existing guidelines. Although the guidelines (APA, 2007a) were designed for the major as a whole, we suggest that the introductory course also cover the same basic core areas as recommended for the major. The core content also builds on and is consistent with the curriculum offered in Advanced Placement Psychology (AP; College Board, 2007b) and *The National Standards for High School Psychology Curricula* (APA, 2005). The College Board develops the AP Psychology course on the basis of recommendations of psychology faculty consultants, and the course content is monitored and assessed by the Educational Testing Service.

The explicit understanding is that students who score high enough on the AP psychology exam receive college credit for introductory psychology. The irony that many AP psychology students are getting a more thorough exposure to the field of psychology than some students who take this course in college is at least partially attributable to the lack of national consistency in the content of the introductory psychology course.

The Psychology Minor

Consistent with the model advocated for the major, the ideal psychology minor should include introductory psychology and coursework in research methods or statistics. As the model shown in Figure 3.1 advocates, methods and statistics are at the center of education in psychology. Students who minor in psychology must have a working knowledge of these disciplinary tools to truly appreciate the material presented in content courses. Some judicious substitutions might be possible here, as could be the case when a student's major area of study includes a course or courses containing research methods or quantitatively based reasoning. If meaningful experience with methods and data analysis are removed, however, then we believe there would be little justification to label this concentration a minor in psychology. Additional coursework in the minor should reflect the content domains presented in Figure 3.1 to the extent department resources and curricular constraints allow.

Impact and Implications of the Proposed Curriculum

What will the impact of the proposed curricular changes be? Put another way, what will these changes prepare undergraduate psychology students to do? At the risk of sounding glib, these changes will prepare them for whatever they decide to do in the future. We believe that a rigorous undergraduate psychology major will prepare students for graduate education in psychology or some other field, just as it will prepare them for a meaningful career. We know that very few students pursue an advanced degree in psychology, but we also know that the psychology major is excellent training for the world of work (e.g., Appleby, 2000, 2007; Kuther & Morgan, 2004; Palladino Schultheiss, 2008; Rajecki et al., 2005). The skills acquired in the proposed core curriculum, both in terms of content and learning outcomes, will increase the likelihood of potential success and personal satisfaction no matter what paths students follow after earning a baccalaureate degree.

RECOMMENDATIONS AND CONCLUSION

This discussion points to several clear recommendations concerning undergraduate education in psychology:

1. In light of the model presented in this chapter, psychology departments should evaluate their programs using quality benchmarks (Dunn et al., 2007).

2. Curricular review should pay particular attention to those areas that have been neglected in the past, which are likely to include matters of ethics, diversity, and integrative experiences.
3. The introductory psychology course should mirror the core model for the psychology major.
4. Introductory psychology should be a prerequisite for all other psychology courses.
5. Psychology majors and minors should enroll in research methods and statistics as soon as possible after completing introductory psychology.
6. Ongoing assessment and evaluation of the undergraduate curriculum in psychology, as well as its learning outcomes, is essential.
7. Future assessment and evaluation of the undergraduate curriculum in psychology, as well as its learning outcomes, is essential.

Dramatic changes in the 21st century threaten the traditional identity of psychology. Despite these changes, we believe that a core of scientific concepts and principles defines the discipline. Nowhere is this more important than in the undergraduate psychology curriculum. We reaffirm the place of scientific psychology in the liberal arts tradition. We advocate a core curriculum emphasizing scientific methodology and ensuring breadth and depth in substantive content areas of the discipline. We stress a clear focus on diversity and ethics throughout the psychology curriculum. The recommended core provides a coherent undergraduate experience for psychology majors and sufficient flexibility to accommodate the unique needs of individual programs and students.

4

PSYCHOLOGY STUDENTS TODAY AND TOMORROW

LINH NGUYEN LITTLEFORD, WILLIAM BUSKIST, SUSAN M. FRANTZ, DENNIS B. GALVAN, ROBERT W. HENDERSEN, MAUREEN A. McCARTHY, MELANIE C. PAGE, AND ANTONIO E. PUENTE

> Imagine that you are a monkey living in a jungle. One day you fall from a branch and plummet into a lake. Unable to swim, you splash and struggle to stay afloat. After a while, you become exhausted and begin to sink. Suddenly a hand reaches in, pulls you out of the water, and places you on the embankment. You are so grateful for being alive that you decide to find someone who needs rescuing. You sit at the edge of the lake, keeping an eye on the calm water surface. After waiting for a long time, you see something splashing wildly in the water. Excited that you finally have your opportunity to be a rescuer, you reach in and pull out . . . a fish.
> —Based on a Traditional Tanzanian Folktale

Who are the students in undergraduate psychology today and tomorrow? What sorts of characteristics do they bring into the classroom? What kinds of key developmental issues do these students face during the college years? What do they need from their experiences to thrive in higher education? Good intentions, without knowing the answers to these questions, will not be enough for administrators, educators, and advisors to be effective in their respective roles. Like the monkey from the folktale, assuming everyone has the same needs can result in harmful consequences.

Tomorrow's students surely will be different from today's students, so identifying, supporting, celebrating, and taking advantage of diversity is necessarily a process of continuous change. Postsecondary institutions need to be inclusive of students from all backgrounds not only to redress past inequalities and promote equality in the future (Adams, 1992) but also to thrive in the global context, to avoid the perils of isolation, and to benefit from the enrichment that diversity infuses into intellectual discourse (Magolda, 2001; Villalpando, 2002). Student diversity is a key resource for enriching learning, teaching, research, and applications of psychological science (Milem, 2003). Having students from diverse backgrounds with different experiences enhances opportunities for students to engage in dialogues in which a wider range of perspectives is represented. The variability among human perspectives within the United States and globally is important and should be included as a vital part of curriculum, research, academic activities, psychological knowledge, and social interactions.

In this chapter, we provide information and suggestions relevant to domains about which postsecondary institutions need to be knowledgeable to ensure that students from all backgrounds, disability statuses, and other personal characteristics subject to stereotyping have access to higher education and opportunities to engage in the intellectual pursuits of our discipline. We address all the domains outlined by the inclusive excellence scorecard (IE; D. A. Williams, Berger, & McClendon, 2005), a comprehensive approach to evaluating diversity progress at higher education institutions. First, we address the *access and equity* domain by discussing the demographic trends and the ways students vary within undergraduate education in general and in psychology. Second, we address the *student learning and development* domain by highlighting the intellectual, interpersonal, and intrapersonal changes students experience in college. Third, we address the *diversity in the formal and informal curriculum* domain by discussing approaches to improving inclusion in the curriculum. Fourth, we address the *campus climate* domain by discussing the multiple components of campus climate and outlining ways to promote positive climate for students from diverse backgrounds including race and ethnicity, gender, sexual orientation, religious identification, age, and disability. Finally, we extend the IE scorecard by discussing the ethical issues relating to the decrease in gender diversity in our profession and the balance between recruiting students to our discipline and informing them about the boundaries of a psychology undergraduate degree.

ACCESS AND EQUITY

Clarice's family life was chaotic, colored by poverty and abuse. Her family moved frequently, one step ahead of the rent collector, often homeless, living in tents, and, for a while, in an old ice cream truck. When she fussed as a young child, her family gave her alcohol to calm her. Her mother is disabled and has depended on her since Clarice was a teenager. With substance abuse problems of her own, Clarice did not finish high school. At 19, clean and sober, she talked her way into a community college, where, with neither a high school diploma nor a general equivalency diploma, she grew more academically skilled in a supportive environment. After completing her associate's degree, she transferred to a large university, where she blossomed. She has been on the dean's list every semester, and faculty recognize her as the kind of student who lights up a class. Clarice is part of a team conducting research in gerontology, and she has realistic aspirations to pursue graduate studies.

Undergraduate Students in General

Clarice is one of many examples of the kinds of people who become successful college students. Undergraduate students today, like Clarice, come from a wide range of backgrounds, and this diversity will increase in the future. Using high school enrollment patterns, researchers have long tracked demographic changes and offered projections for undergraduates who will be entering U.S. institutions over the course of the next 2 decades. Between 1980 and 2002, enrollment in the United States increased for students who enrolled immediately in college after completing high school, from 1.5 to 1.8 million students (Peter & Horn, 2005). In 2005, the year for which the most recent data are available, 1.5 million people enrolled as 1st-year students in 4-year U.S. colleges or universities and 1.1 million in 2-year colleges (Digest of Education Statistics, 2005b).

Between 2004 and 2015, the student population in degree-granting institutions will be more ethnically diverse, with the largest increase in Hispanic students (42%) and the smallest increase in White, non-Hispanic students (6%). Enrollment rates will also increase for American Indian or Alaska Natives (30%), African Americans (27%), Asian or Pacific Islanders (28%), and nonresident aliens (34%; National Center for Education Statistics [NCES], 2006).

Over the past 20 years, women's enrollment in college has increased at twice the pace of men's enrollment. Women earn approximately 60% of associate's degrees and 57% of bachelor's degrees at U.S. institutions (Peter & Horn, 2005). Between 2004 and 2015, the rate of increase in enrollment in degree-granting institutions for women (18%) will continue to be higher than for men (10%; NCES, 2006).

Between 1990 and 2005, enrollment of younger students grew more rapidly than the number of older college students, but this pattern is expected to change. The NCES predicts a proportionately larger increase in enrollment of students over the age of 25 in both community colleges and universities by 2016 (Digest of Education Statistics, 2005a).

In terms of religious affiliation, the majority of college students in the United States identify with Christianity (28% Roman Catholics, 13% Baptists, and 11 % other Christians). About 17% of the students do not claim a religious affiliation, and the number of students who are Jewish, Muslim, and members of other religions each falls at levels below 10% (Higher Education Research Institute, 2008).

Visibility of lesbian, gay, bisexual, and transgendered (LGBT) students has increased, as evidenced by the rising number of campus LGBT centers. In 1994, there were seven such centers with full-time directors compared with approximately 100 in 2006 ("LGBT Centers Today: A Snapshot," 2006). It is impossible to know whether the visibility is due to the increasing number of LGBT students or to increasing cultural acceptance of these students. For example, the number of individuals who accept and support gays has increased (Fassinger, 2008), a trend that is supported by recent legislation that legalizes gay marriage in Massachusetts. Similarly, several nations have provided legal protections for decades and access to marriage since 2001.

Students vary with respect to physical and mental abilities. Approximately 9% of students reported having a disability in the 1999–2000 academic year. The largest percentage of these students reported having a mobility impairment (29%), followed by a mental illness (17%), physical health impairment (15%), visual or hearing problem (12%), a learning disability (11%), or an unspecified disability (15%; NCES, 2003).

Today's students are becoming increasingly linguistically diverse. Many U.S. students speak one or more non-English languages. The percentage of children who speak a language other than English in the home has increased steadily from 8.5% in 1979 to 20% in 2005 (NCES, 2005). The number of students enrolled in U.S. public elementary and secondary schools who did not speak English well increased by 57% between 1995 and 1996 and 2004 and 2005 (ETS, 2008).

Students come from diverse socioeconomic backgrounds, and many work while taking courses in postsecondary institutions. In 2007, 73% of part-time enrolled and 37% of full-time enrolled 1st-year students were employed or were looking for employment (U.S. Department of Labor, 2008). In 2003 to 2004, between 76% and 88% of college students not financially dependent on family worked full time while enrolled (McSwain & Davis, 2007).

Students also enter college with different levels of academic preparation. Almost half of the students (41%) are underprepared for basic college level work. Approximately 40% of students enrolled in two or more remedial courses completed an associate's or bachelor's degree, whereas 69% of students who did not take remedial courses finished (Wirt et al., 2004). However, an increasingly larger percentage of high school seniors are graduating with one or more Advanced Placement (AP) courses (Freeman, 2004).

Finally, the diversity of students also is enhanced by the number of international students enrolled in higher education in the United States and the number of U.S. students studying abroad. In 2006 to 2007, 580,000 international students attended U.S. colleges and universities with most of the students coming from India, China, South Korea, Japan, Taiwan, and Canada (Institute of International Education, 2007a, 2007b). Similarly, in 2006, over 223,000 U.S. students studied abroad, an increase of 8.5% over the previous year (Institute of International Education, 2007c). Most U.S. students travel to the United Kingdom, Italy, Spain, France, Australia, and Mexico (Institute of International Education, 2007d).

Undergraduate Students in Psychology

Within the United States, psychology is the fourth largest college major, with the number of psychology graduates increasing 20% since 1996 (NCES, 2007a, 2007b). In 2005, out of approximately 1.5 million bachelor's degrees awarded, approximately 88,000 were in psychology. The number of high school students taking the AP Psychology test grew from approximately 3,000 in 1992 to over 113,000 in 2008 (College Board, 2008). In 2007, approximately 65% of students entering college received college credit for introductory psychology on the basis of their AP exam score (College Board, 2007a). As the authors of chapter 1 pointed out, undergraduate psychology's popularity as a major is now a global phenomenon as well.

The percentage of ethnic minority students earning bachelor's degrees in psychology increased between 1995 and1996 and 2003 and2004. Hispanic American students demonstrated the largest gains with a 44% increase (5,036 to 7,252), whereas African American students increased by 41% (6,028 to 8,479). Although the number of Native American students graduating with a bachelor's degree in psychology remains small ($N = 596$), there has been a 27% increase over the past decade. The percentage of Asian American students graduating with a psychology degree increased by 18% (3,666 to 4,345), but European American students earning bachelor's degrees in psychology increased only 1% (55,905 to 56,515; American Psychological Association [APA] Task Force on Undergraduate Psychology Major Competencies, 2002a).

LEARNING AND DEVELOPMENT

Maybe I was not encouraged to go to college because only 4 out of 51 students graduating in my class went on to complete a bachelor's degree. I suppose that would be understandable considering how ill prepared we were for higher education. For instance, biology class literally consisted of copied coloring book pages and a few crayons. While in college, I felt myself growing intellectually, and it felt great. By my junior and senior years, I was on the dean's list and held numerous other honors. I was inspired, capable, and eager for graduate school. I remember feeling so lucky that the private college took the risk of accepting me. I was lucky to find my way through a handful of people who were willing to give me the chance that I needed. I completed a master's program and won several research awards. Afterward I entered a doctoral program at a prominent institution, which is one of the best programs in my field. I would not be where I am if I had been evaluated from how I appeared on paper. (W.H.)

Instruction, curriculum, and advising should recognize the diversity of student development trajectories. Like W.H., students bring with them a host of individual differences in terms of their personalities and academic and life experiences (Jones & McEwen, 2000). Complementing these differences is the fact that during their stay in college, students change intellectually, interpersonally, and intrapersonally (Chickering & Reisser, 1993; Choa & Good, 2004; Magolda, 2001). In addition, students often have multiple identities, some visible and some not (e.g., sexual orientation, religious orientation; Abes, Jones, & McEwen, 2007; LaFromboise, Coleman, & Gerton, 1993). Besides accomplishing basic developmental tasks, students seek to resolve their career identities (Bubany, Krieshok, Black, & McKay, 2008). To be effective in their roles, educators and advisors need to vary their approaches to recognize the different types of students and their changing developmental needs.

Teaching and Learning in Developmental Context

As students progress through postsecondary education, they become more independent in their thinking, more flexible and less reliant on dogmatic thinking, more liberal in their attitudes, and broader in their intellectual interests (Chickering & Reisser, 1993). Saenze and Barrera (2007) found that between their first and senior years, students perceived improvements in their relative competency in a wide range of college-related skills, including self-understanding, writing ability, and public speaking ability. All courses should stress student engagement, self-regulation, written and oral expression, and critical thought. A cognitive development perspective is consistent with the quality benchmarks perspective proposed in Dunn, McCarthy, Baker, Halonen, and Hill (2007) and used to best achieve psychological literacy (see chap. 1, this volume), quality instruction and faculty development (see chap. 2, this volume), and the core undergraduate curriculum (see chap. 3, this volume). By assessing the goals of particular courses in a developmental context, course sequences and prerequisites, psychology departments can tailor course demands to the emerging student capabilities.

Student Development and Diversity

Students often have to accommodate multiple identities simultaneously. For example, students need to identify and make meaning of what their ethnicity, sexual orientation, gender, religion, and more mean for them (Abes et al., 2007; LaFromboise et al., 1993). Additionally, from students' perspectives, institutional contexts shift dramatically when students make the transition from secondary school to college and from community college to university. Such changes heavily influence the development of students with disabilities (Spellings & Monroe, 2007). For example, secondary schools assume responsibility for helping students, but in postsecondary education, students assume total responsibility for seeking services. Psychology faculty and advisors need to be aware of the challenges diverse students face and provide support for these students in their quest to become college graduates.

CURRICULAR DIVERSITY

I have always been a small-town girl unexposed to diversity and alternative religions. It was never forced upon me to practice a certain religion or declare myself of a certain race. My only obligation was to just be. If I had not been exposed to different cultures in college, I would be a member of the ethnocentric group that only considers one way of life to be correct. Exposure to diversity motivated me to pursue a doctoral degree because it has taught me that there is knowledge to be gained from all perceptions. (C.H.)

Part of the new generation of students are children of immigrants, who are first- generation college students. Unlike the typical first generation student, we're not only looking for academic guidance and social support but we are also looking to find professors and teachings that integrate various perspectives. It's not just about teaching the typical Western-based theories but about integrating our cultures and beliefs and asserting that our beliefs and customs are not "wrong" or "weird." (A.L.)

It's disheartening sometimes to read research articles that continue to use nondiverse samples. Some researchers might argue that they get a stronger "effect" with fewer "extraneous" variables to consider. It's also disheartening when all you learn in class is about how minority people are scoring lower or doing worse than the majority group. Psychology teachers must challenge students to think critically about these issues. (A.L.)

The call to integrate diversity into the psychology curriculum is not new (Bronstein & Quina, 1988; Whitten, 1993). The diversity movement reflects the origins of psychological science with its long-standing interest in individual differences. One of the strengths of undergraduate education in psychology is its emphasis that students understand, engage, and contribute to the world in which they live by stressing the sociocultural nature of pedagogy. Not making diversity a central part of the psychology curriculum limits the generalizability and applicability of psychological understanding and pedagogy (Puente et al., 1993). More important, students who participate in university-facilitated discussions about diversity issues have better conflict resolution and critical thinking skills, have more positive interactions with peers from diverse backgrounds, and are supportive of civic engagement and social justice (Hurtado, 2007; Laird, 2005; Mayhew & Fernandez, 2007).

Formal Curriculum

Within the psychology curriculum, educators can incorporate diversity into formal courses in three ways: diversity-focused courses, diversity-infused courses, and interdisciplinary courses. Although we discuss these methods separately, we encourage institutions and educators to use all three approaches concurrently. A multimodal approach acknowledges that diversity is an important topic to study in its own right and emphasizes its impact on other psychological and scholarly topics.

Approximately 60% of institutions of higher learning use the *diversity-focused* model, requiring students to take at least one course that focuses on a diversity topic (Humphreys, 2000). Examples include African American, disability, gender, human diversity, religion, and social inequality courses. These courses portray psychology's applicability both to the communities in which instructors and students live and the world at large. They should also address situations that make an individual part of a nonmajority group culture from a scientifically based sociocultural and biological perspective (Gloria, Rieckman, & Rush, 2000).

A *diversity-infused* approach includes diversity as a unifying theme to course materials. This approach places diversity as central to the heart of psychology and on par with other critical topics in the field. For example, a child development or an abnormal psychology course could use textbooks that include a section on diversity and cultural perspectives in every chapter (e.g., Santrock, 2008; Sue, Sue, & Sue, 2006). Although all psychology instructors should use the diversity-infused approach (see resources at http://www.teachpsych.org), integrating diversity into the course content is crucial for those teaching the introduction to psychology course. For over 3 decades, this course has ranked in the top five most popular courses taken by students completing bachelor's degrees (NCES, 2004). It may be the only psychology course most nonpsychology majors will ever take. Thus, it may shape their perceptions of the discipline. The introductory course also is the foundation course for psychology majors, and therefore a diversity-infused introduction to psychology course provides a paradigm for upper division psychology courses to follow. Because of its potential impact on both psychology majors and nonmajors, the content of this course should accurately reflect the centrality of diversity issues to psychological science (for suggestions, see Trimble, Stevenson, & Worell, 2003).

Interdisciplinary courses serve as a third approach to the curriculum wherein psychology faculty, in conjunction with instructors in other academic disciplines, integrate diversity-focused psychological perspectives to address specific topics. For example, psychology instructors could team up with faculty in Chinese studies or anthropology to educate students about the variety of ways humans cope with stressors and treat psychological disorders (e.g., Zhang, 2007). Other examples include teaming up with family scientists and nutritionists to address the obesity epidemic or coteaching with biology instructors to discuss the physical, psychological, cultural, and social factors associated with the AIDS epidemic. Additional examples include race and citizenship in America, interdisciplinary perspectives on sociolinguistics, and the psychology of leadership (for other examples, see Davis, 1995).

Informal Curriculum

Education about diversity, however, should not be limited only to the curriculum. This is consistent with the aspirational outcome of developing lifelong learners who are psychologically literate citizens proposed in chapter 1. Campus and social climate surrounding curricular experiences provide a plethora of informal educational opportunities. Collaborative activities such as group discussions, projects, presentations, and activities may facilitate appreciation for diversity because of more frequent, informal interactions with peers. However, informal curricular activities (out of class activities) also enhance diversity and include community involvement, campus engagement, practica, internships, and research projects. Such activities could be credit bearing (i.e., either required or extra credit) or tied to graduation or experiential demands (e.g., practica) of a degree-bearing curriculum as a means to engage all students.

Delivery and Acceptance of Diversity Instruction

Beyond the formal and informal curricular aspects of diversity, faculty should deliver the curriculum in an inclusive fashion: Teaching should encourage student understanding of access, equity, cumulative advantages, and inclusiveness. Faculty and students also should strive to accept and appreciate diverse perspectives. Instructors need to understand and believe in the value of diversity. Instructors also should be culturally competent and comfortable with teaching students with a wide range of backgrounds and personal characteristics (see APA, 2003; chap. 3, this volume). For example, as a result of lack of knowledge, some instructors might feel uncomfortable when they interact with students with a hearing disability. Similar to members of other groups, people who are deaf have alternated among many descriptors when referring to their cultural group, from *deaf and dumb* to *deaf mute* to *hearing impaired*, to currently *deaf* or *hard of hearing*. It is important for faculty to recognize that the first four labels have negative connotations, whereas the terms *deaf* and *hard of hearing* are more factual. It is appropriate to ask students what terminology they prefer and whether the disability might affect their performance in the class. However, instructors should keep in mind the wide range of disabling conditions and the ways students compensate for such conditions. One student who is visually impaired may need all handouts enlarged and printed on paper; another may prefer them as e-mail attachments, to be magnified and viewed on a computer screen. When instructors include class discussions, they need to ensure that students with speech impairments or sign language interpreters have opportunities to participate fully. Instructors need to be flexible to make sure students with disabilities have opportunities to demonstrate mastery of the material.

Instructors should invite colleagues, community members, and other guests to their classes to present information on particular diversity-related issues on which they have yet to acquire expertise. In addition, instructors need to be able to address the different reactions students might have to diversity-related materials. For example, they need to be sensitive to students from visually recognizable minority groups, particularly when the student is the only class member from one of those groups. Including course materials about diverse cultures can help students from underrepresented groups feel included in the course. At the same time, however, instructors need to be aware that even when not asked to speak about their experiences, some students may feel discomfort when the course content makes their groups the focus of these discussions. Instructors should be attentive to these reactions and offer the necessary support to these students. For example, instructors could have all students provide anonymous feedback about course content and classroom dynamics and offer to meet with individual students. Instructors should discuss multiple types of diversity so that all students can alternate between speaking about their experiences as members of marginalized groups and as members of dominant groups.

CAMPUS CLIMATE

I came from Uganda. I was so afraid of how I was supposed to relate to Americans because I was different. When I came to college, I was just so amazed by the different skin colors, hair, nationalities, and accents. I met students from so many different countries, most of them are now my close friends. I have learned that we are all the same no matter which part of the globe we came from. Working with all these students is one of the reasons why we perform even better in class. This college and all these diverse people made me feel like I blended in from the very beginning. (N.S.)

To succeed in college, students need to perceive that they are integral and valued members of the community. This feeling of belonging depends largely on how students perceive the classroom and campus climate (Hurtado, Griffin, Arellano, & Cuellar, 2008; Kuh, Kinzie, Buckley, Bridges, & Hayek, 2006). For example, Kuh et al. (2006, 2007) found that students who interacted with faculty members outside of class (e.g., discussing course-related materials, conversing about career options, or collaborating with a professor on a project) perceived the campus climate more positively and were more likely to graduate. The size and selectivity of the institution did not predict whether students stayed or completed their degrees. Rather, students' gender, socioeconomic status, and level of engagement contributed significantly and directly to their learning and cognitive development. Thus, these sorts of positive educational outcomes are within the spheres of influence of students, faculty, and institutions.

Although most campus climate research has focused on racial and ethnic groups and gender identification (e.g., Hurtado et al., 2008; Kuh et al., 2006, 2007), the findings appear generalizable to other underrepresented groups as well. Institutional policies and practices need to include input from individuals of diverse backgrounds, ensuring that they are actively involved in creating opportunities for all members of the institution to express their identities. With a clear commitment from community members and the necessary supportive resources, institutions can ensure that opportunities for success are available to all students.

Aspects of Supportive Climate

Supportive climates have multiple aspects. We focus on five of them: compositional diversity; psychological perceptions; social interactions; historical legacies; and social, political, and legal contexts (Hurtado et al., 2008; Kuh et al., 2006, 2007; Milem, Chang, & Antonio, 2005). The compositional diversity of any institution involves having a critical mass of individuals from diverse backgrounds (Milem et al., 2005). Students and family members will look at the compositional diversity to gauge the extent to which the institution values and supports individuals from diverse backgrounds. Physical and intellectual accesses are necessary for compositional diversity (Jaeger & Bowman, 2005) so that education is free of barriers (e.g., financial, physical, and social). For example, institutions can make appropriate technology available to all students, including those who cannot afford their own access or those who live in geographical areas where technological access is limited. Increasing the number of diverse students and faculty members also increases opportunities for interactions across cultural and demographic barriers (Kuh et al., 2006, 2007). Many resources exist to guide institutions to recruit and retain diverse students and faculty (see APA Task Force on Undergraduate Psychology Major Competencies, 2002a; APA's Web site links to associations focused on diverse groups; http://www.apa.org/about/division.html; http://www.teachpsych.org/diversity).

Recruiting a diverse student body is only the first step in developing a welcoming climate: The presence of more people from diverse backgrounds does not automatically precipitate more positive interactions (Hurtado et al., 2008; Milem et al., 2005). The second component of campus climate, psychological perceptions, encompasses students' experiences with and perceptions of differential treatment due to group membership or other personal characteristics subject to stereotyping, and the extent to which institution, faculty, staff, and other students value diversity (Hurtado, 1992). For example, European American students often perceive the campus climate more positively and report fewer experiences with harassment and negative treatment than do underrepresented minority students (Rankin & Reason, 2005). Particularly for ethnic minority students, campus climate is related directly to academic achievement, mental health, and social integration (Hurtado et al., 2008). Psychology departments should recruit, retain, and otherwise support faculty members with the expertise to teach and conduct research in which diversity is a variable of interest (APA, 2003). In addition, the presence of faculty members who speak more than one language recognizes the limitations of communication in English and signals the value of multiple cultural competencies.

The third component of campus climate, social interactions, consists of informal and formal opportunities for intergroup interactions that are either unstructured (friendships and peer interactions) or university facilitated (campus programs and curricula-related activities; Hurtado et al., 2008). Students have positive perceptions of institutions that include diversity-focused courses in their curriculum, intergroup dialogue programs, or service or living learning programs (Hurtado et al., 2008). Dickerson, Bell, Lasso, and Waits (2002) showed that White students are more likely to have fewer non-White friends than African American students are to have non–African-American friends, yet the latter group is often perceived to be more likely to self-segregate. In addition, for cultural minority students, having friends from one's own cultural group can have positive consequences, including feelings of comfort and support when having to deal with negative experiences related to one's cultural background (Dickerson et al., 2002).

The fourth component, historical legacy of inclusion or exclusion, includes acknowledgment of previous institutional and community practices that have favored members from the dominant culture and the examination of how current policies might inadvertently exclude students from some cultural communities (Milem et al., 2005). For example, not being able to use a building because of lack of elevators or ramps would keep a student with mobility issues from attending class in that building. However, these students will probably understand that not all buildings on campus can be retrofitted with ramps, elevators, and accessible restrooms but would expect classes or other programs to be moved to accessible buildings so that they could participate in these offerings.

The fifth component, legal, political, and societal contexts, may be partially beyond the control of individual institutions, but the ways institutions interpret their roles within these contexts can profoundly affect climate. For example, interpreting how affirmative action should be implemented given both state and federal laws or deciding what constitutes a *reasonable* accommodation for students with disabilities or establishing policies for undocumented students may influence the institution's welcoming character (e.g., Grossman, 2001).

Building a Supportive Climate

To foster a supportive learning environment, it is essential that psychology departments incorporate an inclusionary climate in their assessment goals. Climate is the institution's responsibility (see APA Task Force on Undergraduate Psychology Major Competencies, 2002a; Kuh et al., 2008, for institutional inclusionary strategies), but there are discipline-specific strategies that psychology programs can consider. For example, psychology departments might consider recruiting psychology students from underrepresented groups, both from high schools and those students already in college. Toward this end, departments might offer brief, engaging presentations on psychological topics to high school students and to college student groups and campus offices (e.g., Hispanic student organization, LGBT organization, student veterans group, students with disabilities program, multicultural office). Departments can also encourage students to participate in colloquia, brown bag sessions, film series, and invited lectures and display posters with student authors in hallways and on their Web sites. They can also extend *open houses* to high school classes to make field trips where students can tour laboratories, hear lectures, and meet psychology students. When planning colloquia or other student-focused activities, departments should consult and coordinate with the office for students with disabilities to ensure students who have hearing impairments have access to the information. Because students' families can heavily influence their career and academic major decisions, to increase family support, departments should provide information to relatives of psychology students about psychology as a science and the occupational opportunities it affords. For example, many Asian parents discourage their college-age children from selecting social sciences and humanities majors because they assume that careers in these fields lack prestige and are not financially lucrative (Tang, Fouad, & Smith, 1999). To appeal to the importance placed on education and social status by these and other parents, departments should highlight the academic rigor of psychological training and list college professor as one potential career their children could pursue with a graduate degree. If the psychology major is by competitive admission, psychology departments should use flexible and inclusive admission criteria (see Kuh et al., 2007, for more suggestions).

To signal inclusion, departmental newsletters and other publications should use inclusive language. Departments should ensure that artwork, architecture, bulletin boards, brochures, and Web pages accurately reflect the range of student diversity represented on campus (for additional suggestions, see Dunn et al., 2007). They should be mindful, too, of student observances of culturally significant holidays (e.g., not schedule exams on major holy days). Psychology departments might also consider inviting students, staff, and faculty members from diverse backgrounds to provide periodic feedback about departmental access and inclusion efforts.

Excellent Advising Is Central to Climate

A key element of effective college and career advising is to encourage students to become aware of their expectations, strengths, values, challenges, and conflicts, and to develop high but realistic aspirations. For example, if students believe that they will go to a highly competitive graduate program, discuss the prospects of this possibility with them but have specific suggestions for how to make their goals achievable as well as for alternative backup plans. Advisors should also ensure that their students have early access to faculty mentors who can guide them as they begin to pursue research within the discipline.

A student's first year on campus is critical in terms of establishing an identity, choosing a major, and developing the study skills that will serve the student throughout college. Faculty should participate in student campus forums, serve as advisors to student organizations, and invite students to help them with their research. In addition, faculty and advisors should send encouraging e-mails, letters, and comments to students who do well academically.

Advisors should serve as liaisons for students to connect them with the learning community and draw students' attention to opportunities for intellectual engagement, including research and disciplinary networking possibilities. Advisors need to select communication methods appropriate to students' needs (e.g., use interpreters, captioning, and e-mails to converse with a deaf student, and not use e-mails to communicate with a student with dexterity disabilities). Faculty members have similar responsibilities for supporting students in their classes. For example, they could identify well in advance and e-mail struggling students who are not engaged in the learning process to express concern, offer specific assistance, and direct them to resources that will help them succeed. Faculty with students with disabilities should work with the campus disability office to ensure that students have access to all campus resources for learning.

POST BACCALAUREATE ISSUES

Education is very important in today's society, and jobs are harder to obtain without a degree. I believe everyone should be exposed to all cultures to eliminate ethnocentrism and its negative effects. (C.H.)

It is important to have student diversity in all forms because an individual's varied experiences can greatly inform one's view of the world, what one is passionate about, as well as one's direction in life. Real-life knowledge of an issue fosters a deep understanding of the concerns surrounding those factors. In general, it would strengthen the field if more diverse viewpoints and areas of expertise were represented. (M.Z.)

Administrators, educators, and advisors need to strike a balance between increasing the pipeline of psychology majors and ensuring that students know about both the strengths and limitations of a psychology degree. Educators and advisors must continue to recruit students to psychology, but they should provide those students with accurate information about earning potential with a psychology undergraduate degree. Educators and advisors should provide students with the necessary tools to market their skills acquired by earning an undergraduate degree in psychology. For those students who are interested in pursuing a graduate degree, accurate assessments of the likelihood of admission into graduate programs and of earning potential with a graduate degree in psychology must be provided. For example, studies indicate that from 28% to 82% of students wish to pursue an advanced degree (as reported in A. Hall, 1982); however, data suggest that only about 10% of students actually pursue advanced degrees (APA, 2003). In addition, when students do pursue an advanced degree, they often face a high debt load. The median debt level in 2005 for clinical PsyDs, degrees to become licensed psychologists often offered at private universities, was $100,000, nearly double what it was in 1997 (APA, Center for Workforce Analysis and Research, 2007b). The median debt level for clinical PhDs was $55,000, up 50% from 2001. The debt load for research-focused PhDs was less but still substantial ($34,000). Although psychology undergraduate and graduate degrees offer similar opportunities to other social science majors (e.g., sociology) and better opportunities than others (e.g., foreign languages), it must be acknowledged that in comparison with still others (e.g., medicine, law, business) they offer only limited potential for recovering the expense associated with the cost of higher education.

Although students majoring in psychology are becoming more ethnically diverse, a significant gender imbalance exists, with women earning 78% of undergraduate degrees in psychology. Psychologists should recruit and retain more men or the gender disparity may limit the diversity of perspectives in academic discourse and the range of psychological services to meet the needs of people from different backgrounds. Historically, when there has been a decline in a discipline's prestige, value, and salaries, men have left the profession and women have entered it to fill those gaps (APA, Committee on Women in Psychology, 1995).

Psychologists need to ensure that this does not occur in psychology by working continuously as a discipline to increase salaries for students earning degrees in psychology. In addition, they need to expose all students equally to role models within each subfield of psychology as well as to help them acquire skills to be competitive for many jobs that are consistent with a liberal arts degree (e.g., data analyst, editorial assistant). Finally, psychologists need to work with community members from various cultures and with professionals across disciplines to develop their discipline to be relevant to everyone's lives, to enumerate the roles psychologists play in improving communities and society, and to show that all individuals can improve their own lives with more psychological knowledge.

RECOMMENDATIONS AND CONCLUSION

Psychology's undergraduate students will continue to become increasingly diverse in the years ahead. To the extent that administrators and faculty can create classroom and campus climates in which all students feel valued, they will be successful in establishing fertile ground for their students' learning, development, and refinement of cultural competency skills. We offer the following recommendations to help achieve such climates:

1. Administrators should regularly assess the demographic diversity of their student population, report the results to faculty, and use these data to inform strategic planning (e.g., implement policies that feature their institutions' existing student diversity as assets and educational resources while continuing to recruit and retain more students from diverse backgrounds).

2. Individual faculty should be sensitive to the demographics and developmental trajectories of their students and use instructional strategies designed to engage the full range of students in the class (e.g., infuse into courses issues relating to multiple types of diversity and the intersection of diverse identities).

3. Psychology faculty and students should use the empirical findings and theoretical insights of psychological science to inform campuswide and communitywide discussions of diversity-related issues.

4. Psychology curricula should accurately reflect the centrality of diversity issues to psychological science.

5. Department administrators and faculty members should actively create and sustain climates of mutual respect and open communication, recognizing the many factors that contribute to climate.

6. Faculty and administrators with responsibility for faculty development should provide opportunities for faculty members to develop their multicultural competencies and hold faculty members accountable for effectively applying these skills.

7. Advising should accommodate all psychology students throughout their academic careers. Sound advising can be provided through a variety of models, including designating particular faculty members for specialized advising roles

matched to expertise and background, training faculty members in the advising skills they do not already have as researchers and instructors, and integrating professional advisors into the advising system in ways that free faculty members to do the kinds of advising that they do most naturally.

8. Psychology faculty should provide current and prospective psychology students accurate and timely advice about realistic postbaccalaureate employment availability and graduate school admission.

5

WHEN AND WHERE PEOPLE LEARN PSYCHOLOGICAL SCIENCE: THE SUN NEVER SETS

ANN T. EWING, JEFFREY ANDRE, CHARLES T. BLAIR-BROEKER,
AMY C. FINEBURG, JESSICA HENDERSON DANIEL, JENNIFER J. HIGA,
SALVADOR MACIAS III, AND KENNETH A. WEAVER

When and where do people learn about psychology? In this chapter, we suggest that the sun never sets on the teaching and learning of psychological science. The term *psychological science* emphasizes the scientific nature of the discipline. Psychological science is communicated in a variety of formal and informal settings. Formal settings include a wide array of academic institutions and professional development venues, whereas informal settings include popular media, Web sites, podcasts, networking sites, family discussions and religious communities. Psychological science is taught to students across the life span, in a wide range of contexts, at all hours of the day and night, in most parts of the world, and using many instructional modalities. Psychological science is local, national, and international. Psychological science appeals to a diverse audience. In this chapter, we explore quality control of the discipline's content and address the misconceptions that are commonly held by the public. We also describe when and where people learn about psychology, and we conclude with recommendations for the future of undergraduate education in psychological science.

THE CURRENT STATE OF AFFAIRS

Psychological science is taught in various classroomlike settings, but individuals also learn about psychological topics in a variety of settings in and out of the classroom. In the section that follows, we briefly describe both the formal (preschool–college curriculum) and informal (e.g., families, media, folklore) contexts in which individuals encounter psychological information.

Formal Learning of Psychological Science

During the last several decades, the teaching of undergraduate introductory psychology courses to a wide variety of audiences in many types of locations has increased. Five primary avenues for this instruction are precollege, community college, 4-year institutions, departments outside of psychology, and professional development programs.

Precollege Programs

Psychology content is delivered throughout the kindergarten–Grade 12 curriculum in several ways. In pre-high-school the most common method is to include psychological science information in general science courses. Although this content is not generally attributed to psychology per se, information about the brain and central nervous system, sensation and perception, health and wellness, eating disorders, diversity awareness, and even animal behavior is often included in the elementary and middle school science curriculum. One concern is the lack of specific training in psychology that is often prevalent in these pre-high-school teachers.

Most commonly, however, the first explicit exposure to psychological science occurs through introductory psychology courses that are offered as part of the regular high school curriculum. These "regular" psychology courses are different from Advanced Placement (AP) and International Baccalaureate (IB) courses. Regular psychology courses are often year-long high school courses that address topics covering the spectrum found in most AP, IB, or introductory psychology courses. They can also be semester long or shorter courses that cover fewer topics. Teachers of Psychology in Secondary Schools (TOPSS) recommends that teachers of regular high school psychology courses base their course content on the American Psychological Association's (APA's) *National Standards for High School Psychology Curricula* (APA, 2005). These standards suggest teaching at least one unit from each of the five domains of psychology (methods, developmental, biological, cognitive, and variations in individual and group behavior). Psychological science content is also found in nonpsychology high school courses such as family and consumer science, health, and anatomy and physiology. Public, private, and home schools also offer psychological content in direct and indirect ways.

Perhaps the most impressive initiative to deliver college-level psychology instruction to high school students is the AP program sponsored by the College Board. The AP Psychology Exam was first offered in 1992, when approximately 4,000 students took the exam. By 2008, AP psychology had become one of the most popular AP course offerings, and more than 132,000 students took the exam (K. D. Keith, personal communication, June 24, 2008). Worldwide, at least 4,257 high schools offered psychology as an AP course, including countries such as China, Brazil, Pakistan, Mexico, and France.

Dual-credit arrangements between high schools and community colleges have increased dramatically, with 71% of U.S. high schools offering some form of dual-enrollment credit, involving 1.2 million students (Waits, Setzer, & Lewis, 2005.) *Dual credit* means that a college-level introductory psychology course is delivered either by an approved high school teacher (usually with a master's degree or higher) or a community college teacher. Almost all (98%) public community colleges in the United States participate in some form of dual-credit arrangement (Kleiner & Lewis, 2005).

Finally, the IB program includes psychology for students in the 2-year Diploma Programme for high schools. The IB Diploma Programme is aimed toward 16- to 19-year-olds and requires three components of all students: the Extended Essay (a 4,000-word essay on a topic of choice); Theory of Knowledge (an interdisciplinary course focused on critical thinking about the basis of knowledge); and Creativity, Action, Service (a 150-hour service learning component). Furthermore, students take coursework in six different subject areas: Language 1A (which includes the student's first language and literature), Language B (which includes a second modern language study), Individuals and Societies (which includes history and psychology), Experimental Sciences (which includes biology and chemistry), Mathematics, and Arts and Electives (which include visual art, music, a third modern language, and further choices from Individuals and Societies, Experimental Sciences, and Mathematics). Only 2% of U.S. high schools offer an IB program.

Community College Programs

Community colleges play a key role in higher education. As of January 2008, approximately 46% of all college undergraduates were enrolled in community colleges (American Association of Community Colleges, n.d.). Community colleges provide a connection from high school to college through programs that allow students to earn course credits leading to associate degrees and eventually bachelor degrees at 4-year institutions. In addition, community colleges serve as a gateway to higher education for traditionally underrepresented groups. Approximately half of all ethnic minority students who are in college attend a community college. Furthermore, as of January 2008, 39% of all students in community colleges are first-generation college students (American Association of Community Colleges, n.d.) Small classes and ready access to professors make community colleges appealing to students who seek a local and affordable opportunity for higher education.

For many students, the introductory psychology course is their first and perhaps only formal exposure to the science of psychology, and half of those students take that course at a community college (Phillippe, 2000). Moreover, approximately 50% of all psychology majors take at least some coursework at community colleges (D. Smith, 2002). By frequently providing their first taste of the field, community colleges are at the forefront for recruitment and training of future psychology majors.

Finally, community colleges prepare students for the job market. World economic conditions require a workforce with postsecondary education, and employers increasingly rely on students who are served by community colleges. Many citizens who do not have access to traditional 4-year colleges rely on community colleges to meet their educational needs. Community colleges provide numerous opportunities for career changes, lifelong learning, and personal development courses in psychological science.

Four-Year Programs

The APA *Monitor on Psychology* ("Psychology Is," June, 2008) reported that psychology is the fourth most popular undergraduate major at 4-year institutions. In the last 30 years, the number of psychology degrees conferred has increased by more than 75% (U.S. Department of Education, 2007). This rise in popularity occurred even as psychology struggled to find a standard core curriculum (see, e.g., Benjamin, 2001; chap. 3, this volume). The average psychology degree requires 37 credit hours of psychology coursework (Stoloff, Sanders, & McCarthy, n.d.) and is usually classified as a social science. Regardless of the structure of the curriculum, traditional psychology majors often start their training during their first semester in college. Exceptions to this may be students who began even sooner by earning AP, IB, or dual-enrollment credit for the introductory psychology course or students who decide on a major later in the course of their undergraduate education.

Introductory psychology is one of the most frequently selected courses in the undergraduate curriculum, second only to English composition in percentage of credits earned by bachelor's degree recipients (Adelman, 2004). Psychology classes may include traditional lecture and laboratory components, and some institutions now offer online classes that mirror the objectives and coverage of traditional lecture-based courses. Schools such as Drexel University and Troy University offer their entire bachelor of science degree in psychology online. Hybrid (lecture and online combined) courses are also becoming increasingly popular.

In addition to traditional majors, psychology coursework reaches three other groups of students: nonmajors, military personnel, and students studying abroad. Nonpsychology majors usually receive their only psychological science experience as part of their school's general education program, but many other disciplines require a psychology course as part of their major. Students who transfer from community colleges or other 4-year schools generally take their first psychological science course at their first institution. For many students, their first exposure to psychology may be their last. This means that the discipline and its representatives must ensure that there is some quality control implicit in when and where people learn about psychology.

Undergraduate psychological science courses are taught to members of the U.S. military, who receive academic credit for taking these courses in stateside and overseas locations. For example, the U.S. Navy provides professors to teach courses in psychological science to sailors at sea. Traditional students also learn about psychology overseas while participating in study abroad programs. These programs can last anywhere from a few weeks to a full semester or school year. In addition, some schools, such as James Madison University, have alternative spring break programs that require psychology majors to apply knowledge gained in psychology courses in a variety of short-term experiences, either nationally or internationally. Thus, students encounter psychology courses in different configurations and types of institutions all around the world.

Programs in Other Disciplines

Psychology courses are valued and often specifically required in a variety of other disciplines. For example, nursing, education, business, criminal justice, family studies, and mortuary science often require courses such as introductory psychology, life-span development, or educational psychology. In addition, these programs often recommend psychology courses as electives, (e.g., psychopathology, biological psychology, social psychology, health psychology, learning and memory, sensation and perception).

Some departments offer courses incorporating content that is psychological in nature but taught by nonpsychology faculty. For example, degree programs in business, education, mortuary science, and nursing often cover office management, sensitivity training, human growth and development, classroom organization, behavior modification, death and dying, psychopathology, psychopharmacology, and social psychology, among others. Thus, course content based on psychological research and theory is covered in many settings outside of psychology, raising concerns about teachers' expertise, accuracy of material presented, and appropriate recognition of psychological science as the source of the content. Principle C of the APA "Ethical Principles of Psychologists and Code of Conduct" (APA Ethics Code; APA, 2002a) states that "psychologists seek to promote accuracy, honesty, and truthfulness in the science, teaching, and practice of psychology" (p. 3). Countering misinformation and misperceptions is a primary responsibility of teachers of psychology, who must continue to campaign for accurate and ethical instruction in and application of the content of our discipline, regardless of who is doing the classroom instruction.

Psychology in Professional Development

Professional development training targets specific skills to enhance individuals' occupational productivity. Typically, the content of the training is derived from undergraduate psychology courses but reduced to its essentials and presented as a series of recommended applications in a specific setting. These training sessions usually last at least 1 hour but may require a full workday. For example, day care providers may receive information on implementation techniques of guidance and group management (at the appropriate developmental level), child development, or their commitment to professionalism.

Professional development training typically involves face-to-face group sessions, but differences in language, culture, and educational background influence how sessions are conducted. Future growth in online versions of these sessions is expected. Although sessions may occur any time, the training is usually reserved for orientation of new employees, continuing education of workers, or responding to a crisis or awareness of a specific training need. Audiences might include teachers and support staff in schools, paraprofessionals who work in health care, or first responders such as police officers and firefighters. In addition, community health centers have workforces with varied educational backgrounds, and they might receive diversity training or instruction in certain workplace skills such as communication and conflict management. Professional development training in these and other areas may serve as an introduction to the content of psychological science.

Informal Learning of Psychological Science

Imagine this scene: A physician takes her seat on an airplane and strikes up a conversation with a business executive in the next seat. They exchange pleasantries and the executive asks, "What do you do?" The physician replies, "I'm a physician." What is the next question from the executive? It's likely to be something like, "What's your specialty?" Now imagine that the person was a psychologist rather than a physician. How likely is it that she would be asked about her specialty? The executive is more likely to ask, "Are you analyzing me now?" rather than recognize the many ways in which people can study and practice psychology. This vignette illustrates a public perception problem faced by the science of psychology. Many people, perhaps most people, are either uninformed or misinformed about the nature of psychology.

Because of the influence of the mass media, the occupation of psychologist is almost universally perceived by the general public as that of a clinician. Although clinical is the largest specialty field in psychology, only half of all psychologists in the United States are clinical psychologists. Has a community psychologist ever appeared in a TV show or movie? Has a human factors expert ever been the lead character in a novel or a play?

This issue is not faced by most disciplines. People have a reasonably accurate idea of what is included in the fields of history, biology, and chemistry, or at least they are aware of their own lack of knowledge in these areas. Biology and chemistry are perceived to be technically complex and therefore worthy of respect. In contrast, psychology's problem is that it is interesting and imminently accessible to any armchair theorist. Everyone is an "expert" in psychology.

"Real" psychology is typically represented narrowly, or not at all, in the media. Often, portrayals of psychology or psychologists convey an impression that could not be more at odds with the one that psychologists want to convey. Students entering psychology classes are likely to believe that TV and radio "psychologists" are doing what real practitioners do and psychology is limited to counseling others. They are likely to believe that the most influential historical figure in psychology is Sigmund Freud. They are also likely to share stories about what they learned while visiting one of the 3,270,000 sites returned when "dream interpretation" is searched on Google. Furthermore, they believe wholeheartedly in what they learned about themselves by filling out the dime-a-dozen unscientific personality inventories so widely available in magazines and on the Internet. They are eager to start studying astrology, graphology, and a host of paranormal phenomena because they believe that this truly is the "stuff of psychology." Countering misinformation and misconceptions is a primary ethical responsibility of teachers of psychology.

A wealth of valid, empirical psychological content is available in the media, if one chooses to search for it. *Scientific American Mind* is visible at most newsstands. There is an excellent science section (Science Times) in the *New York Times* that has some psychologically related content almost every Tuesday. A growing number of podcasts provide sound psychological information. There are excellent trade books written by psychologists to better inform the public about what psychologists do. Sometimes even *60 Minutes* and other similar TV news programs provide accurate portrayals of the field. Nevertheless, the most common available information is misinformation. Principle A of the APA Ethics Code (APA, 2002a) states, "Psychologists strive to benefit those with whom they work and take care to do no harm" (p. 3). Accurate psychological information can benefit people; inaccurate psychological information can lead to harmful decisions in many realms. Leaving accurate presentation of psychological science to happenstance or to those not trained in the field almost ensures that the public perception of psychology will be distorted, at best.

When introductory courses are taught in fields other than psychology, most of the subject-related knowledge students bring with them on the first day is reasonably accurate. The same assumption cannot be made in introductory psychology courses. According to Principle C of the APA Ethics Code (APA, 2002a), "Psychologists seek to promote accuracy, honesty, and truthfulness in the science, teaching, and practice of psychology" (p. 3). Countering misinformation and misperceptions is a primary responsibility of teachers of psychology. Therefore, it is ethically incumbent on those who teach psychological science to dispel misinformation and teach empirically based psychological science.

Regardless of time and place, at the foundation of psychological science is ethics. Sound ethics makes for good science by establishing standards and guidelines for conducting research and for teaching. Teachers of psychology have an ethical responsibility to provide instruction in psychological science by presenting accurate information, correcting misrepresentations, and monitoring the integration of diversity in both formal and informal settings.

RECOMMENDATIONS

The following recommendations address the diverse nature of the teaching and learning of psychological science. Applications to formal and informal settings are targeted in these recommendations. Each recommendation is consistent with the APA Ethics Code. Regardless of when (kindergarten through graduate school) and where (formal and informal settings) psychological science instruction is provided, adherence to the APA Ethics Code can increase the probability that the instruction and interactions are appropriate and effective.

Recommendation 1: Rename the Discipline of Psychology as Psychological Science

Perhaps the single most prominent action to launch the new blueprint for undergraduate psychology is to recommit the discipline to the underlying belief that psychology is an empirical science grounded in the scientific method. More than any other source of belief or understanding (Peirce, 1972), the scientific method provides the best way to differentiate science from pseudoscience. To this end, we recommend that the discipline of psychology be referred to as *psychological science*. We realize that this is an enormous request that will require great patience and persistence to achieve. This name change would clarify for the public what psychology is and what it is not.

When this change is implemented in elementary and middle schools, a new generation of students will reach high school and college understanding that they are studying science when they take psychology courses. This name change also reflects the history of psychological science from the ancient Greek philosophers to Descartes to the British empiricists to Wundt's first psychology laboratory to the present emphasis on scientific psychology. Psychological science celebrates the breadth of the discipline as evidenced by the many specialties and the scientific basis for all of them. Indeed, this scientific basis ties the specialties together.

To this end, one facet of this recommendation is renaming college psychology departments as departments of psychological science to reinforce the fact that psychology is a scientific discipline and should be identified as such. Change is most often greeted with resistance, but this recommendation can phase in gradually and will catch on just as other new buzzwords have in the past. Psychologists may need to take into consideration the idea that they may not be welcomed in the natural science camp, and some may attribute the effort to change as an indication of a self-esteem problem for psychology. This will not be an easy transition, but it is definitely worth the effort.

Endorsement of this change by leaders in the APA and the Association for Psychological Science will be a necessary component for this type of change to occur. Perhaps the effort could be initiated by the participants in the National Conference on Undergraduate Education in Psychology, which was sponsored by APA. If participants could convince their administrations to change the name of their departments to Department of Psychological Science, the trend could be launched in a reasonably short time frame. Because these participants were selected for their leadership in the area of academic psychology, their widespread influence may be enough to get the initiative off the ground. Similar efforts will gradually change attitudes of other academic decision makers to be more consistent with psychology as a legitimate science.

Recommendation 2: Acknowledge Psychological Science Contributions

The substantive content of psychological science should be recognized as such wherever it is found. Virtually every introductory psychological science textbook defines *psychology* as the "the scientific study of behavior and mental processes." Psychological content is ubiquitous. For example, child development degree and certification programs in education and family studies departments, marketing and management specialties in business departments, and patient care in nursing programs depend on psychological science for their content and intellectual rigor. Many of these disciplines include content that originates from psychological science, such as classroom management techniques, employee incentive programs, child discipline, parenting styles, grief and loss, health management, and eating disorders. When people in other disciplines value and use the research, we recommend that they acknowledge the specific contributions of psychological science.

Although psychological science enjoys a pervasive presence across many disciplines, public perception and professional recognition of its contributions are weak. Psychologists should be integral resources when psychology is taught to students, regardless of context. Part of this recommendation is the creation of a task force to develop specific action plans to encourage the recognition of psychological content in all areas in which it is relevant and to promote the use of psychologists in teaching and consulting roles whenever psychological science is presented, both formally and informally. When students or the public are taught about medical advances, physicians are called on to represent their field. Similarly, psychologists should insist that they be called when psychological science is presented.

Recommendation 3: Identify and Expand Psychological Science in Elementary and Middle School Curricula

Elementary and middle school science and health textbooks often include psychological science content. Exposing young students to this important learning opportunity is good, but they may not realize that the content is psychological in nature. Two related recommendations are (a) psychological information in the curriculum should be appropriately attributed to psychological science, and (b) school curricula should include information labeled *psychological science* so that children can appreciate what the field of psychological science has to offer. Furthermore, we recommend that textbook publishers engage psychologists to develop appropriate curricular materials. This early exposure to appropriately labeled psychological information will facilitate a more accurate perception by the public in future years, promote critical thinking, and inoculate children against psychological misinformation in formal and informal settings. An overall increase in psychological literacy will result.

Recommendation 4: Establish Psychological Science Courses as a Science Requirement

The value of a basic education in science is the acquisition of critical thinking skills and the capacity to apply these logical strategies in novel situations. Evaluating information and its sources, appreciating the complexity of issues, and consuming information critically are timeless skills. The value of an educated citizenry is undeniable. Psychological science is better suited to provide these strategies of critical thinking than are traditional sciences such as biology, chemistry, and physics. At the high school level, psychology courses that follow the *National Standards for High School Psychology Curricula* (APA, 2005) address both the scientific methodology and critical thinking skills found in science courses as well as conclusions drawn from such methodology and reasoning. Students demonstrate greater critical thinking and science reasoning skills after taking undergraduate psychological science courses than after taking chemistry courses (Lehman, Lempert, & Nisbitt, 1988). Compared with courses in psychological science, physics, chemistry, and biology courses spend much time addressing content and findings and conclusions of research and little time teaching students how to evaluate the quality of those findings and conclusions (Macias & Macias, 2009). We recommend that high schools and colleges accept a course in introductory psychological science to satisfy general education requirements in science.

When psychological science courses satisfy science requirements, additional resources available for science education might be dedicated to training teachers and purchasing supplies.

As this recommendation is implemented, high school teachers of psychology should not lose their certification to teach psychology. Teachers of psychology often seek training in statistics and research methodology to bolster their knowledge of the discipline. Allowing these dedicated teachers to document their efforts and to continue providing sound scientific instruction for students will help ensure a successful transition.

Recommendation 5: Expand and Improve Psychological Science Web Resources

How to Think Straight About Psychology (Stanovich, 2007) characterizes psychological science as "a body of knowledge that is unknown to most people" (p. ix). This lack of awareness is compounded by a public perception that psychological science is dominated by Freud and a general belief that psychology is merely a set of commonsense conclusions. Consequently, Stanovich characterized psychological science as the "Rodney Dangerfield of the Sciences." Dangerfield, a popular comedian from the 1970s and 1980s, is famous for the catchphrase "I don't get no respect." Similarly, portraying psychology as parapsychology or pop psychology rather than psychological science explains the discipline's lack of status among the sciences.

Stanovich (2007) provided several examples of misrepresentations of psychological science. Perusing the collection in the psychology section of a bookstore reveals tomes on topics such as parapsychology, telepathy, clairvoyance, psychokinesis, reincarnation, and psychic surgery. With some notable exceptions, radio and TV stations rarely broadcast reports of psychological science, but they routinely present bogus therapies and publicity-seeking personalities not connected to the field. If the public is interested in a particular psychological question, the media will provide a story, often without assistance from psychological scientists.

In his APA presidential address, Zimbardo (2004) extolled the benefits of establishing positive relationships with the media as they "are the gatekeepers between the best, relevant psychology we want to give away and that elusive public we hope will value what we have to offer" (p. 340). He went on to say that it is "essential to our mission of making the public wiser consumers of psychological knowledge to learn how to communicate effectively to the media and to work with the media" (p. 341).

The basis of several recommendations is an insistence that a comprehensive and persistent national effort involving the media needs to occur to improve the perception in the public mind of psychology as a scientific discipline. To support this effort is a recommendation to strengthen the Web presence of psychological science to better (a) educate the public about psychological science, (b) alert the public quickly when misinformation is in the "public eye," and (c) investigate sources and patterns of misinformation reported about psychological science. This Web presence should become as popular and easily recognizable as Google for finding accurate information about psychological science and reporting inaccurate portrayals of psychology. Over time, the ability to differentiate a social psychologist from an industrial and organizational psychologist will be as easy as differentiating a pediatrician from an obstetrician or a dentist from an orthodontist.

One possible form for such a public education Web site is *Psychology Matters* (http://psychologymatters.apa.org/), which presents information gleaned from psychological research on the applications of psychology in daily life. Expanding the site's content about psychological science to include knowledge as well as application and making the content easily accessible to the public are avenues for successful implementation. For example, a list of "Frequently Asked Questions," clearly organized by themes and easily searchable, would provide the public with ready access to answers to their questions. One of the possible themes could be *myth busting* to ensure that the public and the media correctly understand psychological science. One important audience for this content would be teachers of psychological science at all levels who regularly need accurate information to address contemporary issues and answer questions posed by their students.

Second, the Web presence will alert the public when accurate or inaccurate information about psychological science is publicized. Accurate portrayals are identified as such; erroneous or misleading content is presented along with its author and/or source followed by a brief paragraph explaining the fallacies and what the correct content should be. This accurate information would provide psychological science stakeholders with the necessary knowledge to respond to and correct inaccuracies through letters to editors, op-ed articles, discussions in class, and conversations with friends and colleagues. After some time, this content would be reformatted and posted in the educational part of the Web site.

Finally, data on the types, sources, frequency, and prevalence of misinformation about psychological science are limited; thus, the third function of the Web presence is research. A mechanism would be created for psychologists and the public to report the author, source, and content of the misrepresentation, and this information would then be automatically entered into a database. Researchers and policy makers could use the resulting database to grasp more concretely the scope and patterns of the misrepresentations and identify authors and sources consistently reporting erroneous information about psychological science. These analyses would facilitate efforts to contact those writers, commentators, editors, journals, newspapers, magazines, or other media outlets to educate them about psychological science and to increase the likelihood of accurate reporting.

Recommendation 6: Raise Public Awareness of Psychological Science

The final recommendation is that additional resources be developed to acquaint the public with the breadth of psychological science. For many years, APA has made available print and video materials about careers in psychology. For example, there is a DVD and associated brochure called *Psychology: Scientific Problem Solvers—Careers for the 21st Century* (http://www.apa.org/students/brochure). We laud this ongoing effort to provide accurate information about specialty areas. However, the rapidly changing nature of the field and the speed with which presentations begin to look outdated require frequent updates of both the content and presentation medium (e.g., Web sites, podcasts, streaming video, Second Life, Blu-ray). Individuals showcased in these materials should be a diverse group of established professionals as well as younger persons embarking on their careers and representing different ethnicities and cultures. Information about these materials should be distributed widely. One of the best potential vehicles for highlighting these resources may be regular reminders in the various publications and listservs of TOPSS, Psychology Teachers at Community Colleges, Society for Teaching of Psychology, and other psychology teaching organizations.

CONCLUSION

As a result of seemingly unlimited interest and technological advancements, psychological science is taught anywhere in the world at any time of day or night. It is a fascinating field of interest to individuals at many stages of the life span. All psychology teachers have an ethical responsibility to ensure that accurate scientific content is presented with quality. The discipline must ensure its reputation as a science making a difference in the world, adhering to the highest ethical and scientific standards.

6

A CONTEXTUAL APPROACH TO TEACHING: BRIDGING METHODS, GOALS, AND OUTCOMES

STEPHEN L. CHEW, ROBIN M. BARTLETT, JAMES E. DOBBINS,
ELIZABETH YOST HAMMER, MARY E. KITE, TRUDY FREY LOOP,
JULIE GUAY McINTYRE, AND KAREN C. ROSE

WHAT IS THE OPTIMAL PROCESS FOR TEACHERS TO SELECT AND IMPLEMENT TEACHING METHODS TO ACHIEVE DESIRED LEARNING GOALS?

The number and variety of teaching methods are virtually endless and, given technological advances, ever increasing. As an exercise, we eight authors were able to generate a list of over 90 different methods from memory, but there are certainly many more. Given the large number, instructors are faced with the challenge of finding the most effective teaching strategy for their purposes. The need for a comprehensive, empirically based process to guide the selection and implementation of teaching strategies is clear. The purpose of this chapter is to describe such a process. In the first part of this chapter, we introduce a model of teaching that can guide the selection and implementation process. In the second part, we provide a set of examples of how the model can be used to accomplish learning goals.

The large number of teaching methods raises important questions about teaching that must be addressed before we can formulate a process for selecting an optimal method. Why are there so many different methods? Why are there not just one or two best teaching methods that we all should use? With so many, how can instructors choose the best methods to achieve their particular learning goals? We believe that the large number indicates that, despite progress in pedagogical research, we still do not have a comprehensive understanding of the teaching and learning process (Bransford, Brown, & Cocking, 1999; Shulman, 2004; also see chap. 8, this volume). Furthermore, we believe there is a large number because different methods are suited for different teaching purposes or situations. Widely varying purposes and situations arise from the combination of extensive individual differences among teachers, among students, and among teaching environments. Effective instruction depends on designing pedagogy that considers the interaction among these and other factors. In other words, teaching effectiveness is context sensitive or context dependent (Bransford et al., 1999; Daniel & Poole, 2009; Dees et al., 2007; McGovern, 1993).

The context-sensitive nature of teaching and learning has important implications for instructors. To use problem-solving terminology, teaching methods are not algorithms that, if properly followed, guarantee a positive outcome. They are like heuristics, which often lead to positive outcomes but can be ineffective or even counterproductive in some situations. A method that works for one teacher may not work for another; a method that works for one topic may not work for another; and a method that works for a teacher with the students in the 8:00 a.m. section may not work with the students in the 9:00 a.m. section of the same course. There is not a best method for all teachers, all students, all topics, or all learning situations. As a result, teachers must possess an armamentarium of methods and strategies, and they must know how to select and implement the best method to suit different situations. We are not suggesting, however, that all teaching methods will be equally successful. Some teaching methods are generally going to be more effective at achieving certain kinds of learning than others, but there will always be exceptions.

A CONTEXTUAL MODEL OF TEACHING

Selecting the best teaching method is difficult because no teaching method is always effective. Any process for selecting and implementing optimal teaching methods must take into account the context-sensitive nature of teaching and learning. In this section, we propose such a process in the form of a model of teaching. We call it the TACOMA model because we developed it at the National Conference for Undergraduate Education in Psychology, which was held at the University of Puget Sound in Tacoma,

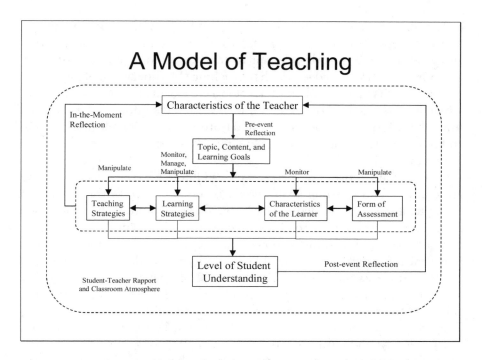

Figure 6.1. The TACOMA (Teaching as a Contextual Outcome of Multiple Agents) model of teaching.

Washington. TACOMA stands for Teaching as a Contextual Outcome of Multiple Agents. TACOMA is designed to provide a comprehensive overview of teaching that will facilitate the selection and implementation of teaching strategies and also assist in assessment of their effectiveness. The model is shown in Figure 6.1.

The ultimate goal of teaching is to develop student understanding, and progress toward that goal begins with the knowledge and decisions of the instructor (Shulman, 2004). This idea is reflected in the top, center box of the model, the *characteristics of the teacher*. These characteristics include the beliefs that instructors have about teaching and learning (Hativa, 2000); their knowledge of how people learn (Bain, 2004; Bransford et al., 1999); how well they know the topic area; their knowledge, experience, and skill with different teaching methods; and their personal preferences on matters such as the amount of control they want to maintain in their class, how closely they wish to interact with their students, and their comfort with technology. For example, teachers who are familiar with Mayer's (2005) theory of multimedia learning will be aware of the complexities and pitfalls of using multimedia effectively. Furthermore, teachers who understand the importance of cognitive load on learning (van Merriënboer & Sweller, 2005) will be less likely to inadvertently overwhelm students in designing instruction. Many concepts within psychology, such as elaborative rehearsal, motivation, and attention, are directly relevant to teaching, and successful instructors incorporate such knowledge into their teaching (Matlin, 2002). Skilled teachers, like experts in any field, must develop a great deal of explicit and implicit schematic knowledge (Bransford et al., 1999). This knowledge is acquired through the scholarship of teaching and learning, review of relevant research, and reflective teaching practice (McAlpine & Weston, 2002; Schon, 1983; Shulman, 2004).

The characteristics of the teacher lead directly to the selection of topics, content, and learning goals, which is the next step of the model. For example, instructors trained in neuropsychology will probably devote more class time to the study of the brain and have greater depth and breadth of content compared with instructors trained in other specializations. Furthermore, the former group will probably demand a greater degree of understanding from students on this topic, and this will influence the design of their assessments. As a second example, consider how different instructors might approach the topic of memory. One instructor might focus on the work of Ebbinghaus; one might focus on the distinction between explicit and implicit memory; and a third might focus on applications of memory research such as eyewitness testimony. Each instructor has made valid but different content choices, and these choices can lead to the different choices about teaching methods and assessments.

Once the topics and goals have been set, the teacher designs and implements instruction accordingly (Forsyth, 2003; McKeachie & Svinicki, 2006; Wiggins & McTighe, 1998). That process is reflected in the next level down in the model. This level has four factors—teaching strategies, learning strategies, characteristics of the learner, and form of assessment—all of which interact with and influence each other. The interdependence among these factors reflects the context-sensitive nature of teaching. Although each individual factor contributes to the success of teaching, the interaction among factors is a greater determinant than any single one.

Teacher strategies includes the selection and implementation of teaching methods such as lecture or service learning and how those methods will be implemented. It also includes how the teacher plans to organize and present information; planning any activities, demonstrations, or assignments for students; the selection of learning resources such as readings, videos, or websites; and the use of technology such as PowerPoint or discussion boards.

Learning strategies refers to the strategies students use to try to learn the course content. This includes the amount and completeness of study and also the level of processing of study, ranging from rote memorization to meaningful semantic processing. This also includes learning activities the student engages in such as note taking, highlighting, and practicing recall (e.g., McDaniel, Howard, & Einstein, in press).

Characteristics of the learner refers to students' prior knowledge and beliefs about a topic, including gaps and misconceptions (Chew, 2005), as well as sociocultural factors such as race, ethnicity, religiosity, and generational cohort (see chap. 4, this volume). Furthermore, Dweck (2002) has shown that students' beliefs about learning and intelligence, such as how fast and easy learning should be and whether learning is a result of inborn talent or hard work, have a powerful influence on achievement and persistence.

The *form of assessment* refers to the activities the teacher uses to measure and evaluate student learning. The form and frequency of assessment can strongly influence learning (Karpicke & Roediger, 2007). There are many forms of assessment, but they fall into two broad categories based on their purpose (Osborne & Wagor, 2004). Summative assessments are used to evaluate student learning, usually for the purpose of assigning grades. They typically occur at the end of a unit of study and often are intended to indicate the total student learning on the unit. These would include exams and writing assignments. Formative assessments are activities that reveal the students' level of understanding to both the teacher and students for the purpose of increasing the effectiveness of teaching and learning. They usually do not contribute to grades or they count very little. Formative assessments usually occur during the course of a unit of study. They allow instructors to monitor student understanding and make necessary adjustments in instruction. They also give students feedback about their own level of understanding in relation to the expectations of the instructor and enable them to make adjustments to their learning strategies. Angelo and Cross (1993) described a wide variety of formative assessment techniques that can be adapted to any teaching method.

The impact of each of the four factors is dependent on the other factors. For example, the form of assessment influences the learning strategies used by the student (Ross, Green, Salisbury-Glennon, & Tollefson, 2006). The challenge of teaching is to oversee this four-way interaction. For example, students may study for a class simply by memorizing all the highlighted terms in the textbook, but this strategy is incompatible with teaching methods and assessment tools designed to promote understanding. In such situations, student learning will be minimal according to the assessment, even if students were genuinely trying (see Daniel & Poole, 2009). Some factors present more of a challenge to manage than the others. Instructors directly control the teaching strategies. For example, they choose whether to use lecture, service learning, or some other method. Instructors also control the form of assessment. They choose what kinds of exams to give, how often they are given, and how much they count toward the grade. The teacher cannot directly manipulate the characteristics of the learner or the strategies of the learners. Students bring expectations about the class and beliefs about the content to the class, and both may be highly inaccurate. Instructors must detect these expectations and misconceptions and try to correct them (Chew,

2005). Students also bring beliefs about the best study strategies to use and judgments about how well they know the material. Once again, these beliefs and judgments can be inaccurate and teachers must detect and try to change them (Dweck, 2002).

The final level of the model is *student understanding*. Student understanding can take many forms, such as explanation, application, interpretation, perspective, empathy, and self-knowledge (Wiggins & McTighe, 1998). Understanding also can involve long-term retention and appropriate transfer of information (Halpern & Hakel, 2003) as well as laying the foundation for further and more insightful learning (Schwartz, Bransford, & Sears, 2005).

Student understanding is the final level of the model because we believe that teaching should be student centered. In other words, the success of teaching should be measured by what the students learn (Bain, 2004; Bransford et al., 1999; McKeachie & Svinicki, 2006). An instructor may select the most up-to-date content, present information clearly, design engaging activities, and use the latest technology, but if the students do not develop the desired state of understanding, then the teaching will not have been completely successful. Instructors, however, can learn from each experience, regardless of how successful, and apply the new knowledge to improve their teaching. This process of continuous improvement is accomplished through reflection.

The model incorporates reflection before, during, and after teaching. Dees et al. (2007) discussed the importance of all three kinds, which they refer to as *preevent reflection*, *in-the-moment reflection*, and *postevent reflection*. Instructors engage in preevent reflection to plan pedagogy. They engage in in-the-moment reflection during teaching to monitor student understanding and make adjustments accordingly. In-the-moment reflection is represented by the arrow circulating between the interaction of the four components of teaching in the middle and the characteristics of the teacher at the top (see Figure 6.1). Teaching rarely, if ever, works out exactly as planned, and postevent reflection is critical for continuous improvement of the teacher's knowledge and skill and for the modification and refinement of the course. Postevent reflection is represented by an arrow from student understanding feeding back to characteristics of the teacher, indicating how each teaching experience enhances teacher knowledge through reflection.

The TACOMA model includes two global variables, classroom atmosphere and student–teacher rapport, which arise from the ongoing interactions between students and teacher. These factors contribute to the overall learning context and influence the impact of all of the other components.

The TACOMA model reflects the complexity of the teaching and learning process. Research supports the inclusion of each of the components of the model as well as the interaction among them as key factors in teaching and learning. We do not claim that the model represents an exhaustive set of all the factors that influence learning, but it can still guide teachers in the planning and the implementation of instruction. For teachers who are having difficulties, it can provide hypotheses about what factors may be undermining instruction. Finally, it can guide future pedagogical research.

GOAL-BASED SELECTION OF TEACHING STRATEGIES

We began this chapter by pointing out that teachers have many teaching strategies from which to choose. Selecting the best method for a particular instructor to teach a particular topic to a particular set of students is challenging, and as the TACOMA model illustrates, implementation of the method is also multifaceted, with no guarantee of success. What, then, is the best way to select a teaching strategy? We believe that the selection of a method should be directly tied to the teachers' learning goals. Teachers should set the desired goals and then choose the method that will give them the greatest likelihood of success (McKeachie & Svinicki, 2006; Wiggins & McTighe, 1998). Tomcho et al. (2008) have provided an extensive review of pedagogical research that links teaching methods to learning outcomes.

In this section, we illustrate the process of selecting and implementing teaching strategies based on learning goals and using the TACOMA model. The model can guide teachers through the implementation process and indicate what factors teachers should consider. For learning goals, we used four goals taken from the APA Guidelines for the Undergraduate Psychology Major (APA, 2007a). This document lists 10 learning goals which are divided into two categories. The learning goals are as follows.

I. Knowledge, Skills, and Values Consistent With the Science and Application of Psychology
Goal 1: Knowledge Base of Psychology
Goal 2: Research Methods in Psychology
Goal 3: Critical Thinking Skills in Psychology
Goal 4: Application of Psychology
Goal 5: Values in Psychology
II. Knowledge, Skills, and Values Consistent With Liberal Arts Education That Are Further Developed in Psychology
Goal 6: Information and Technological Literacy
Goal 7: Communication Skills
Goal 8: Sociocultural and International Awareness
Goal 9: Personal Development
Goal 10: Career Planning and Development

Category I covers knowledge, skills, and values consistent with the science and the application of psychology. Category II covers knowledge, values, and skills consistent with liberal arts education that are further developed in psychology. We selected two goals from each category. For Category I, we chose Goal 3, which deals with critical thinking and Goal 5, which deals with teaching values. For Category II, we selected Goal 8, which deals with sociocultural and international awareness and Goal 9, which deals with personal development. We chose these goals because they are clearly representative of their category and they overlap with other goals in the category. For each goal, we provide two or three teaching methods that research indicates are well suited to achieving that goal. Then, using the TACOMA model, we discuss factors to consider in implementing the method and possible forms of assessment. In choosing teaching methods to discuss, we are not claiming that these are the best methods for that goal, just that instructors can use multiple methods to achieve any particular goal, and these are good candidates. We also do not mean to imply that the teaching methods we discuss can only be used for that goal. A good teaching method can address multiple goals at once.

Promoting Critical Thinking Skills in Psychology Through Lecture, Discussion Boards, or Problem-Based Learning

Goal 3 of the *APA Guidelines for the Undergraduate Psychology Major* (APA, 2007a) centers on the development of critical thinking skills. Halpern (1998) described critical thinking as "evaluating the outcomes of our thought processes—how good a decision is or how well a problem is solved" (p. 451). Critical thinking is the goal of most teaching methods, but the TACOMA model implies that it is not a certain outcome of any particular one. The appropriate method must be selected and implemented for the particular situation. We use the examples of lecture, discussion boards, and problem-based learning (PBL) as possible methods for achieving the goal of critical thinking.

Lecturing is often criticized as a method whereby teachers present information and students passively absorb it, but there are many tasks and activities that teachers can incorporate into lectures that promote the exchange of views and active critical thinking (Halpern, 1998). In fact, Schwartz and Bransford (1998) found that lecture was superior to other teaching methods for helping students think critically about complex information when used in the proper situation.

Teachers might elect to use lecture because it provides them with control of the flow of information and the use of classroom time. To promote the goal of critical thinking, however, the TACOMA model indicates that instructors must consider the interplay among the characteristics of the learner such as attention and engagement, student learning strategies such as elaborative rehearsal, teaching strategies such as class activities and the use of examples, and the method of assessment (Bligh, 2000; deWinstanley & Bjork, 2002; Halpern, 1998).

Online courses and virtual environments such as wikis and Second Life are far removed from traditional lecture, but teachers can still pursue the goal of critical thinking in these environments. Chapter 7 provides a fuller discussion of teaching with technology. We offer the example of an electronic discussion board for promoting critical thinking. With this strategy, students can take more time to carefully compose their ideas and integrate them with the ideas of others more thoroughly than they might in a spontaneous in-class discussion. This opportunity will likely advance their critical thinking about the nature of knowledge and learning and ultimately advance their understanding (McDevitt & Ormrod, 2008). Furthermore, a higher percentage of students can fully participate in an online discussion compared with a traditional in-class discussion. When used in conjunction with a traditional class, postings typically are made outside of class, freeing up valuable in-class time. However, the discussion can be followed up in class.

Participating through a discussion board can develop both communication and critical thinking skills (Jung, Choi, Lim, & Leem, 2002). Students construct arguments, respond to others' postings, and learn how their classmates (and often the instructor) interpreted and responded to their posting. Instructor feedback on the discussion board enhances student learning. Through student postings, instructors gain information about students' understanding of content and are alerted to misconceptions or gaps in understanding. Consistent with the TACOMA model, the instructor can use in-the-moment reflection to make suitable adjustments to teaching methods. Teachers must consider the factors described in the TACOMA model to use discussion boards effectively. When planning discussion boards, instructors should begin with a clear idea of their goals and expectations (e.g., number of original ideas posted or number of responses to others posts). How does the discussion topic link to the expected course outcomes? How will students' contributions be assessed?

As the TACOMA model indicates, students must use proper learning strategies. Discussion boards are ineffective if students simply state opinions, for example, instead of responding critically to issues. Students need to be aware that plagiarism is as inappropriate on a discussion board as it is in other assignments. A number of characteristics of learners and their environments are important to keep in mind when considering this method. Students need ready access to technology. They must learn to log in, navigate the site, and edit their work using the chosen platform. Teachers must be aware of and make accommodations for students with special needs such as visual impairment or limited motor abilities.

The use of technology brings new challenges to teaching as well as opportunities. Instructors should be prepared for the time-consuming task of monitoring the discussion. They should have good institutional information technology support to help with any hardware or software problems that arise. They should have a plan for how they will handle undesirable postings both "on the board" and in assessment.

PBL offers a third approach to developing critical thinking that differs greatly from either traditional lecture or discussion boards. Students are assigned to groups and given an authentic problem that they must solve by finding and synthesizing relevant information. The teacher guides and scaffolds student discovery, synthesis, and application of relevant concepts (Hmelo-Silver, 2004).

PBL requires students to critically analyze real-world problems using psychological concepts. PBL can be highly effective in promoting critical thinking and increasing the appropriate recall and transfer of the information outside of the classroom (Hmelo-Silver, 2004). It also can be effective in addressing common yet tenacious misconceptions students often have about psychology.

Teachers may use PBL to increase student engagement because it highlights the usefulness and applications of psychology. PBL is particularly useful when students may not be inherently interested in psychology, such as when they take a psychology class merely to fulfill a requirement.

The TACOMA model is useful in implementing PBL effectively. Characteristics of the teacher are critical. Teachers must be aware that PBL demands a great deal of advance preparation in developing authentic, interesting problems. The teacher has less control over student activity than in other forms of teaching. Characteristics of the student also play a major role in the effectiveness of PBL. Students may like PBL if they find the problem is interesting, but if they do not, then they may see the activity as a waste of time. Students may also try to use learning strategies, such as memorization, that are inconsistent with PBL. They may not like working in groups. Assessment is also a difficult issue in PBL. Individual assessment may penalize groups that divided responsibilities. On the other hand, group assessment may reward members of groups who did not contribute as much. For these reasons, instructors typically use a combination of individual and group assessment.

Teaching Values in Psychology Through Case Studies and Group Work

Goal 5 of the APA *Guidelines for the Undergraduate Psychology Major* (APA, 2007a) focuses on the development of values that are considered to be the foundation of psychological science: valuing empirical evidence, tolerating ambiguity, and acting ethically. One useful teaching strategy for understanding these values is the examination of case studies. A second useful teaching strategy is group work in which small groups of students can share perspectives on complex ethical issues. The two methods can be easily and effectively combined so that groups of students discuss key case studies.

Cases can be used as a starting point for reading, analyzing, and discussing ethical problems. They allow the student to consider the complexities of ethical thinking and behavior in familiar (e.g., educational settings) and unfamiliar situations (e.g., research and clinical settings). Cases can be constructed to meet specific student learning goals and crafted to simulate real-life situations by providing a background, characters, settings, and details designed to engage students and to have them reflect on particular ethical issues. Excellent sources for previously constructed cases exist (see Lucas & Bernstein, 2005). In conjunction with other methods such as directed discussion and debates, the case study method can promote active learning as well. Case studies provide a useful mechanism for highlighting the ambiguity associated with ethical decision making, and this notion of ambiguity often runs counter to students' unrealistic perceptions that what is judged to be ethical is always clear-cut. Faculty can vary the level of ambiguity by having a preferred solution (closed case study) or leave the case open to a variety of solutions (open case study; Herreid, 2007). This method can be used in both small and large classes and can stimulate lively discussion in either (Silverman & Welty, 1990).

For case studies to be effective in meeting student learning goals, it is important that they be engaging, realistic, and focused directly on specific learning goals (McKeachie & Svinicki, 2006). Of equal importance, according to the TACOMA model, is consideration of the context in which they are used. For example, when considering cases in the classroom, the teacher must monitor discussion carefully to ensure that goals are met. Characteristics of the learner such as learner diversity, developmental level, and tolerance for ambiguity also have potential to impact learning outcomes. Learner diversity can focus the lens through which students perceive the details of the case. And although cases should be challenging, cases that are too complex can diminish engagement and ultimately, student understanding. Similarly, when students find it difficult to tolerate ambiguity (often seen in introductory and lower division classes), it may be best to use a combination of closed and open cases, thereby building up to greater levels of ambiguity (McKeachie & Svinicki, 2006). Assessment of effectiveness can be accomplished in a variety of ways, including formative assessments such as in-the-moment reactions and measures of participation (quality and quantity of participation) as well as summative assessments gathered through formal testing.

Group work is a second strategy that can be used to meet the learning outcomes put forth in Goal 5. Transitioning from a discussion of values to immediate application of the material through a related group assignment increases student engagement with the material and enables the instructor to work more closely with students. In addition, working in groups allows a student to approach a task with peer support in a smaller, less intimidating context than the larger classroom setting. Group work can take on many forms (e.g., collaborative learning, cooperative learning, and jigsaw) and be designed to be short-term, completed within a single class period, or long-term, completed over the course of the semester.

Like the case study method, group work can be constructed to meet specific learning outcomes associated with the development of values. However, it offers additional advantages in light of the TACOMA model, particularly for the components of learning strategies and learner characteristics. Group work allows the use of diverse learning strategies and also engages students in ways that are not possible when students work alone. Consider first that group work can be structured to model as well as practice higher order ethical thinking. For instance, in conjunction with case studies, group activities can be structured to weigh evidence, identify ambiguities, recognize different perspectives, and consider ethical issues in light of professional standards across a variety of situations. Student groups then share their findings with the class, and here similarities and differences across cases can be integrated into the discussion. Second, because of peer support, group work presents opportunities for challenging students in ways that are different from when students work alone. Using a long-term activity, students can find their own examples of ethically challenging or troubling events with which psychologists have had to contend (see Pope & Vetter, 1992) and then evaluate these events in light of ethical values. Finally, for sensitive ethical issues or for students who are reticent about speaking in class, working in groups may be an ideal way to engage students in discussions of values and may give them confidence to speak their minds when encountering real-world ethical dilemmas.

According to the TACOMA model, it is important to consider contextual variables that may affect group learning. Barkley, Cross, and Major (2004) outlined several practices that increase the effectiveness of group work across situations. Specifically, students need a clear, meaningful task in which to engage that is linked to student learning goals. It is crucial that groups are constructed so that all members have the opportunity to contribute and that they are able to complete the task in the allotted time. Characteristics of the learner should also be considered when constructing groups. It is best to construct groups that are heterogeneous with respect to gender, ethnicity, and other demographic variables (Halpern, 2000; Millis & Cottell, 1998), especially if sociocultural awareness is a learning goal. In-class group work can be used to provide formative feedback, which allows the instructor to make adjustments to teaching strategies. Group work content can be included in formal testing for summative assessment.

Despite the usefulness of both case studies and group work for developing values, there are a number of potential drawbacks. Construction of cases, as well as modification of preexisting cases can be time intensive. Developing in-class group activities also requires careful preparation, and they consume class time. Social loafing is a potential problem (Kerr, 1983; K. Williams, Harkins, & Latane, 1981). To address this, instructors can require students to turn in separate papers as well as emphasize the need for equal "air time" during the presentation. Social loafing also can be countered by assigning both a group grade and an individual grade. Further, group work decreases an instructor's level of control in the classroom. Level of comfort with these aspects has the potential to impact strategy effectiveness and ultimately influence student outcomes. For many faculty, the benefits of active student engagement with the material outweigh such drawbacks.

Promoting Sociocultural and International Awareness Through Service Learning and Cultural Awareness Activities

Goal 8 of the *APA Guidelines for the Undergraduate Psychology Major* centers on sociocultural and international awareness, specifically that students should "recognize, understand, and respect the complexity of sociocultural and international diversity" (APA, 2007a, p. 21). We focus on two teaching strategies, service learning and cultural awareness activities, both of which involve learning outside the classroom. Service learning encompasses a wide range of community service opportunities, whereas cultural awareness activities require an affiliation with an individual or group from a different cultural context. According to the TACOMA model, the challenge of teaching is managing the interplay of teaching strategies, learner strategies, learner characteristics, and assessment. The challenge is even more complex as academic work extends beyond the classroom.

Many psychology faculty want students to see the relevance of course content and apply course concepts to real world issues. Service learning is an excellent teaching strategy for accomplishing this goal (Heffernan, 2001). In service learning, students learn concepts through active service in the community. This strategy allows students to apply knowledge as opposed to simply receiving it and in doing so fosters both the motivation to learn and critical thinking skills (Beckman, 1997; Klinger, 1999). Service learning has multiple benefits to the institution and to the community, such as building true community partnerships (Roschelle, Turpin, & Elias, 2000; Valerius & Hamilton, 2001).

For service learning to be most successful in meeting course objectives and fostering student learning, it must involve a community activity that (a) addresses specific learning objectives for the course, (b) targets a community need, and (c) is seamlessly and consistently integrated into the course (Ozorak, 2004). These characteristics are what distinguish it from volunteerism or community service in which students engage in the community without a direct link back to academic content (Cauley et al., 2001). In addition, service learning requires careful orientation of the students as well as the community partners, and faculty must develop meaningful reflective assignments in order for students to make the connections between their experiences and the academic course content. Osborne and Renick (2006) have provided a list of best practices for service learning programs.

Cultural awareness activities are a second strategy for promoting an understanding of sociocultural diversity. Instructors design activities in which students choose an affiliation opportunity with another cultural group. For example, Mahan (1982) reported on successful semester-long cultural awareness programs for student teachers in which the learning goal shaped the class activities. The activities included attendance at cultural activities, in-depth interviews, dining at the home of a member of another cultural group, attending a church service, riding school bus routes, and involvement with community organizations. The instructor has the option of using service learning or community involvement experiences as cultural awareness activities. The goal is to help students take another's perspective, which can lead to attitude change and empathy (Pope-Davis, Breaux, & Lie, 1997). Such activities are meaningful to students because the activities offer the students the opportunity to reflect on the origin of their beliefs and to appreciate how they can change.

Faculty must ensure that students select cultural awareness activities that are meaningful and meet the objectives of the assignment. Referring to the TACOMA model, the characteristics of the learner are paramount in this approach. Faculty should consider how students approach the activity (e.g., with proper respect and openness) and should ensure they are safe in their new setting. For example, in order to increase awareness of diversity of religious beliefs and practices, an instructor at a college with students who are predominantly White, affluent, and Southern Baptist might assign students to attend a service of a religious group that is unfamiliar to them. The students can be given the option of attending a Greek Orthodox service, an African Methodist Episcopal service, a Catholic service in a Hispanic neighborhood, a Muslim service, a Native American Indian religious ritual, a Jewish service, or a Quaker meeting. As is true for all cross-cultural experiences, it is important that students review the group's customs and norms in advance and realize that they need to be respectful of those norms. Students should avoid calling undue attention to themselves as visitors and should understand that it might be inappropriate for them to participate in some aspects of the service. It is sometimes helpful for the student or the instructor to contact the group's leader in advance to discuss these issues. The faculty should include options that students feel comfortable with but that also push them beyond their latitude of familiarity and comfort. Some students, for example, may be intensely uncomfortable interacting with groups of individuals from a different cultural background but may benefit from an interview with one member of that cultural group. Assessment should be based on deep reflection on the experience and integration with the psychological literature. Students should be allowed to express any anxieties and negative emotions they may have experienced. Giving students the grading rubric in advance clarifies the objectives of the assignment and provides a framework for how students should write about the experience.

Although both techniques have numerous advantages, quality implementation of service learning and cultural awareness activities can be time intensive for the faculty member and the students. Students are learning outside of the carefully controlled boundaries of a traditional classroom, and as a result, faculty have little control. Faculty should be vigilant for unforeseen difficulties and misunderstandings.

The TACOMA model emphasizes that implementation also can be influenced by characteristics of learners, such as readiness to engage in the community, how comfortable they feel with the setting, and maturity in handling social and cultural encounters. A poorly designed and implemented activity can confirm stereotypes and lead to student resistance (Jackson, 1999). Students can have strong emotional reactions to people who are different from them, and these reactions are more likely for students with less multicultural experience (Biernat, Vescio, Theno, & Crandall, 1996). Therefore, it is important to consider providing alternative assignments. Faculty may design different activities for students who already have considerable experience interacting with people from other social groups compared with students from a relatively homogeneous student body who perhaps have less experience. Flexibility, therefore, becomes crucial. Despite potential drawbacks, well designed service learning and cultural awareness activities are excellent ways to enrich student learning of course content while expanding social and cultural awareness.

Promoting Personal Development Through Portfolios and Student Presentations

Goal 9 of the *APA Guidelines for the Undergraduate Psychology Major* (APA, 2007a) focuses on personal development. Specifically, students are expected to "gain insight into their own and others' behavior and mental processes and apply effective strategies for self-management as they strive for self-improvement" (p. 21). Two teaching strategies that can promote these goals are portfolios and presentations.

With portfolios, students collect artifacts that represent their best work according to criteria set by the student or the instructor. The portfolio can represent the work in a single class or across their entire course of study (Tillema, 2001). Portfolios are flexible both in terms of their format and the learning goals they can facilitate. Portfolios can increase student learning and critical thinking but increasingly are being used to provide both the student and the faculty an in-depth understanding of students' knowledge, skills, and professional attitudes (Keller, Craig, Launius, Loher, & Cooledge, 2004).

Tillema (2001) studied the impact of reflective learning portfolios in which students collect key artifacts of learning and achievement and then give their personal evaluations of the significance of the work. The portfolios provided students with useful insights into their own learning that allowed them to improve their effectiveness and redirect their efforts if needed. Similarly, Brown (2002) found that portfolios improved students' self-knowledge but also found that they enhanced communication and organization skills.

Larkin, Pines, and Bechtel (2002) used a career exploration portfolio to help students think about the fit between their own interests and abilities and potential careers. Consistent with Goal 9, portfolios give both students and faculty a developmental view of the students' work as well as ideas for future learning needs and goals.

As a teaching strategy, the portfolio requires a clear explanation of the scope of the task and its relevance to course goals. In accordance with the TACOMA model, the instructor can alter the criteria for work to be included in the portfolio according to the learning goal. If the goal is concrete and specific, such as including five pieces of original writing, then instructors can set rigid criteria. If the goal is to give students insight into their own learning and abilities, then the student should be allowed some freedom to decide what should be included (Tillema, 2001). Instructors may see resistance on the part of the students because portfolios can require a great deal of reflection and effort. Development of portfolios should be integrated into the regular class work and the culture of the department as much as possible (Keller et al., 2004). Students may be given feedback at various points such as at the end of a learning unit or at the completion of an educational program. The chance for repeated reflection affords students the opportunity to identify their personal and professional values, empowers them to set goals for themselves, and allows them to appreciate the skills they have acquired.

The criteria for evaluation should be set a priori, and the instructor should be prepared to give process feedback about the portfolio. Portfolios are often evaluated by multiple people, and the establishment of reliability and validity of assessment is critical (Keller et al., 2004). Keller et al. (2004) have developed rubrics for reviewing and evaluating psychology portfolios.

Student presentations are a second strategy that can be used to meet the outcomes of personal development set forth in Goal 9. The usual rationale for assigning presentations is to actively engage students in honing their communication skills while mastering a particular content area, but the process of deciding what to include and how best to present information in a limited amount of time also enhances metacognitive skills. Furthermore, preparing and making presentations require self-regulation in setting and achieving goals. *Self-regulation* refers to the ability to regulate one's attention, select goals, find the means to attain those goals, and cope with problems in reaching these goals (Lerner, 2002). Students also gain the valuable skill of synthesizing information and making connections. Motivation is likely to be high because students often are allowed to choose their topic and use creative license to make it their own (Deci & Ryan, 1985).

With presentations, the teaching strategy is for students to learn concepts for themselves and then teach other students through their presentations. The TACOMA model can help teachers to design the presentation assignment to optimize learning for both the presenter and the audience. Whether students work individually or in groups, it is critical that students be given clear instructions on the purpose and format of their presentation. They need to have a goal that will shape their presentations. For example, should the presenters provide a handout for the rest of the class, and if so, how detailed should it be? Likewise, the instructor can require presenters to end with "food-for-thought" questions to encourage discussion and to help students to think critically. Giving students the grading rubric at the outset reduces anxiety because the goals are clear and they can use it as a guide as they are preparing. Peer feedback also may be included as a way to actively engage the audience and to provide useful information from a student perspective.

A shortcoming of presentations is that students may not be equally engaged or interested in the topics they are responsible for presenting, which can lead to varying levels of quality in the presentations. If the class is to be tested over the material in the presentations, then the uneven quality can cause resentment of the teaching method. Student presentations also may fail to include critical information or include misinformation because the instructor does not directly control where the students get their information and what they choose to include or omit. However, these shortcomings can be minimized with clear instructions, guidance, and grading criteria. The benefits to students in terms of self-regulation, communication and metacognitive skills often outweigh the drawbacks.

RECOMMENDATIONS AND CONCLUSION

We end this chapter with a set of recommendations:

1. Teaching strategies should be driven by desired learning goals.
2. Consistent with the TACOMA model, instructors should recognize that students bring prior knowledge, beliefs, expectations, and their own learning strategies to the teaching situation, and these factors interact with instructors' choices about content, pedagogy, and assessment to determine how well students perform and what they learn.
3. Consistent with the TACOMA model, instructors should use formative assessment to monitor student learning to determine whether teaching methods are being effective and to make necessary adjustments.
4. Teaching should be recognized and rewarded as the complex, dynamic, and skilled activity that it is.
5. Psychology faculty should be encouraged to conduct both laboratory and classroom research to investigate teaching and learning in general and to examine whether particular teaching methods are effective in different situations and for achiev-

ing particular learning goals. They should document and share results publicly through presentations and publications.

6. Greater resources should be allocated for faculty development of teaching. This should include improved faculty development programs, incentives of time, money, travel support, and scholarly recognition for classroom research.

7. Psychologists should share their knowledge of effective teaching and learning with campus stakeholders such as students, colleagues, and administrators, particularly directors for centers for teaching and learning.

When nonteachers think about the hardships of being a teacher, they probably think of grading papers and dealing with difficult students, but the TACOMA model illustrates a more fundamental challenge. When teachers select and implement teaching strategies, they must manage a complex interplay of factors in order for students to achieve a learning goal. In this chapter, we have described the TACOMA model, which illustrates the context-sensitive nature of teaching and can help instructors to implement teaching strategies successfully. We then discussed the importance of linking selection of teaching methods to learning goals. Using the learning goals endorsed by the APA, we illustrated how teaching methods can be chosen according to learning goals and implemented with the guidance of the TACOMA model.

The subtext of the TACOMA model and the discussion of implementing teaching strategies to achieve learning goals is that teaching presents as complex a problem in research and application as found in any area of psychology. Teaching knowledge and skill develop across the entire career through research, study, and reflective practice. Instructors, especially new ones, benefit from institutional and peer support in developing teaching skills. Acts of teaching scholarship should be recognized and rewarded. Teachers of psychology have an advantage over teachers in other fields because so many topics central to teaching, such as learning, motivation, and problem solving, are within the domain of psychology. Teachers of psychology have an obligation to share this knowledge with both colleagues and students.

New teaching methods are developed each year, and new technologies have quickened the pace. As we develop and test these new methods, we should abandon the notion that a method is either always good or always bad. The TACOMA model tells us that we should not expect to find a method that is effective in every situation. We should expect to find that new methods work well in some situations but not in others and that they promote some kinds of learning goals more than others. For any method to be successful, it is up to the teacher to make decisions and adjustments based on the interaction of multiple factors.

7

TEACHING AND LEARNING IN A DIGITAL WORLD

KEITH MILLIS, SUZANNE BAKER, JUDITH E. OWEN BLAKEMORE,
FRED CONNINGTON, YOLANDA Y. HARPER, WEI-CHEN HUNG,
ART KOHN, AND JEFFREY STOWELL

How is technology changing undergraduate education? There can be little doubt about the power of technology to change the world. As technology has become smaller, faster, and more affordable, people have altered the way they obtain information, organize their lives, and communicate.

Technological changes have also created an entirely new set of educational tools for teaching and learning. The instructor now has instant access to multimedia, software, and vast online resources, and can use student response devices such as clickers to monitor student knowledge, mood, and opinion. Publishers, private companies, and individuals are creating teaching tools that simulate psychology laboratories, day care centers, and even therapy sessions. Intelligent tutors use natural language to mentor students in real time. Tools such as wikis, Facebook, and Del.icio.us extend the boundaries of the classroom, and virtual world technologies might even one day replace the traditional classroom, enabling classes to meet in an entirely virtual world.

Clearly, new technologies have the potential to affect education in dramatic ways. For example, new technologies have expanded the capability of distance education courses. Once relegated to simple correspondence courses or telecourses, distance education can now be more convenient, compelling, and cost-effective. As a result, distance education is becoming more popular and may significantly change the model of higher education. New technologies also give one the ability to address important issues such as diversity and accessibility in effective new ways. At the same time, they also raise ethical issues that need attention.

The question is no longer whether technology will be a major force in psychology education. The question now is whether psychologists will be prepared to make optimal use of technology for creating the next generation of well-equipped citizens. Our goal for this chapter is to review some of these educational tools and consider ways in which they might affect teaching and learning. We also touch on other issues: challenges to implementing new technologies, ethical concerns, and how new technologies might be used to achieve inclusive excellence.

TECHNOLOGY, PEDAGOGY, AND STUDENTS

Although the various stakeholders in education (students, instructors, parents, administrators, and policy makers) hold different goals and viewpoints, they share at least one wish: to promote durable and meaningful learning. Technological advances have great promise, but their ability to promote learning depends on a number of related multidimensional factors. Figure 7.1 illustrates that the impact of technology on learning depends on the interactions among characteristics of the technology, the student, and the pedagogy. We acknowledge that this is a simplified model that leaves out many factors (e.g., content, culture, the instructor, physical environments), but we present it as a starting point. Technologies vary on a number of attributes, including accessibility, presentation format of the content, use of multimedia, and cost. Students vary on age, socioeconomic status, computer literacy, prior knowledge, interests, and cognitive and memory constraints. *Pedagogy* refers to the varieties of teaching methods (e.g., lecture, Socratic dialogues, problem-based learning).

Meaningful learning with technology requires understanding the mutually reinforcing relationships between all three elements taken together. For example, if a software program can present only text and graphics, then students who learn best from interactive activities will probably not benefit as much from this technology as students who do well from reading. Therefore, one starting point in evaluating technology in the context of teaching and learning is to examine how the technology can adapt to the characteristics of the student. For example, a computerized tutoring system may adopt

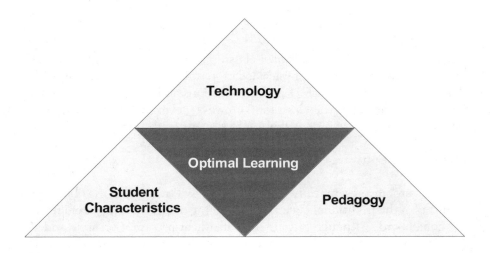

Figure 7.1. A simplified framework for discussing the impact of technology on teaching and learning.

the pedagogy of using personally relevant information in examples if it detects that the student is losing interest.

This framework is important for understanding the role of technology because new technologies are being used by instructors, often without deep consideration of their effectiveness or how they should be implemented optimally. Technology is not an educational panacea and does not automatically make teachers more capable. For example, one of us (Keith Millis) had students make Web pages for a history of psychology course. The students were required to include links from their Web pages to others in the class so that they would acquire deep knowledge of the entire domain by interacting with each other. Unfortunately, students did not include many links in their pages and spent most of their time building their own pages and learning the software. This example illustrates that although the Web page technology afforded collaborative learning by enabling links, it was up to the instructor to make sure that true collaborative learning occurred.

We believe that technology has the potential to provide students with learning opportunities to gain the knowledge and skills needed to survive an increasingly complex world. However, the bottom line is that teachers need to be versed in best practices in the use of technology. Their students also need to become well-informed users of technology; the *American Psychological Association (APA) Guidelines for the Undergraduate Psychology Major* highlight the importance of technological literacy as a vital component of an undergraduate liberal arts education (APA, 2007a). In the pages that follow, we discuss ways that technology is affecting today's classrooms, followed by a brief discussion of newer and emerging technologies.

OPTIMIZING THE TRADITIONAL CLASSROOM

The definition of a *traditional* classroom as a place where teacher and student interact in the same physical location is changing as technology makes classroom experiences, such as group discussions and lectures, available outside of the confines of the classroom. However, even within the traditional classroom, technology is contributing to student learning in new ways.

Presentation Software

Classroom presentation software, such as PowerPoint, has become a mainstay of the traditional classroom, replacing overhead transparencies and the chalkboard. Although criticized for its linear presentation style and all-too-frequent inappropriate use (Tufte, 2004), research suggests that multimedia presentations (images, words, sounds) can improve student learning and satisfaction. Combining visual and auditory modes creates multiple cues for storing and retrieving information (Mayer, 2005; Paivio, 1986) as long as the depictions are relevant to course content (see Ludwig, Daniel, Froman, & Mathie, 2004, for review and best practices). New features in presentation software include greater flexibility in the order of content presentation and easier integration and management of content.

Student Response Systems

Unfortunately, there may be a gap between what instructors think they are communicating and what is actually being understood by the students, especially in large classes (Caldwell, 2007). Instructors now can peek into students' minds by using electronic student polling and assessment devices, known as *clickers*, or polling software installed on laptops and other mobile devices. Instructors can ask opinion or knowledge-based questions to which students respond electronically. Polling systems tabulate student responses and immediately display them to the class. Polling systems have a number of positive attributes. Using electronic polling, students respond more honestly to knowledge-based questions than when using traditional methods such as hand raising (Stowell & Nelson, 2007). The immediacy of feedback can increase students' self-awareness about their learning progress. This is crucial because students are notoriously poor at accurately gauging their own understanding (R. H. Maki, 1998; Palincsar & Brown, 1984). Furthermore, depending on the polling results, the instructor may choose to change the content or mode of teaching on the fly. Another advantage is that polling allows, and possibly empowers, shy or anxious students to participate in a nonthreatening manner. We should note that the largest effects of student response systems on learning occur when they are used in conjunction with peer instruction (Duncan & Mazur, 2005). For example, the instructor might first poll students on a conceptual question before having them work in small groups to explain and justify their responses. The instructor might then poll the class a second time, revealing the correct answer. The uses of student response systems mentioned here highlight how technology can be used with different pedagogies for reaching different types of students.

Online Testing

Online testing is similar to electronic polling but is typically used for summative assessment. Online testing frees up class time for other activities and can take advantage of distributed practice effects by breaking content into manageable chunks on which students can be tested frequently (Glenberg, 1979; Roediger & Karpicke, 2006a). Instructors can also allow students more flexibility in their exam schedule by making online tests available for windows of time.

Course Management Systems

Traditionally, instructors used course management systems (CMS; e.g., Blackboard and Moodle) for distance learning, but now they are using them to manage face-to-face courses too. CMS provide efficient ways to manage the administrative functions of teaching (e.g., controlling access to content, assignment submissions, grade books) and to promote interactive learning. CMS typically have sophisticated systems for testing as well as for anonymous surveys (e.g., for course evaluations). They offer internal e-mail, discussion boards, and other forms of electronic communication. Students can work collaboratively in private discussion groups. Students can submit assignments online that instructors retrieve, grade, and return electronically.

STRETCHING THE WALLS OF THE TRADITIONAL CLASSROOM: DISTANCE LEARNING

Today's online courses are nothing like the televised or correspondence distance learning courses of the past. Unlike correspondence courses, contemporary online courses usually begin and end with the regular academic semester and have specific deadlines for exams and assignments, much like their face-to-face counterparts. There can be a good deal of student–instructor and student–student interaction mediated through electronic communication. However, unlike synchronous two-way video courses in which students watch the instructor live, but at a distance, or even the traditional college class, online courses are generally asynchronous. That is, students can log in and complete their work at any time of the day or night, vastly increasing students' and instructors' convenience and flexibility. Unlike any of their distance predecessors, online courses are operated within CMS that support teaching and learning in increasingly sophisticated ways (e.g., bulletin boards, blogs, chat rooms, podcasts, PowerPoint presentations, videos, links to Web pages).

Distance learning is spreading (Allen & Seaman, 2005, 2007). More than two thirds of all institutions of higher education in the United States offer some online courses, and about half of these institutions offer complete degree programs online (Allen & Seaman, 2007). This trend is also evident in undergraduate psychology courses (Piotrowski & Vodanovich, 2004).

Can students be effectively educated through the Web? There is some controversy surrounding online courses, perhaps especially about fully online degree programs. There are certainly reports of resistance from faculty to offering online courses and a sense from some faculty that somehow online courses cannot be as "good" as face-to-face courses. Indeed, at the Puget Sound conference there was a formal debate about whether students could receive a quality education online. Faculty representing the "no" side argued that the traditional face-to-face context provides interpersonal experiences that help students learn and develop a meaningful sense of self and social connectedness. They suggested that students gain many more benefits from their college years than simply content knowledge and skills to prepare them for a profession. The traditional college education can be a developmental experience, helping younger students prepare for adult life.

On the other side of the debate was the recognition that these courses are already widely available and increasing, and that online courses often serve a particular group of students. Older students, those with employment and family responsibilities, and students who live far from available or affordable higher education are particularly likely to enroll in online courses (Allen & Seaman, 2007). Also, it was pointed out that there can be a genuine sense of community among students who are enrolled online. Researchers have reported high levels of interaction using electronically mediated communication and have documented instances of humor, sarcasm, expressing agreement with and support of other students, and referring to the group as a whole (Garrison, Anderson, & Archer, 2000; Rourke, Anderson, Garrison, & Archer, 1999; Zhu, 2006). The faculty who favored distance education in the debate also mentioned advances in CMS that enable meaningful learning experiences. In sum, there was no clear winner of the debate. Clearly, faculty attitudes toward and perceptions of online courses vary considerably (e.g., Gibson, Harris, & Colaric, 2008; Maguire, 2005).

What does research tell one about the effectiveness of online education? Several meta-analyses and narrative reviews based on hundreds of empirical studies (e.g., Bernard et al., 2004; Lou, Bernard, & Abrami, 2006; R. H. Maki & W. S. Maki, 2007; Sitzman, Kraiger, Stewart, & Wisher, 2006; Zhao, Lei, & Yan, 2005) have indicated that academic performance in online courses is similar to that in face-to-face classes, but there is a great deal of variability. Sometimes online courses produce much better outcomes than comparable face-to-face courses; sometimes they have much poorer outcomes; and in some cases there is little difference between them. Because of this variability it is important to ask what features of online courses are associated with better outcomes. Interestingly, as technology has improved, so has performance in distance courses, with more recent courses having better outcomes than older courses (Zhao et al., 2005). In addition, better outcomes are associated with highly involved and interactive *live* instructors providing regular feedback, the opportunity for students to interact with each other, the use of engaging media, and regular active-learning assignments (Bernard et al., 2004; R. H. Maki & W. S. Maki, 2007; Zhao et al., 2005). As conveyed by Figure 7.1, the impact of distance learning surely depends on the types of pedagogies that it can support together with the characteristics of the student.

How can teachers assess online courses to improve them? Resources exist to help faculty develop effective online courses. One widely used system is Quality Matters (QM), which is run by MarylandOnline, a statewide consortium of colleges in Maryland. QM provides criteria to evaluate the design of online and hybrid courses, either by self-review or peer review. The standards include "course overview and introduction, learning objectives, assessment and measurement, resources and materials, learner engagement, course technology, learner support, and accessibility" (see the QM rubric at http://www.qualitymatters.org). Qualified peer reviewers who have experience in teaching courses in the discipline can assess the depth and quality of content. We encourage further development of similar rubrics to evaluate the design and quality of online courses specific to psychology under the leadership of organizations such as the APA.

What are the major challenges for instructors who would like to teach online? The most prominent challenge is that online courses require more faculty time to learn the pedagogy appropriate to online teaching, to develop new courses, and to master new and continuously changing technology. Teaching online takes more time relative to teaching in the face-to-face classroom. One recent study did a careful examination of the time it takes to teach a previously developed and taught course and concluded that it took about 20% more faculty time to teach online. The author concluded:

> For the first time, research has shown that successful distance education is contingent upon smaller, not larger, class sizes—nearly half the size of its traditional ancestor. Online teaching should not be expected to generate larger revenues by means of larger class sizes at the expense of effective instruction or faculty over-subscription. (Tomei, 2004, p. 44)

Are there any tips for faculty who are considering teaching online? At a minimum, we suggest talking with someone at their institution who already does and seriously considering that person's advice. Many institutions also provide faculty development programs or courses (some of which are themselves at least partly online) to assist faculty in developing the necessary skills. In addition, the Sloan Consortium (http://www.sloanconsortium.org) is just one of several Web sites that provide resources on effective practices in online teaching. Last, there are also publications for helping faculty incorporate learning activities in their online course (e.g., Shank, 2007).

LOOKING TOWARD THE FUTURE: NEW AND EMERGING TECHNOLOGIES

Educators, computer scientists, cognitive scientists, and textbook companies are creating an explosion of new computer-mediated technologies. In the section that follows, we describe some of the technologies that could impact the future of undergraduate psychology education. When considering use of these technologies, instructors will need to consider the extent to which the technology supports social connectedness, collaboration, and active learning, and the amount of structure provided for specific learning activities. Other, more practical considerations include cost and degree of accessibility and usability by the specific student population.

Available Commercial Multimedia

Before a faculty member or department rushes out to buy an expensive software product, we suggest first making a call to a major book publisher. Many publishers provide their customers with a free collection of lecture aids, including animations, videos, and PowerPoint lectures. Publishers also augment textbooks with e-books. In an e-book, publishers migrate an existing textbook into an electronic form such as PDF files and then add a collection of Web links and dynamic media elements. Publishers and other private companies have also developed a range of electronic ancillaries that include page-turning tutorials, virtual laboratories where students can replicate classic research, and video jukeboxes where students can interactively do research within video archives. Most of these products support popular courses such as Introductory Psychology, Social Psychology, Abnormal Psychology, and Developmental Psychology.

Some textbook publishers and private companies produce stand-alone course-in-box software. These tools provide premade lectures, an electronic textbook, a laboratory component, and a recitation forum, which is mediated by the instructor. These products may have the potential to significantly improve the quality of some online courses but may run the risk of homogenizing psychology courses.

Using Technology to Promote Collaborative Learning

Whether in traditional classrooms or learning through the Web, collaborative learning can facilitate the development of higher order skills, such as critical thinking and problem solving. When students work together to determine solutions to complex problems, they frequently work at a level that exceeds the ability of any one individual in the group (Dunlap & Grabinger, 2003; Halpern, 1998). Technology can assume the supporting role through which communication (e.g., e-mail, threaded discussion, chat room) and scaffolding (e.g., links, prompts, feedback) occurs. Tools such as e-mail, real-time communication (e.g., instant messaging, Web conferencing), and asynchronous discussions (e.g., threaded discussions, blogs) are often used to promote group interactions and provide questions and clarifications. Students can use threaded discussion, blogs, and e-mail to make comments, ask questions, or describe events to establish a learning rapport and build a learning community. In addition, students can use chat rooms, instant messaging, and Web conferencing with the instructor or peers to clarify tasks and determine the content most relevant for the class assignments. Instructors can also incorporate these tools to monitor and comment on students' progress toward learning outcomes and content knowledge. Recent open (and often free) editing systems (e.g., wikis) and digital portfolio systems (e.g., LiveText, ClassCentral) offer structured environments in which students can organize thoughts, represent knowledge using multimedia, link relevant project works, and demonstrate learning outcomes. These tools enable students to see the use of knowledge and form connections to prior knowledge, making learning more durable. They also allow instructors creative options for assessing, monitoring, and facilitating student progress.

Virtual Worlds and Learning Environments

In a virtual world, the user creates an *avatar*, a character that represents them in a simulated space. Avatars can move through the virtual world and can interact with each other and with objects in the world. Examples include Second Life (http://www.secondlife.com), ActiveWorlds (http://www.activeworlds.com), and Whyville (http://www.whyville.net). Some virtual worlds (e.g., Whyville) provide a structured space, including ready-made buildings and environments. Others (e.g., Second Life) allow users to create objects, structures, and even entire virtual communities. These may be virtual recreations of the real world or they may be objects, environments, or settings that could never exist outside virtual space.

Some virtual worlds essentially present a *blank slate* environment, which can be used by the instructor for learning activities and class experiences of various types. For example, they can be used to facilitate social connectedness and collaboration by providing a space for online meetings or office hours or as a space for student group meetings or collaborative work. Interactions in a virtual world may help build a sense of community in classes that otherwise may not meet in a face-to-face setting (e.g., Steinkuehler & Williams, 2006). Use of virtual worlds can broaden the campus community by enabling collaboration at a distance, for example, between students at different campuses or even internationally. Psychology faculty might use virtual worlds to provide students with opportunities for role-playing to practice skills or as a platform to create objects and environments (e.g., creating a working model of the brain and nervous system or a virtual lab for data collection). Student-designed research can examine social interactions in virtual world settings (e.g., Yee, Bailenson, Urbanek, Chang, & Merget, 2007). Most virtual worlds used for education allow for a great deal of creativity on the part of the instructor to design activities appropriate for the particular content, student population, and learning goals being addressed. However, the lack of structure puts the burden on the instructor to design appropriate activities that use this developing technology in ways that result in learning.

Intelligent Tutors

Intelligent tutoring systems (ITS) are computerized programs that mimic human tutors by tailoring instruction to the individual (Graesser, Chipman, & King, 2007; Koedinger, Anderson, Hadley, & Mark, 1997). ITS have various attributes that may be attractive to educators and students. First, ITS promote deep learning by employing a number of well-established learning principles, such as anchored instruction, collaborative problem solving, scaffolding, and question answering. Second, ITS induce impressive learning gains (Graesser et al., 2007). Third, many ITS hold dialogues between the tutor and student using natural language, which is natural to the student and effective for increasing learning (VanLehn et al., 2007).

ITS and other media platforms increasingly use animated pedagogical agents to deliver content; provide help; and serve as teachers, models, guides, and peers (Graeeser, Jeon, & Duffy, 2008). Like avatars, these pedagogical agents come in a variety of shapes and sizes (e.g., a person, an insect, an object). They might talk, point or gesture, understand, reflect, respond to the learner's input, show personality, and display emotion (Yilmaz, Ören, & Aghaee, 2006). A system may use only one pedagogical agent or several. If there is more than one, then they may interact with one another in engaging and pedagogically effective ways. For example, one agent may be a student modeling desirable behaviors (for the human student) in front of a *teacher* agent. Given the system, the human then might be interacting with a virtual community of agents. Not only are pedagogical agents engaging to students, they also offer flexibility beyond that of a prerecorded message because they can respond dynamically to meet the current learning demands of the student.

Other New Technologies

There are many different types of technologies in various stages of development that can potentially shape the future of education. Bonk (2004) and the *Horizon Report* (New Media Consortium and the Educause Learning Commission, 2008) summarize many of these technologies, including educational and serious games. These games immerse the students in a virtual world in which the students must achieve goals, and they learn while interacting with virtual and (possibly) real characters. The games are typically used for training, education, simulation, and advertising (Prensky, 2000). One advantage of educational games is many students find them extremely engaging to play. Teenage gamers play an average of 20 hours per week (Yee, 2006). Therefore, students may be more likely to engage in out-of-classroom work if it involves a well-crafted educational game. However, there are challenges to building educational games. Besides monetary resources, a key challenge is to weave the curricular material into the game while preserving engagement and pedagogical effectiveness.

Other types of technologies being developed include virtual reality, immersive learning environments, interactive simulations, wearable computing, and ubiquitous learning in which learning takes place anywhere at anytime (S. Thomas, 2006). A student using virtual reality to learn how neurons communicate with one another might "swim" within synapses by using virtual reality goggles and haptic gloves. In wearable computing, students and teachers will be equipped with small mobile microcomputers, microphones, and cameras so that they can communicate with one another and access the Web in real time using different modalities. With ubiquitous learning, students learn in a game-like environment using cell phones, PDAs, televisions, and computers. One potential advantage of wearable computing and ubiquitous learning is to engender collaborative problem-solving activities in the real world.

Currently, empirical validation of the educational value of many of the new and emerging technologies described previously is in its infancy, but it is quickly growing. Psychologists are increasingly exploring cognitive constraints and molecular factors that enhance learning in electronic environments (see Mayer, 2005, for a compilation of this research and relevant learning principles). This research examines the impact of various configurations of multimedia presentations on learning. It remains unclear the extent to which this research generalizes to complex learning environments, however. For example, educators have only just begun to examine teaching and learning in virtual worlds (e.g., Antonacci & Modaress, 2008; Dickey, 2005; Neulight, Kafai, Kao, Foley, & Galas, 2007; M. Peterson, 2006). Many of the relevant unanswered questions relate to the relationships among technological factors, student characteristics, and pedagogical techniques depicted in Figure 7.1. How does student engagement in a virtual world compare with the real world? Which activities in virtual worlds contribute to learning, and which do not? What student populations are virtual world activities best suited for? For example, do more introverted students who tend to "hang back" from collaboration and social interaction in a face-to-face setting feel more comfortable in a virtual setting, where interaction is one step removed from the real world? Other challenges also exist. Can virtual worlds be accessible to all students? How do instructors enhance collaborative learning? These and other questions need to be addressed by psychology instructors wishing to use this technology in optimal ways.

USING TECHNOLOGY TO ACHIEVE INCLUSIVE EXCELLENCE

Technology provides avenues for faculty to be more inclusive than ever before. The Internet has increased the availability of new information about various cultures to faculty and students. It is possible to connect with people around the world to provide educational insight into diverse perspectives. Students who would normally not be able to leave their homes as a result of a disabling condition, or any number of personal, social, political, or economic reasons, may learn from others online with perspectives they would not have otherwise known existed. Other students might be more willing to travel to other countries and further enrich their educational and career experiences or engage in a variety of intercultural exchanges toward developing international and intercultural competencies.

Instructors can use these emerging tools to support students who come from diverse backgrounds and abilities. Simulations, online tools, and online data create new options for students with various disabilities. For example, technology gives students the flexibility to listen to or view lectures as many times as needed, resulting in increased comprehension and retention. Such opportunities can be especially valuable for students studying in environments in which the language of instruction is not their native language. Devices such as digital pens aid students in writing classroom notes by retrieving the notes electronically over the Internet; these notes can then be synchronized with video and audio recordings of class presentations.

Teachers can also use these tools to assist students in the development of multicultural competencies. These environments provide an opportunity to learn culturally specific knowledge and values as well as culturally appropriate interpersonal and language skills before entering a real-world setting in which these skills are required. Virtual environments could also help students consider how others may perceive their behaviors in intercultural contexts. Where appropriate, psychology teachers will be able to use virtual environments to teach students about different perspectives by having them represent themselves in any way imaginable, allowing them to try on different identities (e.g., Bainbridge, 2007; Yee et al., 2007). The choices students make and how these choices impact their experiences can be a stimulus for discussions among peers and faculty.

All stakeholders in education are ethically bound to ensure the availability of technologies that aid students with disabilities. Such technologies include voice recognition software, screen readers, audio and e-books, computer-based tools to assist with organizing writing, text-to-speech software, handheld scanners, real-time captioning, digital Braillers and screen enlargers (Parette, Wojcik, Peterson-Karlan, & Hourcade, 2005). The National Center on Accessible Information Technology in Education's AccessIT Web site (http://www.washington.edu/accessit) provides practical guidance on using electronic and information technology for students and employees with disabilities in educational institutions at all academic levels. The AccessIT Web site provides free curricula for educators. Here faculty will find publications on universal Web design, accessible instructional software, assuring that informational technology in distance learning courses is accessible, providing accessible technology in labs, accessible file formats, and so on.

INSTITUTIONAL CHALLENGES FOR ADOPTING NEW TECHNOLOGY

The issue of how and whether technology should be implemented at an institution is important, especially when institutions face budget cuts. If an institution is allocating precious resources toward purchasing state-of-the-art software, then besides achieving whatever the software is meant to do, the institution expects that the software will be used by the target audience (students, teachers, staff). Learning and using new software programs, such as CMS, can be extremely daunting and time consuming. Who makes the decision whether to acquire and use new technology?

Typically the impetus for adoption of new technology in an institution will come from either the leaders at the top or the instructors and students from within. One advantage of the leadership model is the leaders can choose to provide the resources, such as professional development, to effect change in a positive manner. When choosing new technologies, leaders tend to favor standardized technology because it is cost effective and time efficient. Standardized technology reduces compatibility issues, training time, and avoids unnecessary duplication. However, leaders have the burden of choosing the most appropriate technologies to meet the institution's mission and of providing the resources for training faculty and students in those technologies.

Alternatively, technological change that comes from instructors and students spreads across an institution haphazardly. However, one advantage here is that there is little need for administrators to convince individuals to use the technology. Another is that those who learn the technology can assist and serve as role models for others. The disadvantages of this model are that the use of technology is limited and that there is no comprehensive plan for the use of technology. Regardless of the model of implementation, teaching with new technologies should be attractive to a younger generation who might be more familiar with the technologies that instructors now consider innovative.

TECHNOLOGY-RELATED ETHICAL ISSUES

Emerging technologies raise a host of new ethical issues, including privacy rights (e.g., instructors can monitor who is online), intellectual property (e.g., who owns multimedia products produced by faculty and students), and various forms of academic dishonesty (e.g., a student may surreptitiously have another student take his or her online exam). Institutions define and encourage ethical behavior by providing honor codes and guidelines, but the instructor is an important role model for students' ethical standards and responsible use. Therefore, professionalism begins with the instructor. We believe that instructors should try to understand the mind-set of their students when confronting ethically questionable behavior. Current students may not understand that unauthorized sharing of information is unethical because they have developed in a society in which sharing of intellectual property (e.g., music) is done without regard to proprietary rights.

Ethical issues should be presented as part of a larger picture that includes responsible use and professionalism. Most businesses and educational institutions have an acceptable use policy that dictates the responsible, appropriate use of technology. Professionalism dictates that behaviors relating to the field should be consistent with the goals of the profession, and ethical considerations are personal decisions about what is right or wrong. Hinman (2002) outlined the broader view of ethical standards. He identified five values that apply to students, faculty and administrators. They include respect, trust, honesty, fairness and responsibility, all of which should be modeled and reinforced by instructors and expected of students.

RECOMMENDATIONS AND CONCLUSION

A complete review of the issues related to technology in the teaching of psychology is beyond the scope of this chapter. However, there are key areas in which action by individual faculty, departments, institutions, the APA, and other professional organizations could make substantial contributions to the responsible selection, adoption, implementation, and ongoing use of current and emerging technologies. We base our recommendations on the assumption that new technologies will continue to appear and be used in educational settings, with or without the guidance from expert educators, researchers, and psychologists.

We recommend the following for faculty support and development:

1. Departments, institutions, and professional organizations should provide support for training faculty in the use and responsible implementation of technology. Examples of support may include course releases, administrative support, funds for technology training, software, hardware, and travel funds to professional conferences dealing with technology.
2. Before adopting software, faculty should examine preview copies and consider software reviews that are published in *Teaching of Psychology* and other journals to make sure the software is effective as indicated by empirical research.

We recommend the following for technology and learning outcomes:

1. Researchers should conduct rigorous empirical studies on the effectiveness of new technologies and how they interact with student characteristics and pedagogical techniques to provide optimal learning (e.g., the use of appropriate control conditions, meaningful dependent variables).
2. A comprehensive Web site should be established to assist psychology instructors in the wise use of available technologies. This Web site could be modeled after the *Assessment CyberGuide for Learning Goals and Outcomes in the Undergraduate Psychology Major* (APA Task Force on Undergraduate Psychology Major Competencies, 2002a) and could include a matrix of available technologies and types of learning outcomes the technologies afford, as informed by empirically based research.

We recommend the following for online courses and programs:

1. APA should develop and offer targeted support for online instruction in psychology similar to other outreach efforts that APA has made to high school (Teachers of Psychology in Secondary Schools) and community college (Psychology Teachers at Community Colleges) educators.
2. APA should establish a set of recommendations for online instruction in undergraduate psychology comparable to the report from the Task Force on Distance Education and Training in Professional Psychology (APA, 2006b; http://www.apa.org/ed/graduate/distance_ed.pdf).
3. Sponsors of online courses and programs should maintain the same quality standards expected of traditional face-to-face

classes and programs as established by the *APA Guidelines for the Undergraduate Psychology Major* (APA, 2007a) and available benchmarks for quality undergraduate programs (Dunn, McCarthy, Baker, Halonen, & Hill, 2007).

4. Departments and programs should establish ways to ensure that faculty and students are competent in technology used for online courses.

We recommend the following for accessibility and inclusive excellence:

1. Developers of technology should design their products to be accessible to faculty and students with disabilities according to international guidelines such as those established by the World Wide Web Consortium.

2. Instructors should use technology to be inclusive of minorities, those with disabilities, and underserved populations, and to use technology in creative ways to foster understanding of cultural diversity.

We recommend the following for ethics:

1. A task force should be created to review and update APA ethical standards to cover the use of existing and emerging technologies.

2. Instructors who choose to incorporate new instructional technologies should be aware of the potential benefits, limitations, and ethical issues associated with their use.

In this chapter we presented an optimistic perspective on the use of technology in education. We believe that technology holds great promise for the future of education. However, there are several obstacles to overcome. One is the digital divide—the haves and the have-nots. Technology is not cheap, and not everyone can afford a laptop or a broadband Internet connection. Therefore, technology can be exclusive for some instead of being inclusive for all. Faculty should be aware of this fact when requiring technology for their classes. Another is resistance from faculty to adopt, learn, and use the new technologies. Not only is learning new software time consuming but it will also likely change the content and feel of an existing course, which can be anxiety provoking for some faculty. Incorporating new technology may require an attitude change on part of the instructor from being a "sage on the stage," where he or she is the authority, to a role as a "guide on the side," where he or she plays a supportive role, helping students learn by using the technology. Finally, technology requires the support of administrators as well as ongoing technical support. Using technology is an ongoing commitment, a commitment that is sometimes costly, sometimes frustrating, but, we hope, rewarding.

8

PROMISING PRINCIPLES FOR TRANSLATING PSYCHOLOGICAL SCIENCE INTO TEACHING AND LEARNING

FRANK C. WORRELL, BETTINA J. CASAD, DAVID B. DANIEL,
MARK McDANIEL, WAYNE S. MESSER, HAROLD L. MILLER JR.,
VINCENT PROHASKA, AND MARTHA S. ZLOKOVICH

Psychology is a science, teaching is an art, and sciences never generate arts directly out of themselves. An intermediary, inventive mind must make the application.
> —James, *Talks to Teachers on Psychology, and to Students on Some of Life's Ideals* (pp. 7–8)

Where do effective teaching and learning come from? Possible sources include trial and error, word of mouth, the research literature, and even dumb luck. Our predecessors who took on the improvement of teaching and learning at the St. Mary's conference in 1991 (Mathie et al., 1993) advocated the use of active learning, which promised to be sufficiently flexible and rigorous to produce better teaching and learning across a variety of contexts. In light of the present variegated educational landscape, however, we sought an answer that is more sensitive to local terrains. Thus, our view from the University of Puget Sound (UPS) takes a novel approach. We focus on a dynamic model (see Figure 8.1) that can be used to frame teaching and learning practices across content domains and contexts. A foundational premise of the model is that teaching and learning are forms of work and doing either effectively will require much effort. But the focus is not simply on doing more

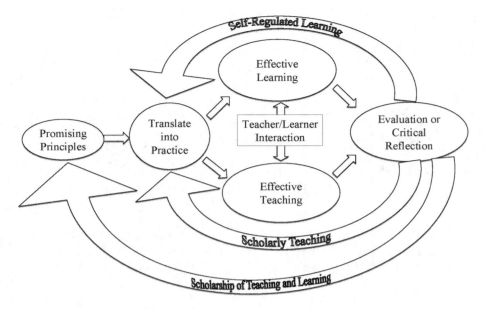

Figure 8.1. A dynamic process model of teaching and learning.

work. Instead, we suggest a process that will make the work of teaching and learning more effective, a process that will have important and desirable outcomes for teachers and learners.

Any form of work is principled. In other words, we can identify some principle or set of principles that explain why the work produces specific outcomes. As psychological scientists, we seek principles that are useful for the work of teaching and learning. Rather than claim that there are best practices, we more modestly identify several *promising principles* from the extant literature—principles that are promising candidates to be translated into more effective practices of teaching and learning. We consider them promising because they have passed at least one of two crucial empirical tests. The first (and often the easier) is that they have survived laboratory experiments designed to disprove them. The second is that they have survived experiments conducted in real-world classroom settings.

Although there are many promising principles that meet our criteria, we highlight only a few of them. In the pages that follow, we describe the structure and dynamic nature of the model in some detail. We then offer examples of how promising principles may be translated into learning and teaching practices that produce outcomes suitable for evaluation and critical reflection. There are at least two important implications of the model. The first is to recognize that the world is not divided into teachers and learners. Each person, within the same skin, is both. Sometimes we teach and sometimes we learn. What this implies is that the practices of learning and teaching that the model includes apply to everyone. For this reason, people who are lauded as fine teachers often disclose that they are avid learners or admit to having learned something new from a class or a particularly curious student. The other implication is ethical. The model attempts to capture a process that teachers and learners should engage in if they care about teaching and learning. Thus, the model is meant to be lived early and until the last breath is drawn.

A DYNAMIC MODEL OF TEACHING AND LEARNING

The model in Figure 8.1 presents participants at every level of analysis as active and interactive. For example, learners must work to develop and use new strategies and evaluate their relative effectiveness, as must teachers. Laboratory researchers must consider issues specific to learners and teachers with an eye to real-world generalization when developing appropriate research methodologies. Similarly, those who conduct research studies in real-life contexts must necessarily attend to learner and teacher variables and their interactions.

The model can be viewed from the perspective of the learner, the teacher, and others interested in pursuing related inquiry and practice. The promising principles described in a subsequent section and in Table 8.1 are the starting points for the model. Part of their promise is that they can be approached from different levels of analysis. As previously noted, we do not mean to imply that effective teaching and learning cannot arise from other sources (e.g., mentoring, trial and error, direct observation). But we believe strongly that the greatest likelihood of improving teaching and learning lies in practices grounded in empirically derived principles.

However, principles alone are not sufficient to guarantee effective teaching and learning. The principles must be *translated into practice* through the interaction of teacher, learner, context, and content. Thus, translational research is at the heart of our model at all levels. In order for promising principles to have utility in practical contexts, teachers, learners, and researchers must adapt them to their particular goals and resources. Teachers must be creative when making the leap from the laboratory-based literature to their classrooms, just as researchers must be creative when approximating the complexity of the teaching and learning environment. Successfully translating principles into practice leads to effective learning for students and effective teaching for teachers.

For students, *effective learning* includes increased domain-specific knowledge and metacognition (i.e., the ability to articulate what one does when one learns). As students reflect critically on their learning, a feedback loop (labeled self-regulated learning in Figure 8.1) is created. Reflection changes what learners contribute to future learning environments, in essence modify-

TABLE 8.1
Promising Principles Translated Into Classroom Techniques

Translation into practice	Example
Desirable difficulties	
Generate answers based on scaffolding, rather than the teacher providing all answers.	To learn the names of famous psychologists, students generate the names from one- to two-sentence descriptions of the psychologists, with their initials provided by the instructor.
Interleave learning by alternating content presented, types of problems solved, or skills practiced by students rather than focusing on one topic or skill at a time.	Present 12 short descriptions of experiments, and ask students to identify the hypothesis for Experiment 1, the independent variable for Experiment 2, the dependent variable of Experiment 3, and so on.
Induce cognitive equilibrium/dissonance by providing information likely to be unfamiliar to most students, then helping them to incorporate this new information into their previous knowledge.	Ask students to write down how the sex of a baby is determined, then describe how the sex of a fetus is determined by both the sperm's X- or Y-carrying chromosome transmitted at conception, as well as testosterone production and absorption in the first weeks of embryonic development. Relate all of this to what students already knew.
Deep explanatory processing	
Ask questions that elicit explanations rather than simply explaining every concept. Develop questions that elicit complex answers, not easy, shallow answers.	Rather than asking what percentage of adolescents smoke cigarettes, ask why adolescent girls have surpassed adolescent boys in their cigarette-smoking rates.
Connect new information to prior knowledge when presenting new material in class or in the readings.	Have students write a list of four methods for improving their memory of textbook material, and then share their methods with the rest of the class. Based on their answers, expand on and add to their current knowledge of how to improve their memory.
Organization effects	
Outline important points from the assigned reading.	Provide a scientific article on a topic to be discussed in class, and require students to read it and bring a typed outline with main headings and subheadings to class.
Develop concept maps to visually represent important concepts and their relationships to one another.	Have students draw a concept map for a particular concept in which they integrate materials from class and text.

Spacing or distributed learning	
Space learning over time rather than lumping all learning into one study session.	Ask students to prepare for a quiz by spending 20 minutes in the morning, 20 minutes at midday, and 20 minutes in the evening studying. Specifically ask them not to study for the allotted 60 minutes all at one time.
Testing as a teaching device	
Quiz to promote reading by giving quizzes after assigned reading should have been completed.	At the beginning of class, give a 1–5 question short quiz on the reading that students should have completed before class.
Metacognition	
Teach students to delay judgment of their own learning until after a meaningful delay. This prevents them from confusing comprehending at the moment with remembering and understanding later.	Ask students to use the quizzes at the end of each chapter. Ask them to read, then after at least a 1-hour delay, to answer the questions.
Provide feedback to students on the efficacy of their learning efforts.	Ask students to use the quizzes at the end of each chapter. Ask them to read, take the quiz, then go back to the text to read about any question they missed and determine why their answer was incorrect.
Transfer appropriate processing to new contexts	
Teach students metacognitive skills that they can transfer to new learning situations.	Let students know that an upcoming essay exam will require them to learn and apply the assigned reading to a specific case study. Explain that they will be required to discuss the material at the level of Application, according to Bloom's (1956) taxonomy. If they are able to prepare more effectively for the essay exam, they should be able to prepare more effectively for essay exams requiring application in other courses as well.
Teacher and learner as holistic agents	
Motivate students to complete and study the reading.	Provide students with a 10-point contingency for completing online prelecture quizzes.
Build rapport with students by letting them know the teacher is attempting to learn about them as individuals.	Learn students' names as early in the semester as possible.

ing their status as learners. Thus, students develop self-pedagogy as they learn to self-regulate their learning. For teachers, *effective teaching* includes improved metacognition about teaching, a wealth of domain-specific knowledge, and awareness of research and theoretical developments in pedagogy. As teachers evaluate and critically reflect on their teaching, a similar feedback loop develops, labeled *scholarly teaching* (Buskist & Davis, 2006).

The *teacher–learner interaction* is an essential component of the model. The teacher's role includes providing the learner with opportunities for translation through direct instruction on strategies, initial contingencies for engaging in new strategies, and opportunities for feedback to enable learners to refine the use of specific strategies and assess their effectiveness. Not all learners will benefit in the same way from each strategy in every context or with all subject matter. The learner, however, must be motivated to faithfully engage the process and expend the effort essential for success. The teacher thus serves as a bridge between the learner and successful strategies found in the research literature.

Finally, the model urges teachers at all levels to contribute their evaluations, critical reflections, and data to the *Scholarship of Teaching and Learning* (SOTL). Thus, SOTL creates a translational feedback loop with the promising principles (reciprocally translating between science and practice). In this way, teachers communicate their findings to learners, other teachers, and researchers. In turn, researchers, both basic and applied, should realize that high-quality practices are not only an outcome of the use of promising principles but also a wonderful source of new principles. Teachers who are not directly involved in SOTL can develop partnerships with researchers who are so that the data generated by teachers' efforts through scholarly teaching eventually contribute to the promising principles.

TRANSLATION INTO PRACTICE

At all levels of teaching and learning, the translation process is best understood as a process involving ineluctable interactions among several important factors, including characteristics of teachers and learners, context, and content.

Teacher Characteristics

Critical to whether and how a principle translates successfully into practice are characteristics of the teacher, such as familiarity with the principle, past experience, teaching philosophy, domain knowledge, and confidence. Teachers also need to consider their willingness to take risks and to devote discretionary time as well as their abilities and preferences. In translating principles into practice, teachers become learners and, as such, may benefit from workshops and conferences, advice from more experienced colleagues, and from organizations such as the Society for the Teaching of Psychology.

Student Characteristics

The diversity of learners, including their levels of preparedness, past experience, academic motivation, and personal interests, is a crucial consideration (see chap. 4, this volume). Students may need explicit instruction about the time they are likely to need for reading and other learning activities and perhaps even how to read and learn effectively. The teacher may find it useful to explain the logical bases and empirical support for practices that are being recommended. Students have already developed their own strategies for successful learning in some classroom contexts (Ross, Green, Salisbury-Glennon, & Tollefson, 2006), but some of these strategies may be detrimental to their success in other contexts. Informing students about criteria for identifying successful practices may help them revise or abandon counterproductive strategies.

Context and Content Characteristics

Translation also must consider local conditions that might be barriers to effective and efficient practices. For example, an overcrowded classroom or one with fixed seating may be a serious barrier to the successful use of some principles. Aspects of the course content, including unfamiliar terminology, directness of application, and connections to existing knowledge, are also relevant considerations. Moreover, teachers should ensure that their objectives are congruent with the subject matter being taught.

The interactive nature of the translation process means that one size will certainly not fit all. The translation of principles into techniques necessarily implies unique combinations of the characteristics already described as well as their interactions (Daniel & Poole, 2009). Successful translation may require precise prescriptions that take into account the variety and fluidity of teaching styles, learners, motives, goals, and resources that may potentially interact in a particular context. We view teaching, learning, and their interaction as personally empirical: Each teacher and learner must discover what works for the task at hand and then, perhaps spontaneously, adapt to be successful (Ross et al., 2006). Failure to take these characteristics into account may result in practice that does not meet its objectives and leaves learners and teachers frustrated by the wasted time and effort.

IDENTIFYING PROMISING PRINCIPLES

Literally hundreds of findings across domains of psychology may be applicable to classroom practice and learning. From the cognitive psychology literature alone, several research groups have derived lists of recommendations for educational practice (e.g., Halpern & Hakel, 2003; Lifelong Learning at Work and at Home, n.d.; Pashler et al., 2007). However, the process of translating laboratory findings into teaching and learning in a classroom context has not been as rigorously pursued, making it difficult to identify principles that may apply to a variety of teaching and learning contexts. Principles extracted from the extensive, predominantly laboratory-based literature may be promising, but learners and teachers need to translate them in terms of their particular goals, contexts, and resources. Translations into practice should include a critical evaluation of the implementation and its resulting impact to provide suggestions for modification and further refinement of practices and principles, as indicated in Figure 8.1.

As previously noted, good teaching and meaningful learning both require effort, feedback, and critical reflection. Rather than attempting to identify translations that are effortless, we point to principles that, when translated, reward the work of teaching and learning by helping teachers and learners target their efforts toward desired outcomes. Indeed, the popular quest for a method of teaching that results in effortless learning violates our claim that individuals must actively work at learning. Often, students expend effort using strategies that, at best, waste time or, at worst, have a negative impact on learning (Gurung, 2003, 2004; Gurung & Daniel, 2005). Unfortunately, teachers may do the same. Our goal is to encourage the emergence of a clearinghouse of effective, empirically grounded principles to serve as a base on which to structure demonstrably effective practices. Following is a brief description of sample principles that have solid grounding in the basic experimental research literature. Table 8.1 includes these principles and suggestions for how they might be translated into effective teaching and learning.

SOME PROMISING PRINCIPLES

The principles that follow are not intended to be exhaustive. These principles were chosen because they have a well-established empirical base.

Desirable Difficulties

Learning, retention, and transfer can be enhanced by introducing desirable difficulties into the instructional process (e.g., presenting two topics in interleaved fashion or asking students to generate information that integrates concepts across two or more topics; see also Table 8.1). Though interleaving and integration across concepts make the initial acquisition of the target information more challenging, these difficulties enhance performance on criterial questions several days after the lesson (Richland, Linn, & R. A.

Bjork, 2007). Generally, desirable difficulties stimulate active engagement that would not ordinarily occur, and this supports retention, transfer, or both (R. A. Bjork, 1994; R. A. Bjork & E. L. Bjork, 2006; McDaniel & Einstein, 2005). We recognize that the learner ultimately must be able to meet the difficulty that is posed (otherwise learning could be stymied) and that the difficulty may slow the pace at which students produce correct answers. However, gains typically appear in long-term retention.

Spacing

Reviewing key content with delays between repetitions produces positive benefits for long-term retention as opposed to massing repetition or relying on a single presentation (for a review, see Cepeda, Pashler, Vul, Wixted, & Rohrer, 2006). For example, material on the action potential of a neuron might be revisited some days after its initial presentation (for a classroom example, see Reynolds & Glaser, 1964).

Organization

Organizing content can be extremely effective for promoting retention and recall. Organization involves relating and structuring individual facts and concepts into integrated and coherent representations that can be viewed as schemata, mental models, or situation models that allow learners to draw on previously learned information (Dean & Kulhavy, 1981; Moore, Hauck, & Furman, 1975).

Deep Explanatory Processing

Deep explanations foster development of a complex understanding of the topic (Pashler et al., 2007). Deep explanations reflect well-reasoned arguments, logic, use of causal mechanisms, and persuasive assembly of evidence. For example, when introducing students to the limitations of correlational evidence, it is useful to discuss the research conditions necessary for drawing causal inferences (even from correlations), rather than simply stating the oft-repeated phrase *correlation does not imply causation*.

Transfer-Appropriate Processing

Maximizing performance on summative assessments in an academic course requires that study and learning strategies are appropriate for transfer to the type of assessment selected for the course. Although this principle is straightforward, its consequences often are underappreciated. For example, study that involves elaborative processing of individual facts will enhance performance on tests that focus on individual facts but penalize metacognitive awareness and performance on tests that focus on conceptual relations. Conversely, elaborative processing of conceptual relations will enhance performance on tests that focus on such relations but may penalize performance on tests that focus on the retention of individual facts (Metcalfe, Kornell, & Son, 2007; Thomas & McDaniel, 2007).

Testing as a Learning Tool

Testing is not a neutral event. Requiring retrieval of information from memory in the form of a test is a potent memory modifier that produces robust long-term retention relative to repeatedly studying the information (Karpicke & Roediger, 2008; Roediger & Karpicke, 2006b). Thus, quizzes (even low- or no-stakes quizzes) enhance learning and retention of course material (McDaniel, Anderson, Derbish, & Morrisette, 2007).

Metacognitive Monitoring

Metacognitive monitoring refers to learners' assessments of their knowledge levels and ability to remember information on criterial assessments. Promoting accurate metacognitive monitoring results in learners being able to more effectively assess what they know and do not know, leading to the development of more efficacious study habits (Schunk & Zimmerman, 1998).

A CAUTIONARY NOTE

Translating research-based principles into the practice of teaching and learning is not straightforward. The perils associated with translations of research-based principles into teaching and learning practices are illustrated by a problem that lurks in many psychology textbooks. Typically, these textbooks contain a variety of so-called pedagogical tools for students that take the form of signaling devices such as headings, bolded terms, and marginal inserts. The value of signaling devices is convincing in laboratory studies (e.g., R. F. Lorch & E. P. Lorch, 1996; Mautone & Mayer, 2001), especially for readers who do not spontaneously organize their reading or who cannot easily discern the most important information. However, the utility of signaling devices may not generalize to use in the classroom. For example, when used in the college classroom, self-reported usage of text-embedded signaling devices was neutrally or negatively associated with exam performance (Gurung & Daniel, 2005).

EFFECTIVE TEACHING

Several efforts have sought to identify the qualities of effective teachers (e.g., Bain, 2004; Buskist, 2002; McKeachie & Svinicki, 2006) and the practices they use (see chap. 6, this volume). We contend that effective teachers approach their teaching the way scientists approach their research (i.e., they use the scientific method by proposing and testing hypotheses). Effective teachers strive to be scholarly in their approach, basing their practices on empirically tested principles. They engage in self-reflection and critical evaluation of their practice. In other words, scholarly teachers examine their teaching goals and methods in great depth, experiment with new approaches, and assess the effectiveness of each approach with effective learning as the desired outcome.

Thus, effective teaching is a continual, lifelong process, and teachers at all levels have an ethical imperative to examine and improve their teaching practices. As previously stated, the process may begin with identifying promising principles from the research literature on how students learn (Figure 8.1). The teacher then develops learning activities and other teaching approaches that instantiate one or more of the promising principles. The application of principles to practices is not a one-size-fits-all process. When developing lesson plans, effective teachers must consider the contextual factors that potentially impinge on their practice, including, for example, the characteristics of their students (see chap. 4, this volume), educational institution (see chap. 5, this volume), classroom configuration, learning objectives for the specific course, and desired curricular outcomes (see chap. 9, this volume).

Teachers' assessment of their own teaching is as crucial to maintaining the flow of our dynamic model as is assessment of student learning. Without evaluation of teaching practices, neither teachers nor researchers can distinguish what works from what does not work in reaching learning outcomes. The model includes two potential feedback loops or paths that the results of teaching assessment might follow, both of which are vital to continuously improving teaching and learning.

One path focuses more narrowly on using evaluation and critical reflection to improve a teacher's own practice, that is, to adopt scholarly teaching. Faculty members' assessment of their own teaching requires them to reflect on how their own experiences, willingness to take risks, abilities, and preferences affected their choices in the classroom. After a teacher tries a new method, the teacher's metacognitive task is to determine whether the practice worked. Did the teacher accomplish the predetermined goals for student achievement? How might he or she improve the technique next time? Do the data support trying the technique in other sections of the same course or even in other courses? Was the class time intellectually stimulating and enjoyable for the teacher's students and for the teacher? Were all groups of students engaged?

A second path involves teachers using their evaluations of practice to build the empirical literature on applying promising principles to classroom settings. Regrettably, scientists often do not apply science when studying teaching and learning. For example, researchers have observed that too few submissions on SOTL include pretests, baseline data, or control or comparison groups (e.g., Richlin, 2001, 2006), thereby limiting their potential for satisfying peer review and contributing to promising principles. We propose that educators interested in SOTL assure that these types of measures are included whether they intend to use the assessment results for improving their own teaching or for wider dissemination.

TRANSLATING PROMISING PRINCIPLES INTO EFFECTIVE TEACHING

To make the model concrete, consider how a teacher at a small liberal arts college (let's name her Bettina) would use our proposed model to improve her teaching. To identify promising principles, Bettina scans the literature on evidence-based principles for improving student learning. She notices that *testing as a learning tool* is a promising principle and one that might suit the context in which she teaches. For example, trying risky new methods is not supported in her college, and she does not want to dramatically alter her present curriculum and support materials. She recognizes, however, that using quizzes to improve learning could be translated into her current classroom practices.

At this point, Bettina is confronted with a host of decisions about translating this promising principle into her teaching. She must decide about quiz format (multiple-choice, short answer), timing (before class, during class, outside of class), frequency (every class, once a week), delivery system (paper and pencil, online, interactive response systems such as clickers), and so on. Her particular translation will depend on a combination of her intuitions, the constraints of her teaching context, and perhaps even additional perusal of the research literature.

Bettina decides to use prequizzing when introducing new topics. It shows promise for helping students to identify material they do not know and to activate any relevant prior knowledge. She also decides to use postlecture short-answer quizzes to reexpose students to key content and promote retrieval practice. After implementing this new technique for a semester, Bettina finds that her students are performing better on exams than in past semesters, and she decides to integrate the quizzing methods into her courses. After a couple of semesters, Bettina might engage in SOTL by publishing a brief report of her data and reflections on the successful use of quizzing (e.g., Leeming, 2002).

Suppose, however, that with continued use of pre- and postlecture quizzing, certain aspects of Bettina's translation become increasingly problematic. Students resist so much quizzing, and Bettina finds that prequizzing is taking up more class time than she envisioned. Accordingly, she decides to drop prequizzes but retain postlecture quizzes. In later classes, she observes that eliminating the prequizzes has not had a negative impact on her students' learning. Bettina discusses this issue with her colleague David, an instructor at a nearby state university. Like Bettina, David introduced pre- and postlecture quizzes. However, when he removed prelecture quizzing, his students' exam scores went down, and he reinstituted them. For David's students, prelecture quizzes provided motivation for reading the text each week, which resulted in higher exam scores (see Brothen & Wambach, 2004; Daniel & Broida, 2004).

Bettina's and David's unique translations of a promising principle resulted in more effective teaching. Their evaluations produced iterative improvements that were particularly effective for their respective pedagogical contexts. At this point, if so inclined, Bettina and David might conduct a study in their classes to evaluate more objectively whether quizzes are an effective translation of the basic principle. Individually or in collaboration, their research could then inform the larger scholarly community of their results (e.g., McDaniel, McDermott, Agarwal, & Roediger, 2008).

TRANSLATING PROMISING PRINCIPLES INTO EFFECTIVE LEARNING

Our model assumes that fostering the development of sound principle-based learning strategies by students and promoting sound principle-based pedagogies by teachers are equally important. A growing literature supports the use of training in metacognition to improve classroom learning. How might such training increase the effectiveness of student learning? The literature on metacognitive strategies (sometimes referred to as *self-regulated learning*) may be traced back to Dewey (1933) and has increased substantially in the past 30 years (e.g., Montalvo & Torres, 2004; Ross et al., 2006; Schunk & Zimmerman, 1998).

For example, a teacher might initially assess the metacognitive abilities of students in her classes using scales developed for this purpose (e.g., Niemivirta, 1998; Pintrich & DeGroot, 1990; Wolters, Pintrich, & Karabenick, 2005). After the teacher conducts the preassessment, results are shared with students to enhance their awareness of the strategies they are already using. The teacher then engages the students in questioning whether their strategies are the most effective and efficient ones to use. The teacher then encourages students to develop hypotheses for improving their metacognition, citing some of the promising principles and helping students to focus their hypotheses on one or more of these. The teacher could go further by introducing *concept mapping* as an example of how to integrate, test, and review material from the lectures, the textbook, and any additional readings or video sources (Hilbert & Renkl, 2008; Nesbit & Adesope, 2006; Novak, 1990).

Students are shown examples of concept maps and then instructed to construct their own for a specific topic in the class. Each student can proceed by identifying and selecting relevant material and organizing it in a meaningful way for him or her, using verbal, spatial, and visual means to enhance its construction. At this stage, the maps are submitted to the teacher or to merged collaborative groups to identify inaccuracies or omissions. Later, students reconstruct their maps from memory and have the opportunity to fill in omissions and correct misconceptions. The maps may be valuable to the teacher as the means for identifying what students deem important and also assessing their understanding of relationships among concepts. Of critical importance, however, is the students' acquisition of a new practice (or the opportunity to refine an already existing practice) by which to increase the effectiveness of their learning.

RECOMMENDATIONS AND CONCLUSION

Our model of learning and teaching is applicable to a complex terrain. It does not specify conditions for optimal implementation, nor does it require preconditions other than some familiarity with one or more of the promising principles and a willingness to translate them into practice as a learner or teacher or both. We recognize that effective teaching and learning have long occurred, but we think that anyone, even those already effective in teaching or learning or both, may use the model with positive results. We also recognize that engaging in the process proposed in the model is time consuming and may be more difficult to implement by early career teachers and scholars working in contexts in which SOTL is not valued or rewarded. However, we enthusiastically encourage those teachers who are not hampered by organizational structures to apply the model in order to directly contribute to SOTL, and thus to enlarge and refine the base of promising principles. Ideally, as the number of researchers actively engaged in SOTL increases, the reward structures for faculty and institutional definitions of scholarship will change (Edgerton, O'Meara, & Rice, 2005).

Our examples of the model's application should not be viewed as prescribing a particular translation of a specific promising principle. Instead, they are intended to inspire individual teachers and learners, who will ultimately shape the practices that make teaching and learning more effective. Similarly, the following recommendations are meant for various stakeholders.

For teachers and learners:

1. Use the proposed dynamic process model (Figure 8.1) to guide teaching and learning practices.
2. Collect baseline and control or comparison data to enhance reflection and scholarly teaching and to facilitate contributions to SOTL literature.

3. Encourage students to invest efforts in developing metacognitive strategies and using all classes in becoming more independent and self-regulated learners.

For educational institutions and professional organizations:

1. Provide formal training in teaching and ongoing professional development for all teachers in higher or tertiary education settings on content and process knowledge.
2. Make scholarly teaching the standard practice in tertiary education settings.
3. Provide support for the pursuit of high-quality scholarship on teaching and learning, with an emphasis on translational research.
4. Create more outlets for translational research on teaching (e.g., increase the publication frequency of existing teaching journals and begin a new journal, tentatively titled *Psychology of Teaching*).
5. Create reward structures that support translational research as much as non-teaching-related research.
6. Facilitate and reward collaborations between scholarly teachers and researchers to build the knowledge base in SOTL with an emphasis on applying laboratory findings in real classrooms.
7. Publish casebooks on translating promising principles into effective teaching and learning.
8. Initiate a Promising Principle of the Year award and featured session at teaching conferences.
9. Produce an entertaining TV or DVD series for students on self-regulated learning. Emulate popular TV programs such as *Pimp My Ride* by transforming an unsuccessful student into to a successful learner through implementing evidenced-based strategies.
10. Form a committee dedicated to undergraduate education with teaching as a major charge.

For policy makers and grant-making institutions:

1. Provide funding for formal teacher training and ongoing professional development.
2. Provide funding for institutional and translational research in SOTL.

We hope the recommendations, taken collectively, will produce climates—family, local, state, regional, national, and international—that are more favorable to effective teaching and learning by means of the model we offer here. Nothing would please us more than to meet the model in altered form as it is changed and adapted according to specific contexts and thereby see it take on a life of its own. Indeed, we would consider that happy development to be further evidence of effective teaching and learning.

9

DESIRED OUTCOMES OF AN UNDERGRADUATE EDUCATION IN PSYCHOLOGY FROM DEPARTMENTAL, STUDENT, AND SOCIETAL PERSPECTIVES

R. ERIC LANDRUM, BERNARD C. BEINS, MUKUL BHALLA, KAREN BRAKKE, DEBORAH S. BRIIHL, RITA M. CURL-LANGAGER, THOMAS P. PUSATERI, AND JAYE JANG VAN KIRK

What are the desired outcomes of an undergraduate education in psychology? It is vital to identify the desired outcomes that benefit departments, students, and society, because the pursuit of these goals helps psychology educators achieve the best possible learning experience for their students. When psychology educators meet their instructional and educational goals in a high school, community college, college or university setting, knowledge of psychology and human behavior adds richness to the fabric of society. Psychology educators invest daily in the development of intellectual capital and professional abilities of their students while simultaneously fostering personal development through enrichment and growth. Their current knowledge of human behavior places them in a formidable position to harness psychology to anticipate and resolve problems for the greater good of all. Psychology educators hold stewardship responsibilities, regardless of the venue of delivery or a student's desires to effect change locally or globally. Furthermore, our stewardship extends to those students who take just the introductory psychology course and to those completing a bachelor's degree in psychology.

Psychology educators have an obligation to stand accountable to their multiple stakeholders for their educational practices both at the departmental and institutional level, and to remain ethically bound to provide effective teaching and learning experiences. Their commitment to improving psychology education serves a dual purpose—to ensure that effective teaching and learning occurs and to empower students with a psychology education that prepares them for success in their future aspirations, regardless of the postbaccalaureate path.

We purposely take a different approach to what might be expected of an *outcomes* chapter in a review of undergraduate psychology education. We address methods that departments and educational institutions use to assess the outcomes of psychology education from the standpoint of departmental performance and student achievement. We identify goals of the undergraduate experience held by psychology faculty, employers, and students and we examine current indicators of postbaccalaureate success through educational outcomes. We then place our students' achievements in a broader context of societal demands and global expectations. We conclude this chapter with specific recommendations and a call to action.

WHAT ARE THE DESIRED OUTCOMES IN UNDERGRADUATE EDUCATION FOR FACULTY, DEPARTMENTS, AND SPONSORING INSTITUTIONS?

The call for greater accountability and transparency from institutions of higher education has increased since the turn of the 21st century. In the United States, the Spellings Commission report "urge[d] the creation of a robust culture of accountability and transparency throughout higher education" (U.S. Department of Education, 2006, p. 21) and recommended that "postsecondary education institutions should measure and report meaningful student learning outcomes" (p. 24). The Association of American Colleges and Universities (AAC&U) called for reforms in higher education (AAC&U, 2002); proposed a core set of knowledge, skills, and values that students should achieve in college (AAC&U, 2005); and endorsed a set of principles and actions for addressing the call for accountability (AAC&U and the Council on Higher Education, 2008). Psychology, as a discipline, is poised to evaluate its standing on these national issues and to report on what has been successful, as well as to offer necessary recommendations for further advancements to achieve comprehensive educational goals.

Internationally, most countries in the European Union have joined the Bologna Process (or Accord) to collaboratively articulate shared standards and articulation agreements for all academic degree programs across all participating countries (European Commission, 2007). The recognition of shared standards and the articulation of agreements between other countries enable students to transition seamlessly to other academic institutions and continue their educational pursuits. The impact of such global actions on American students' educational opportunities is uncertain. Where American education will seek to position itself relative to these international standards will impact American psychology educators' standing and functioning within the global academic community. Given international agreements related to the Bologna Process and the Spellings Commission report, some form of standardization of core knowledge and skills may be in American psychology educators' future. At the graduate level, the search for the core curriculum has occurred for some time (Benjamin, 2001). If American psychology educators fail to act, others may act on their behalf and then they may lose the ability to control the destiny of psychology education.

Departments of psychology are experiencing pressures both from students to prepare them for their future and from the public for greater accountability and quality assurance for the successful entry of graduates into society and the workforce. We urge departments to continue to take charge of their curricula and their students' learning by advocating for basic psychological literacy as an important learning outcome of introductory psychology courses (see chap. 1, this volume) and by designing their advanced courses and curricula in ways that support both the *American Psychological Association (APA) Guidelines for the Undergraduate Psychology Major* (APA, 2007a) and the core recommendations presented earlier in this volume (see chap. 3). The guidelines (a) establish psychology as a scientific discipline, (b) set forth goals and expectations for assessment plans, (c) articulate goals and outcomes for investigation and assessment of effective practices, (d) extend the *National Standards for High School Psychology Curriculum* (APA, 2005) to fit postsecondary settings, and (e) designate consistent standards for distance learning courses and programs to promote comparable expectations. The guidelines contain 10 goals and 52 suggested learning outcomes in two major categories: (a) knowledge, skills, and values consistent with the science and application of psychology and (b) knowledge, skills, and values consistent with a liberal arts education that are further developed in psychology.

We also urge departments to adopt rigorous assessment strategies that demonstrate the effectiveness of their introductory and general psychology courses and major programs. Because psychology programs can have a variety of emphases (e.g., research, human services, business applications), assessment instruments must reflect departmental goals and institutional context. Each program in psychology should consider how best to align the department's assessment strategies with the institution's mission and strategic planning priorities of its home institution. Assessment cannot succeed with a one-size-fits-all approach. For example, Borden and Owens (2001) provided a detailed overview of 27 assessment instruments and services that can be used for assessing institutional quality.

Current best practices in assessment capitalize on a seamless relationship between teaching, learning, and assessment. The APA Task Force on Strengthening the Teaching and Learning of Undergraduate Psychological Sciences (2008) argued for a coherent curriculum in psychology using Bloom's taxonomy (Bloom, 1956) of learning outcomes as an organizing scheme. Chapter 3 presents a similar argument. Within a coherent curriculum, departments can develop strategies that use outcomes for program improvement. For example, assessment within an integrative capstone experience can inform faculty about necessary changes to improve course complementarity (Dunn, McCarthy, Baker, Halonen, & Hill, 2007) and to measure student learning in basic level courses (e.g., Sullivan & Thomas, 2007) across the curriculum. Students can be educators' partners in assessment, for example, by collaborating with faculty, as exemplified by capstone experiences that directly involve students in program assessment (Morgan & Johnson, 1997; Zechmeister & Reich, 1994).

Assessment should improve education practice by helping to establish standards of performance against which one can measure student learning (Halonen, Harris, Pastor, Abrahamson, & Huffman, 2005). We recommend that the organizational framework for assessing student development be the *APA Guidelines for the Undergraduate Psychology Major* (APA, 2007a). This document provides a clear starting point for developing metrics that effectively assess student performance. For example, models of learning presented in earlier chapters can provide frameworks for studying individual student achievement. Recently, Halonen et al. (2003) developed a rubric for the assessment of Goal 3 (Critical Thinking Skills in Psychology). We welcome research to develop assessment rubrics for each of the 10 guidelines and, ideally, multiple measures for each of the 10 guidelines.

Careful comparative assessment of student learning outcomes can provide useful feedback to faculty so that they can document which educational practices are effective for enhancing student learning. Another important component of assessment occurring at the departmental level includes such factors as program development, faculty characteristics, and student development. Dunn et al. (2007) proposed a set of quality benchmarks for psychology faculty to consider when evaluating the effectiveness of their departments. We recommend that departments and faculty consider the use of these benchmarks for a twofold purpose: (a) to open discussions for meaningful self-assessment and (b) to be used by external consultants conducting program reviews as appropriate.

We make one other recommendation here, albeit gently, regarding educational practices within departments of psychology. We recommend that a national conversation begin on the accreditation or certification of undergraduate programs of psychology offering the bachelor's degree. Our primary motivation for this discussion is quality assurance. It is important to remember that "the founding premise for accreditation traditions in the United States was to ensure voluntary compliance of standards of educational institutions and programs" (Dooley, 2005, p. 299). The APA has a long history of accreditation at the doctoral level (Benjamin, 2001; Crawford, 1986). As pointed out throughout this and in other chapters in the volume, it is apparent that the stakes are high for undergraduate education in psychology. Accreditation can have numerous benefits according to Crawford, including (a) giving prospective students an idea of the quality of programs to which they may apply, (b) providing useful information to state credentialing bodies as a standardized index of preparation, (c) motivating self-study of the program considered for accreditation, and (d) ensuring to the general public that the program is effective.

However, this conversation on the desirability and feasibility of departmental accreditation must be open to evaluating the considerable drawbacks, including the following: (a) Accreditation by itself does not guarantee quality, (b) there are substantive costs accrued within the accreditation the process, (c) accreditation many generate unfunded mandates, (d) there is the potential for increased levels of bureaucracy and paperwork, and (e) accreditation potentially limits programmatic creativity and flexibility (W. Dixon, personal communication, August 3, 2008). At this time, we are not calling for the accreditation or certification of undergraduate programs or for the credentialing of undergraduate students in psychology. We are recommending, however, that a conversation begin on this topic at the national level to meaningfully consider and weigh the potential benefits and drawbacks of accrediting undergraduate programs in psychology. The authors of chapter 1 evaluated the European and Australian strategies for quality assurance as closer to an accreditation approach. Comparing and contrasting these approaches with the ever-changing American approach could be a starting point with multiple outcomes for such discussions.

WHAT ARE THE DESIRED OUTCOMES FOR UNDERGRADUATE STUDENTS IN PSYCHOLOGY?

Students are the primary stakeholders of psychology education (see chap. 4, this volume, for a fine-grained analysis of who psychology students are today and who they will be tomorrow). Consider, for example, that most people during their work life will have three to five different careers involving 8 to 10 jobs (L. Peterson, 1995). Psychology educators need to prepare their students for dynamic changes in both personal and professional settings that will continually change and that will require them to adapt as they mature. Psychology educators need to provide their students a solid foundation of psychological literacy that will contribute to their lifelong learning in a variety of contexts.

When a student takes a psychology course, there is a clear expectation that the centerpiece of the course will be domain-specific content knowledge. Psychology is such a wide-ranging science that no single student (or psychology educator) can master its entire breadth. However, the *APA Guidelines for the Undergraduate Psychology Major* (APA, 2007a) articulate certain core theories, concepts, skills, and values that permeate the discipline and are considered essential to a quality undergraduate education. Additionally, students should be able to articulate and apply the knowledge, skills, and values consistent with their coursework. Psychology graduates, with their domain-specific knowledge and their liberal arts education, should be equipped to address some of society's most pressing issues, such as those pertinent to physical and mental health. Furthermore, these important professional and personal skills, in addition to the knowledge gained by a psychology baccalaureate through the *APA Guidelines for the Undergraduate Psychology Major* (APA, 2007a), are applicable for those who pursue a graduate education in psychology and for those who seek employment with a bachelor's degree in psychology.

What, then, is unique about psychology that can be applied to so many circumstances? The discipline is one that combines the problem-solving power of scientific research and analysis with sensitivity to the complexity of human thought and behavior. Disciplined observation, problem solving, and communication are part and parcel of education in psychology, as they are in many other disciplines. However, the study of psychology applies these processes directly to the challenges humans face daily. Psychologists focus their lens on the correlates and consequences of human behavior. Their topics of study—aggression, prejudice, emotional health, prosocial behavior, and productivity, to name a few— are ubiquitous in their daily encounters with all of those around us.

Professional Skills

A graduate's knowledge base in psychological science can serve as one component of readiness to enter the workforce or to pursue continued education, but perhaps of equal or more importance are the skills developed as part of a liberal arts education in psychology. Perhaps most apparent are those skills that will contribute to success in the workplace as well as in postgraduate education. In a study of 210 senior-year psychology majors from 12 departments of psychology in the United States during the spring 2008 semester, 33.8% of seniors indicated that they had applied (or would apply soon) to a graduate program in psychology (Landrum, Klein, Horan, & Wynn, 2008). In that same study, 45.3% of seniors indicated that they planned to attend graduate school in psychology; the gap in percentages represents those who do not apply immediately after graduation but may apply eventually. Thus, from this study, the majority of students do not apply directly to graduate schools in psychology or have the intention of going eventually. The majority of psychology graduates go directly to the workforce or other professional preparatory programs, such as specialized counseling and medical fields, business administration, and education. Nevertheless, in many ways, being successful in the workplace requires similar skill sets as being successful in the graduate school. There are common skills that psychology education attempts to impart to students, including thinking and language skills, information gathering and synthesis, research methods and statistical skills, interpersonal skills, and ethics and values that apply to many diverse settings (McGovern, Furumoto, Halpern, Kimble, & McKeachie, 1991).

Data from employers as well as graduates themselves indicate that there is a core set of required skills that are considered vital for success in acquiring and advancing a career, and these reflect the APA *Guidelines for the Undergraduate Psychology Major* (APA, 2007a) learning goals and outcomes. Appleby (2000) suggested five major categories of skills: social skills, personal skills, communication skills, information gathering and processing skills, and numerical/computer/psychometric skills. When Landrum and Harrold (2003) surveyed employers of psychology baccalaureates, employers indicated the following are the top 10 most important skills and abilities (starting with most important): listening skills, ability to work with others as part of a team, getting along with others, desire and willingness to learn, willingness to learn new and important skills, focus on customers or clients, interpersonal relationship skills, adaptability to changing situations, ability to suggest solutions to problems, and problem-solving skills (successfully implementing solutions to problems). Taking a different approach, Gardner (2007) studied the reasons that collegiate employers fire new hires, and the top reasons are lack of work ethic or commitment, unethical behavior, failure to follow instructions, missing assignments or deadlines, inappropriate use of technology, and being late for work. Psychology educators should work to incorporate aspects of career planning and development in each course as relevant and impart to their students a work ethic that poises students for success in the workplace while also teaching students what not to do.

Evidence presented by the AAC&U, Spellings Commission, and students themselves indicates that the degree to which psychology baccalaureate students in the United States are prepared for professional life may not match with students' expectations and skill levels. Employers who participated in a recent survey (AAC&U, 2008) indicated that approximately one third of college graduates who applied for positions in their companies did not possess the skills and knowledge needed to succeed in entry-level positions. Large percentages of these employers further indicated college graduates were not well prepared in global knowledge (46%), self-direction (42%), writing skills (37%), critical thinking skills (31%), adaptability (30%), and self-knowledge (26%). The recent Spellings Report stated that "employers complain that many college graduates are not prepared for the workplace and lack the new set of skills necessary for successful employment and continuous career development" (U.S. Department of Education, 2006, p. 12). In addition, psychology students indicated that their undergraduate education in psychology was only slightly related to their current positions and reported being less satisfied and less prepared than the majority of their peers in other majors (Borden & Rajecki, 2000). The disconnection between the popularity of the psychology major and the potential for dissatisfaction with the outcomes of a psychology education indicated by employers, educators, and the students is important to study and monitor for the future health of psychology programs. Our colleagues in chapter 4 even framed such monitoring as an ethical obligation psychologists have to their students.

In fact, some in the private sector are already addressing the gap between the skills required on the job and the skills new employees bring to the workplace. The Career Readiness Certificate Consortium (2005) uses WorkKeys subscales (reading information, applied mathematics, and locating information), and each test taker receives a gold, silver, or bronze designation for each subscale. These scores are portable, and 15 states in the United States currently issue Career Readiness Certificates. Students need to understand that if they do not acquire the necessary skills during their undergraduate education, future employers may require additional education and training. Faculty members need to recognize that if students fail to achieve necessary competencies in the skills employers value, then faculty have failed to prepare their students for postbaccalaureate success, and others are obligated to fill the gap.

Personal Skills

In addition to the professional skills acquired through their education in psychology, students need to understand that psychology has wide-ranging applications in their personal lives. The student case studies in chapter 1 and the anecdotes in chapter 4 illuminated these applications well. Psychology educators expect students to think critically when presented with information and to differentiate between empirically based psychological information and pseudoscience. Given the large volume of information individuals receive from multiple media sources, psychology students need to be able to evaluate the validity of the source of information and the potential accuracy of that information. Often, decisions related to one's work or personal life require one to make judgments based on diverse sources of information. Understanding the difference between correlation and causation, for example, can influence the kinds of conclusions drawn about the information encountered. Some of those decisions can have immediate and long-term consequences. Whether psychology students become corporate leaders, educators, policy makers, health care providers, or caretakers and caregivers for their own families, being proficient in assessing information can have far-reaching impact on their own lives as well as the lives of others. Equally as important as the cognitive attributes that characterize psychologically literate individuals are the affective competencies that such literacy can help psychology students develop. Examples of such competencies are those involved in coping, self-regulation, and healthy relationship building. Learning positive interpersonal skills such as these can contribute greatly to long-term quality of life on a daily basis.

As diverse cultures work more closely with one another, it is important that psychology educators provide their students with exposure to multiple perspectives. Psychology educators need to ensure that students are acquiring sensitivity for and an appreciation of sociocultural and international diversity for interpersonal success and possess the ability to function effectively in a global society. Psychology students need to know that, regardless of the boundaries between countries and cultures, exposure to different perspectives helps individuals to understand multiple approaches to investigating and explaining behavior, sometimes depending on the cultural context. In this way, the goals of psychology should include teaching students to be sensitive decision makers because they have been trained to recognize, respect, and understand the complexity inherent in sociocultural and international perspectives. As psychologically literate citizens, students should be able to identify and advocate for the role of psychology in improving daily life in multiple arenas. Students who develop a foundation of psychological literacy and values structured by ethical principles will be more likely to make decisions that are appropriate for their individual circumstances.

Outcomes for Nonmajors

An estimated 1.2 million to 1.6 million students enroll annually in an introductory psychology course (Steuer & Ham, 2008). Psychology educators' opportunity to mold and shape future ambassadors of psychology rests not only in the education of students who major in the discipline but also in their one-time opportunity (in many cases) to influence those students whose only exposure to psychology will be the introductory psychology course. Although APA has approved a set of *National Standards for High School Psychology Curricula* (APA, 2005), there is currently no equivalent document indicating what students should learn from a college-level introductory psychology course.

The recommendations from chapter 3 call for greater consistency of content and learning outcomes for the introductory psychology course. However, only a few studies have attempted to assess outcomes for this course (e.g., Halonen et al., 2005; VanderStoep, Fagerlin, & Feenstra, 2000), and these attempts have been limited to assessment within a single institution.

We urge the development of assessment instruments that departments can use to determine whether students are achieving the learning outcomes recommended for introductory psychology. Other disciplines have already developed similar instruments for their introductory courses, such as the Force Concept Inventory used in physics education (Hestenes, Wells, & Swackhamer, 1992). The set of assessment instruments we propose should not only assess content knowledge, as is already assessed through instruments such as the Advanced Placement Psychology Test and College Level Examination Program, but this set of instruments should adequately measure the basic skills of psychological literacy as articulated in chapter 1.

It is evident from the previous discussion that the outcomes that can be achieved from an undergraduate education in psychology are of wide application and are capable of preparing students for professional and personal success throughout their lives, regardless of whether they continue in the field of psychology. What psychology educators need to do with some urgency is to ensure that these outcomes are being addressed in the psychology curriculum. In addition, psychology educators need to foster better self-awareness in their students of the skills they have developed through their major so that they may articulate them more clearly to prospective employers. Just as departments and the discipline are asked to become more accountable in the educational enterprise, so must students be accountable. The departments and disciplines carry the responsibility of providing the resources of knowledge, and the students carry the responsibility of recognizing that their motivation for what and how they learn will indeed be critical in shaping many aspects of their future.

WHAT ARE THE DESIRED OUTCOMES FOR UNDERGRADUATE PSYCHOLOGY STUDENTS IN SOCIETY?

Although learning outcomes for individual students remain a primary concern for psychology educators, they instruct and nurture individual students within a larger social fabric. Brofenbrenner's (1979) model of ecological development is instructive here in that it presents the person within a pattern of concentric circles representing ever more inclusive spheres of social influence beginning with those systems in the immediate environment— family and friends, and continuing with community institutions such as neighborhood, media, and health service entities, all enveloped by the *macrosystems* of cultural values, national policy, and economic conditions. If one views each student of psychology as a developing being within Bronfenbrenner's model, then one recognizes that, cumulatively, such individuals both influence and are influenced by each of these systems. For example, students who have been exposed to the content of psychology in one or more courses may be able to apply their knowledge appropriately and effectively to improve daily life. The proximal contexts for becoming psychologically literate citizens include the evaluation of information, development of interpersonal effectiveness, enhancement of coping skills, positive parenting and family development, and fostering an environmentally sustainable lifestyle. Those who teach psychology have a responsibility to guide their students so that they may respond both *reactively* and *proactively* to the many demands of societal systems.

Increased Accountability

The climate of increasing accountability that has been discussed in this chapter and elsewhere represents one way in which economic and other forces have demanded appropriate response from the APA and undergraduate psychology departments in terms of demonstrating the value of their product. Educational researchers and employers agree that jobs require cross-discipline knowledge, cognitive abilities, and interpersonal and intercultural skills, and that individuals and communities reach higher quality productive lives with advanced social responsibility, personal ethics, and motivation for continued engagement. Further, students, parents, and the taxpaying public represented by the U.S. Department of Education expect direct indicators that institutions of higher education can address the needs of their constituents and patrons (AAC&U, 2005). Numerous beneficiaries want higher education institutions and students to succeed in postsecondary education and desire evidence to that effect. The question remains as to how the educational community will most appropriately assess these goals given the diverse circumstances in which psychology undergraduate education takes place. One starting point for the consideration of such efforts would be to consult the valuable resources provided by Dunn, Mehrotra, and Halonen (2004).

In response to these calls for accountability, the APA *Guidelines for the Undergraduate Psychology Major* (APA, 2007a) describe the competencies that psychology majors should achieve from their degree programs. In addition, students who complete even one psychology course should develop sufficient psychological literacy skills applicable to real-world problems; students should also be prepared to advocate for the importance of psychological science and practice. We encourage psychology programs to collect and report assessment outcomes in response to the call for accountability, as mentioned earlier in this chapter.

Embracing Diversity

In the 21st century, the U.S. population will be diversely represented by individuals from a variety of communities. The fundamental demographic shift underway in the United States represents an unprecedented (self-determined) progression to a multicultural society. In 2000, the ethnic and racial makeup of the United States consisted of 71.4% European Americans, 12.4% African Americans, 11.8% Hispanics, 3.9% Asian Americans and Pacific Islanders, and 0.7% Native Americans (Hollmann, Mulder, & Kallan, 2000). According to the same authors, the projected demographic change of the population in 2050 is expected to be 52% European Americans, 13.2% African Americans, 24.3% Hispanics, 8.9% Asian Americans and Pacific Islanders, and 0.8% Native Americans. By 2100, it is anticipated that the demographic makeup will be 40.3% European Americans, 13.9% African Americans, 33.3% Hispanics, 12.6% Asian Americans and Pacific Islanders, and .7% Native Americans. In other words, by the year 2100 there will no longer be a majority ethnicity in the United States, but a nation of pluralities. Diversity encompasses more than just ethnic and racial diversity, however. Educators need to keep in mind the diversity of their students in all forms, including the diversity of sexual orientation, age, disability, and other personal characteristics. To serve the many forms of diversity, including the anticipated demographic shift, our communities, institutions, and corporations will need to prepare for and seek a diverse and culturally literate workforce to address the unique needs of the individuals within these communities.

Regardless of the nature of the work or community service setting, essential skills include the ability to engage in culturally-sensitive communication, flexible use of critical thinking, and the ability to work in teams. In addition to recognizing similarities and differences across cultural groups, psychologically literate citizens should be able to recognize how their attitudes and beliefs can influence their perceptions and interactions about individuals different from themselves and possess the ability to adopt *best practices* from cultures and social groups other than their own. Such knowledge can only be gained when institutions make efforts to integrate and employ the constructs of multiculturalism throughout education. Psychologically literate individuals are involved in work affecting all segments of the population. Not only will they conduct the research but they will also need to possess the experience, history, and training to address the problems of their respective communities. In short, the faces of psychology as researchers, teachers, and practitioners should reflect the faces of the community.

However, the ethnic diversity of the general population is not currently proportionally represented among the ranks of psychology graduate students. For instance, when examining doctoral degrees conferred, Snyder, Dillow, and Hoffman (2008) found 6.4% of doctoral recipients were African American compared with 12.4% of the population. Although Hispanics consist of 11.8% of the population, only 5.8% of doctoral recipients in psychology were Hispanic (using the most current data at the time of this writing). Several factors may contribute to this disparity. For example, the career path for ethnic minority students may be influenced by factors related to degree of acculturation. Tang, Fouad, and Smith (1999) found that Asian Americans tended to choose careers because of factors related to acculturation, family background, and self-efficacy, thus leading them away from service careers commonly pursued by psychology majors and toward "higher status" careers in medicine, law, or business. Although much still needs to be done, professional agencies such as the APA, Teachers of Psychology in Secondary Schools (TOPSS), Psychology Teachers at Community Colleges (PT@CC), and the National Institute of Mental Health have made some inroads into addressing these issues.

For example, in 2004 TOPSS established a recruiting project for ethnic minority high school students. The goal was to introduce and encourage the students to pursue psychology and careers in psychology. As a joint venture of TOPSS, the APA Membership Committee, the APA Office of Ethnic Minority Affairs, and PT@CC, the project linked minority high school students with peers from 2-year and 4-year universities and local ethnic minority faculty. High school students received exposure to a number of successful role models within the field of psychology. These efforts need to be continued, expanded, and evaluated so that psychologists may identify best practices in this very important area.

Ethical Practice

One of the most challenging and complex demands that psychologists face as they move through this century is the many ways in which psychology education can support ethical decision making and behavior in the face of many different complex, challenging contexts. As such, preparing psychology students for the moral and ethical challenges that they will encounter in their lives represents a demanding responsibility for psychology faculty. Investigators of cognitive and moral developmental stages demonstrate that moral thinking and ethical behavior follow a predictable trajectory but require challenges and guidance for students to produce sophisticated solutions to ethical dilemmas. Recall Perry's (1970/1999) descriptions of initial stages of polar thinking about right and wrong by young college students, demonstrating a lack of reflective judgment and preponderance of dualistic thinking. After recognizing multiple points of view and believing that all points of view are equal, students learn to compare the pertinent merits of opposing explanations. Finally, students improve their ability to think within the framework of contextual relativism. Mature thinkers learn to respond similarly to well-defined versus poorly defined conditions. Students in undergraduate psychology programs should demonstrate advanced divergent thinking and reflective judgment necessary to respond to personal and societal ethical dilemmas.

Ethical practices include not only the more traditional contexts of research and practice in psychology but also the more subtle and yet pervasive situations that involve, for example, personal integrity and sensitivity to the multiple factors that underlie others' perspectives or actions. The ethics that guide a community or culture at any given time represent a consensus of its members, and as such, undergo continuous debate and change. Yet, students should be capable of distinguishing universal moral principles such as compassion for others from cultural codes and practices that emphasize one type of ethic over another such as justice over care. Every psychology student is (or should be) presented with a range of ethical considerations as part of his or her undergraduate education. Questions of confidentiality, benefit versus harm, integrity of data, justice, deception, and other issues apply not only to research and practice within the field but also to ethical behavior in many walks of life. To the extent that psychology students are brought to reflect on these matters and recognize their generalizability, they can provide informed, reasoned voices for positive ethical development as society evaluates new and existing dilemmas.

Psychology's Impact: Economic and Public Policy

In the late 20th and early 21st centuries, the economies of many countries have become increasingly knowledge based. This type of economy demands that a critical percentage of the population possess certain technological competencies that are based on societal expectations and societal demands for productivity. Persons must locate, use, and evaluate information of different types and from different sources, manage personal and institutional records and finances, and effectively communicate with others about these processes to sustain local and global economic engines. Individuals possessing these abilities will thereby be able to act proactively to societal challenges. Furthermore, individuals educated in psychology can shape public perception and policy relevant to the discipline. This responsibility emphasizes the role of psychology's ambassadors, whether that status is achieved with the completion of one course or the undergraduate psychology major, as the case studies and anecdotes in chapters 1 and 4 illustrated.

Psychology's Impact: Health Care

Problems of psychology permeate modern life, and this is no more apparent than in modern health care. A 2006 National Institutes of Health Fact Sheet indicated that "50%–80% of the quality of our health and health care is rooted in behavioral, social and cultural factors" (¶ 7). In coming years, psychologists may represent an essential component of cross-disciplinary collaborations that address the behavioral health issues facing the world.

At the community level, a public educated in psychology will make informed decisions regarding access to and use of behavioral and mental health services that reflect multicultural sensitivity. In addition, psychologically literate individuals will have the knowledge base to make informed evidence-based public policy decisions that are relevant to behavioral issues in health- and well-being-related educational policy, promotion of preventative health care and healthy behaviors, family leave and child care policy, and so on.

Psychology's Impact: Internationalization

As the previous examples illustrate, improving psychological literacy is vital to the public good as people move into an era of increasingly complex and global and community systems. People live in a highly mobile world. It appears now, as compared with previous generations, people's personal, professional, and academic lives extend across multiple countries and cultures. Thus, the globalization or internationalization of psychology is essential to maximizing the transferability of learned knowledge and skills, with the goal of a common understanding of human needs and endeavors and a common understanding of human behavior that transcends national boundaries. Thus, students emerging from this new vision for the future of psychology must not only be more psychologically literate but also have tangible benefits acquired from their education that will make them effective and productive members of the global society.

Well-educated students, whether they major in psychology or take only one course, will be better able to understand the place of psychology as a science in today's world and understand what kinds of contributions they can make to society. By promoting accurate public perception of psychology, these psychologically literate community members and ambassadors of psychology will be the societal leaders who will then be able to generate and gather empirical evidence supporting effective policy decision making, legislation, and funding.

RECOMMENDATIONS AND CONCLUSION

We recommend that local psychology departments review the recently developed quality benchmarks (Dunn et al., 2007) to continuously improve program assessment. As national benchmarks emerge from ongoing study, we also recommend that external program reviewers use such quality benchmarks as one possible rubric to assess departmental and program effectiveness.

We recommend that psychology educators work to develop a system for the assessment of specific student outcomes that is more broadly defined than tests of knowledge (e.g., Sternberg, 2004). Students need to be able to demonstrate to others not only their acquired knowledge but also well-developed skills and abilities attained (some employers and states now do this with Career Readiness Certificates). In some form, this could result in certification of students on the basis of accomplishments in multiple areas of the *APA Guidelines for the Undergraduate Psychology Major* (APA, 2007a).

To better understand the outcomes and accomplishments of an undergraduate education in psychology we recommend that the APA Center for Workforce Studies expand its scope to include comprehensive studies of psychology baccalaureates, systematically tracking psychology baccalaureates so that psychology educators can better understand the long-term impact of their educational practices in psychology.

To better understand the impact of psychology education at all levels and for students who do not major in psychology, we recommend that a task force (or other appropriate body) be appointed to study the impact of psychology education when exposure to psychology is limited to just a few courses and especially for those students whose only exposure to psychology occurs in a single introductory course. This task force should be directed to develop a means to assess the impact of the introductory course, and especially to understand how the limited exposure of nonmajors to psychology courses impacts attitudes and beliefs about the discipline of psychology and, more broadly, a greater understanding of human behavior.

From a societal perspective, we recommend that a conversation begin on a national level concerning the accreditation or certification of undergraduate program in psychology. The overarching goal of these conversations should be quality assurance. There are multiple institutional, political, and economic roadblocks for even considering accreditation, but we recommend that, at the very least, the conversation begin.

We recommend an increased effort to achieve greater understanding of the career development of psychology students. With a greater awareness of their own contributions to psychology, psychology students become more effective ambassadors to society in telling the story of what psychology brings to the improvement of everyday life.

Although these may seem like daunting goals, achieving these goals is essential for the future of psychology students and the discipline. Today's students are tomorrow's psychology educators, researchers, practitioners, and consumers of psychological knowledge. Furthermore, today's students, regardless of whether they major in psychology, comprise the global citizenry. Perhaps Ernest Boyer said it best in *Scholarship Reconsidered: Priorities of the Professoriate* in 1990:

> The aim of education is not only to prepare students for productive careers, but also to enable them to live lives of dignity and purpose; not only to generate new knowledge, but to channel that knowledge to humane ends; not merely to study government, but to help shape a citizenry that can promote the public good. Thus, higher education's vision must be widened if the nation is to be rescued from problems that threaten to diminish permanently the quality of life. (pp. 77–78)

10

PRINCIPLES FOR QUALITY UNDERGRADUATE EDUCATION IN PSYCHOLOGY

DIANE F. HALPERN, BARRY ANTON, BERNARD C. BEINS,
DANIEL J. BERNSTEIN, CHARLES T. BLAIR-BROEKER,
CHARLES L. BREWER, WILLIAM BUSKIST, BETTINA J. CASAD,
WALLACE E. DIXON JR., YOLANDA Y. HARPER, ROBIN HAILSTORKS,
MARY E. KITE, PATRICIA PUCCIO, AND COURTNEY A. ROCHELEAU

As members of the Steering Committee for the 2008 National Conference on Undergraduate Education in Psychology, we realize that the future of our discipline depends on quality undergraduate programs that prepare students for advanced study in psychology. Our concern with quality education in psychology extends far beyond the future of the discipline. Psychology continues to be one of the most popular majors on college campuses, but most undergraduate psychology majors do not pursue graduate study in psychology. They select psychology as their major because they are interested in the subject and they believe that a major in psychology will provide them with the knowledge, skills, and values they will need to enter and succeed in the workforce and to thrive in their daily lives. Our recommendations for quality principles for undergraduate education in psychology are designed to ensure that psychology students are prepared for the challenges they will

These principles and recommendations do not constitute the policies of the American Psychological Association (APA) or commit APA to the activities described herein.

encounter as workers, family members, and concerned citizens in the new global century.

Within the context of contemporary challenges and changes, we offer recommendations for all of the stakeholders in higher education. These recommendations are designed to foster exemplary outcomes to meet the rapidly accelerating demands of this millennium. We crafted our recommendations to benefit both psychology majors and nonmajors who will need to acquire personal and profession skills to compete and to cooperate in the global society. Our goal is to educate students to be psychologically literate citizens who can apply their understanding of psychological principles and methods to the many demands they will encounter during the following decades. Today's students must prepare themselves for a world in which knowledge is accumulating at a rapidly accelerating rate and in which old problems such as poverty, racism, and pollution join new problems such as global terrorism, a health crisis created by alarming increases in obesity, and the growing gap between the very poor and very rich. All of these problems require psychological knowledge, skills, and values for their solution. Necessary skills and values include being able to work cooperatively, think critically, communicate effectively, understand various types of diversity, lead effectively, act ethically, and develop creative solutions to existing problems as well as those that will emerge in the coming decades.

We call on all of the stakeholders in undergraduate education—students, faculty, departments, academic administrators, public policy makers, and the general public—to adopt the following principles for quality teaching and learning. Knowing that educational institutions have diverse missions and student populations, we are not overly prescriptive or specific in our recommendations. Moreover, we are not recommending specific courses; the relative mix of teaching, research, or service in which faculty should engage; or the level of academic preparedness expected of students. Likewise, we do not suggest a single model for assessing gains in student learning. Instead, we focus on broad principles that apply across the vast variety of institutions with psychology programs in the United States and around the world. A program could be a major, minor, or group of courses that make up a certificate or area of specialization. Many of our recommendations apply to all quality educational programs. Thus most departments and programs on college and university campuses can adopt the quality principles with minimal revisions in their programs.

Psychology is a liberal arts discipline grounded in research methods typically associated with the physical and biological sciences. Psychology is a bridge between the social sciences and physical sciences that facilitates the exchange of ideas with many of our sister disciplines on both sides of the bridge. A well designed major will prepare students for a wide variety of possible futures, including careers that begin immediately after graduation, careers of the future that do not now exist, and graduate and professional school. We recognize the role that psychology plays in general education programs and in the core curriculum of other departments such as nursing, education, business, and child development. Psychology is poised to benefit from the increasing trend toward interdisciplinary coursework being offered on many campuses because it depends heavily on biology, neuroscience, sociology, education, and many other academic disciplines. Our recommendations for quality principles are broad in their applicability and do not constrain creative thinking by any of the stakeholders in higher education.

The following quality principles for undergraduate education in psychology are designed for creating a world-class educational system that provides students with the workplace skills needed in this information age; a solid academic background that prepares them for advanced study in a wide range of fields; and the knowledge, skills, and abilities that will enhance their personal lives.

QUALITY PRINCIPLE 1: STUDENTS ARE RESPONSIBLE FOR MONITORING AND ENHANCING THEIR OWN LEARNING

The entire educational enterprise centers on the learner and ways to make learning effective, durable, and transferable across academic domains and to out-of-school contexts. The most important variable in learning outcomes is what students do to making learning effective, durable, and transferable. Recommendations for this principle are provided in the following numbered points with explications.

1. Students should know how to learn.

   Knowing how to learn includes the use of learning strategies such as spacing study sessions; processing information for meaning; generating responses to enhance memory; explaining what one knows using visual–spatial, verbal, and kinesthetic strategies; and becoming actively engaged in the effortful process of learning. Students can reasonably expect faculty and support staff at their institution to be able to assist them in learning to learn.

2. Students should assume increasing responsibility for their own learning.

   Students should develop the skilled habit of metacognition, which includes knowing when they need help with learning and when they are learning well on their own. Early in the semester, students who need assistance with learning should seek help from their professors and others on campus who can support learning (e.g., staff at student learning centers).

3. Students should take advantage of the rich diversity that exists in educational institutions and learn from individuals who are different from them.

    Projections from the U.S. Census Bureau (2008) suggest that there will be no single majority group in the United States by the year 2050, a time when most of today's students will still be in the workforce. Demographers expect other regions of the world to become increasingly diverse as well. People vary in multiple ways, including extent of ability, race, ethnicity, country of origin, age, religious beliefs, sexual orientation, and socioeconomic status. The diverse characteristics of other students and faculty members provide learning experiences for the real-world tasks of understanding people who view events in the world from varying perspectives. Learning from other students and diverse faculty is an important component of a quality education.

4. Students are responsible for seeking academic advice for tasks such as selecting courses in the approved sequence that satisfy the institution's requirements for the major and general education. They are also responsible for seeking advice about planning for a career that is both realistic and tailored to their individual talents, aspirations, and life situations.

    A corollary of this principle is that faculty and staff will be available and knowledgeable about requirements for the major and about career options for majors in psychology.

QUALITY PRINCIPLE 2: FACULTY STRIVE TO BECOME SCIENTIST–EDUCATORS WHO ARE KNOWLEDGEABLE ABOUT AND USE THE PRINCIPLES OF THE SCIENCE OF LEARNING

Students need knowledgeable and caring faculty to achieve student learning goals. Thus, the quality principles for faculty in higher education and other places where students learn are closely tied to the principles to which students aspire. Recommendations for this principle are provided in the following numbered points and explications.

1. Faculty should act ethically and provide instruction in the ethical standards that undergird the discipline.

    Faculty in psychology should model ethical behavior in all of their interactions with students, in their research and in all aspects of their professional and personal lives. Faculty should provide students with practice in thinking through both new and old ethical dilemmas. As a means of developing ethical standards in students, faculty provide students with a framework in which they can analyze new and emerging ethical issues such as the use of memory-enhancing drugs, the incarceration of pregnant women who engage in practices that are likely to harm their baby at some later time, and whether teens should be held liable as adults for criminal behavior.

2. Faculty should understand and apply a variety of learning principles and modes of learning, such as spaced practice, generation of responses, active engagement by students, group exercises, and explaining as a way of understanding, among others. Expertise in one's specialized subdiscipline in psychology is not sufficient to promote quality learning. A large and growing literature applies empirically derived outcomes from the science of learning to college settings and other places where people learn (e.g., high schools, media at home, and at work).

   Faculty need to know how to teach the information in their specialty content areas and in general psychology in ways that promote deep understanding, long-lasting knowledge, and the ability to apply what is learned to disciplines outside of psychology and in settings outside of the formal classroom. Faculty need to know how to alter their teaching, depending on faculty and student learning goals, background preparation of their students, institutional mission, and personal preferences.

3. Faculty should make the same commitment to using the science of learning in their teaching as the discipline requires of scientist-practitioners who use the scientific findings of psychological research in their practice with clients and other aspects of their professional lives.

   There are numerous ways to meet the objective of this principle. Faculty may collect teaching-related data to determine the effectiveness of various modes of teaching. In addition, they may become familiar with the scholarly literature on effective teaching and learning at their level of education. We encourage all faculty to do both and to apply their knowledge of how people learn to enhance learning.

4. Faculty should engage in continuous, iterative inquiry into the success of their instruction in generating appropriate learning, using that evidence to refine instructional practices in ways that enhance the success of future students.

   Once evidence-based teaching practices are implemented, faculty need to ask how many of their course goals are met and how many students are meeting the identified goals. Over time each course needs to have some students achieve all of its goals, and the percentage of students who achieve excellence in the goals should increase. Faculty need to use both the experience of other instructors and principles of learning to identify and implement more effective teaching practices, as indicated by successful student learning. Continuous adaptation of teaching practices to generate appropriate student success is an essential feature of excellent instruction.

5. Faculty should teach critical thinking by identifying the critical thinking skills and abilities they wish to promote in their classes and in the psychology major as whole. Faculty should periodically review these skills and abilities throughout the term and through all years of undergraduate education.

Today's students get their information from a wide variety of places, including both credible and less than credible Web sites. The Internet is filled with misinformation (unintentional inaccuracy), disinformation (intentional inaccuracy), propaganda, and just plain nonsense. Students are bombarded with advertisements that now blink on their supermarket shopping carts and are projected onto the night sky. More than ever, the most important outcome for an undergraduate education is the ability to think critically. Faculty should teach for critical thinking by identifying the skills and abilities they wish to promote in their classes and in the major as a whole. After identifying these skills and abilities, faculty should periodically review them throughout the term and at graduation (or the end point of their psychology program, if it is not graduation).

6. Faculty should ensure that students develop basic skills in communication, numeracy, and working cooperatively with others.

The ability to think critically is an essential outcome of a quality education, but it is not the only basic skill that should be developed through challenging coursework. Other essential skills include effective writing, fluent speaking, and thinking with numbers, which can be incorporated in classes within and outside of the major. Faculty should think about their students' development of these skills and provide systematic learning opportunities so that students can build on earlier skills as they become more proficient.

7. Faculty should ensure that diversity issues are infused throughout the curriculum, with deliberate inclusion in most, if not all, courses.

Culturally competent faculty will be (or will strive to become) at ease with and knowledgeable about the full range of students, staff, and other faculty on their campus and will communicate that knowledge to their students. Psychology educators are not providing students with a quality education if they avoid or deny the importance of diversity as a central topic in psychology. They cannot teach about topics such as human development, love and sexual attraction, motivation, mental disorders, effective treatments for mental disorders, health and well-being, or the multitude of other topics in psychology without including diversity issues. Diversity is not simply an add-on to an otherwise overcrowded curriculum; it is central to understanding psychology. Inclusive excellence in academia exists when diversity and educational quality efforts are fully integrated and embedded into the core of academic mission and institutional functioning both inside and outside of the classroom (Williams, Berger, & McClendon, 2005).

8. Faculty should develop competence in commonly used technologies and foster competence with these technologies in their students.

Today's students are *digital natives*, a term that is used to highlight the fact that they have never known a time when computers were not used for finding information, communicating with people around the world, or for playing games and listening to music. Despite their birth status as having been born during the decades of increasing use of computers, many students are not proficient in using word processors, spreadsheets, presentation software, and other common programs that will be indispensible to their work lives. Students who do not have these necessary skills must be identified and strongly encouraged to learn the essential tools of their trade— the computer programs that are needed for success as students and later as workers. Regardless of their level of expertise, student interests and abilities have been shaped by their technology related experiences. Faculty should recognize that technology is a language that we must use to communicate with our students.

QUALITY PRINCIPLE 3: PSYCHOLOGY DEPARTMENTS AND PROGRAMS CREATE A COHERENT CURRICULUM

Quality teaching and learning for undergraduates take place in an organizational context. Psychology departments and programs should be organized to support the learning goals of students and faculty. Recommendations for this principle are provided in the following numbered points with explications.

1. The scientific underpinnings of psychology should be reinforced throughout the curriculum.

   We urge departments to consider ways to communicate the scientific basis of psychology to present and prospective students, to faculty in other departments on campus, and to the general public because of common misunderstandings about the nature of psychology. There are several ways that the scientific bases of psychology could be made more prominent. These include changing a department's name to Psychological Science, seeking greater affiliation with departments in schools of science, or other ways that are appropriate for each department's structure, history, and setting. Research methods are at the heart of psychological inquiry and knowledge. They distinguish psychology as a science from psychology as a pseudoscience. For this reason, students should complete coursework in statistics and research methods as early in each student's course of study as possible. When students acquire knowledge about the research basis of psychology early in their education, statistics and research topics can be included in subsequent courses throughout the curriculum.

2. Every major should include courses from the four basic domains: biological bases, development, learning and cognition, and sociocultural influences. These perspectives should also be included in the introductory course.

   Regardless of the structure of an individual department's curriculum, the major should incorporate these four core perspectives on psychology. Because the introductory course is the only formal exposure to psychology that many educated citizens will have, this course must reflect the nature of psychology as a scientific discipline and include sections from each of the four basic domains.

3. The psychology major should provide an applied experience, if possible.

   Learning is more durable and more likely to transfer when applied to relevant, real-world problems. Student internships, externships, volunteer activities, work in a research laboratory, along with certain types of paid employment allow students to apply what they are learning to real-world problems. We recommend a required applied learning experience in the major, whenever this is possible.

4. Curricula in psychology should be designed to include coursework in writing and speaking across the curriculum and courses that teach students how to think critically across a broad range of

situations (see the *American Psychological Association [APA] Guidelines for the Undergraduate Psychology Major*; APA, 2007a).

The psychology curriculum as a whole should be designed to foster high-level learning outcomes that include essential skills such as thinking critically, learning effectively, writing well, and speaking fluently. The development of these essential skills should be coordinated across classes and systematically developed in the curriculum. Psychology departments should identify courses that enhance each of these skills and should assess learning gains for students who take those courses.

5. Courses should be sequenced in ways that are developmentally appropriate.

Students develop their ability to handle advanced concepts and procedures as they progress through the curriculum. For this reason, we recommend a broad course that introduces the discipline to students, followed by statistics and research methods as soon as is feasible for a department's local conditions (e.g., within the constraints of transfer agreements between community colleges and 4-year institutions), and lower division courses should be followed by the advanced requirements of upper division courses. A comprehensive introductory psychology course should be the required prerequisite for all subsequent psychology courses. The introductory psychology course is one of the cornerstones of social science general education programs, and as such, it needs to represent the entire field of psychology accurately and reinforce the basic premise that psychology is a scientific discipline. A developmentally appropriate curriculum supports cognitive development in psychology students.

6. Members of psychology departments should agree on the desired learning outcomes for the major and, possibly, for a minor concentration or other similar psychology program.

Clearly articulated learning outcomes promote development of a coherent curriculum in which students understand what they should learn and in which students and faculty can examine what students actually have learned. Psychology educators cannot improve undergraduate education without assessing what and how much students know when they complete a psychology program. Learning outcomes can be assessed by numerous methods. Faculty members must become familiar with some of the ways academic learning outcomes are assessed, the strengths and weaknesses of each method, and how to select among the possible methods in ways that will improve teaching and learning.

7. Graduate programs should make a commitment to quality undergraduate education by requiring formal instruction in teaching for all their graduate students, including those students who do not intend to seek academic positions.

    Psychology faculty receive most of their advanced education in graduate programs in psychology, which is where they should receive instruction in how modes of teaching lead to quality learning. Instruction in teaching is needed by all graduate students, whether or not they intend to become academic psychologists. Most doctoral students will teach in formal or informal settings at some point in their later careers. These graduate programs should not simply rely on a mentoring relationship with a single faculty member to foster teaching skills. Although mentoring relationships are highly desirable, they are not sufficient for teaching graduate students about the science and art of teaching.

8. As a contribution of psychology to the public good, courses should include knowledge and skill acquisition that is relevant to students' lives.

    Students should walk away with knowledge and skills that they can implement in their personal lives, families, career, and community contexts.

QUALITY PRINCIPLE 4: ACADEMIC ADMINISTRATORS SUPPORT AND ENCOURAGE QUALITY PRACTICES IN TEACHING AND LEARNING

Academic leadership can play a pivotal role in encouraging quality practices that enhance teaching and learning. Quality institutions have high-quality leaders who encourage and support the learning activities on their campuses. Recommendations for this principle are provided in the following numbered points with explications.

1. Faculty should be encouraged to engage in the scholarship of teaching and learning.

    The scholarship of teaching and learning is gaining increased credibility as a legitimate form of scholarly activity on most campuses. But inquiry into practices that support excellence in teaching and learning will be sustained only if these activities are supported by the academic administration. Scholarship and excellence in teaching and learning should be rewarded in ways that are appropriate for each campus. Regardless of an institution's mission, some amount of high-quality research on topics that promote teaching and learning needs to be recognized for its scholarly contributions.

2. Teaching assignments should take into account the needs of each campus, but institutions should not ask faculty to teach subjects in which they have very little background, knowledge, or preparation.

   Everyone loses when faculty are inadequately prepared for the courses they teach. If there is a need for faculty to teach in subject areas that they are not prepared to teach, they need to be given time and support to gain the necessary knowledge. Support may include, for example, paying for an advanced (or basic) class in the needed content area, sending faculty to conferences where they can learn about the needed area, and arranging mentoring with someone who has the necessary expertise.

3. Psychology departments need adequate support for their laboratories and laboratory-based classes.

   As teachers of a scientific discipline, psychologists need space and equipment for data collection and analysis, and students need laboratory courses that teach these skills. Adequate investments in laboratory space and equipment as well as routine upgrading of equipment, computers, and software are essential for a quality undergraduate education. The support of laboratory space for student learning and faculty research is a tangible commitment to psychological science.

4. Academic administrators should encourage faculty members to engage in lifelong learning to stay current in their field.

   The knowledge base of psychology is constantly changing, and new technologies are used in teaching and in research. New methods of data analysis and collection are changing the nature of psychology. Academic administrators should support the learning activities of faculty by funding advanced coursework and attendance at symposia, conferences, and other places where faculty can stay abreast of the rapid changes in their field. In many instances, adjunct faculty teach for decades at the same institution, so administrators who care about the quality of instruction their students are receiving will also extend some continuing education benefits to their long-term adjuncts as well as tenure-track faculty.

5. Administrators who support faculty experimentation to enhance teaching and learning must ensure that faculty are not punished if student evaluations are uneven.

In general, learning will be enhanced when faculty try different modes of instruction, with the goal of selecting appropriate modes that depend on the propensities of individual faculty (e.g., some may prefer to do mostly lecturing; others mostly group work around problems they pose in class), the nature of the students in their classes, the types of class, and the learning goals of both the faculty members and the students. Faculty will engage in a variety of modes of instruction only when there is a clear understanding that if student ratings of faculty effectiveness temporarily drop as a result of the experimentation (e.g., an attempt at cooperative learning does not work as well as expected), there will be no negative consequences for their promotion, tenure, or salary decisions. Faculty members must be free to experiment with different teaching and learning approaches without fear of reprisal. For these reasons and others, student evaluations should not be used as the sole criteria for promotion and tenure.

QUALITY PRINCIPLE 5: POLICY MAKERS AND THE GENERAL PUBLIC UNDERSTAND WHY PSYCHOLOGICAL LITERACY IS NECESSARY FOR INFORMED CITIZENS AND AN EFFECTIVE WORKFORCE

Principles for quality in teaching and learning need support outside of academia. We need public policies and an informed public to support efforts for quality improvement in undergraduate education. Recommendations for this principle are provided in the following numbered points with explications.

To bring about change in the perceptions of the general public and policy makers, all psychologists should develop the concept of psychologically literate citizens and convey this message so that policy makers and the general public will understand that the need to be psychologically literate is similar to being able to read or use numbers in thinking.

1. Psychologically literate citizens have a well-defined vocabulary and basic knowledge of the critical subject matter of psychology.

Psychologically literate citizens value the intellectual challenges required to use scientific thinking and the disciplined analysis of information to evaluate alternative courses of action. They act ethically. They recognize and foster diversity. They are insightful and reflective about their own and others' behavior and mental processes. Psychologically literate citizens know how to cooperate and to help a group come to consensus, and they can discriminate between science and pseudoscience. They can apply their knowledge of psychology to a broad range of situations such as making educational decisions, assisting with plans for someone with advancing Alzheimer's disease, using appropriate disciplinary practices with their children, and using leadership skills in group settings. There are endless ways that literacy in psychology will advance individuals, families, and larger groups. The general public and policy makers need to understand and value what psychologists know and do.

2. We call on the media for accurate depictions of psychological science and on policy makers to use our findings to inform public policies.

   For the most part, the general public, including policy makers, misunderstands psychology, thinking that it is entirely a profession that helps emotionally disturbed people cope with their problems or perceiving it as a way of dealing with the paranormal. These misunderstandings are not surprising given the widespread images of psychologists in the media where they are very rarely shown as scientists and practitioners who apply psychological research. We urge the media to present a more accurate depiction of the science of psychology, and we urge public policy makers to use psychologists' research findings when crafting public policies and deciding how to act in the public good.

Taken together, these principles offer recommendations that will have positive and long-lasting effects on the millions of students worldwide who enroll in undergraduate psychology classes throughout the world. They will advance psychology in ways "that benefit society and improve people's lives" (APA mission statement, 2008, http://www.apa.org/about/mission.html).

CONCLUSION: HOW TO MEET THE CHALLENGE OF PREPARING COLLEGE STUDENTS FOR LIFE IN THE 21ST CENTURY

DIANE F. HALPERN

From the capital of Guam to what is celebrated on Boxing Day, today's students know that the answer is a click away. The easy availability of factual knowledge has changed what students need to know. Of course, factual knowledge is still needed, because no one can think critically about any topic without it, but unlike their parents' generation, today's students need to be able to discern the difference between facts they need to know and facts they can access easily on the Internet when needed. There are other important cognitive skills that are far more important for the millennial student than for students as recently as 10 to 15 years ago. Even though it has always been important to know how to recognize and avoid unnecessary or misleading information, the massive quantity of information that bombards today's students means that they need to be constantly vigilant about the quality of the information they are receiving and deciding what *not* to read or learn.

Consider, for example, that a simple search on a Web browser for *psychotherapy* brings up over 17 million entries in a fraction of a second, and this information can be accessed from all but the most remote regions of the world. Some of the entries, which are disguised as informational sites, are advertisements designed to sell something to anyone whose cursor wanders onto their Web site. Some of the psychotherapies that are encountered during a routine search are, in fact, pseudotherapies that can do more harm than good. How can anyone who is looking for information about a topic as basic as psychotherapy know how to eliminate many millions of Web pages to find the relevant and credible information he or she needs to know? The cognitive skills needed for eliminating information are qualitatively different from the ones needed when the parents and professors of today's students were in school, when the primary task was to find enough information.

Today's students are living at a time when new information is replacing the old at a rapidly accelerating rate. With so much changing, *lifelong learning* is no longer a slogan. Millennial students must realize that formal and informal educational experiences will be a part of their lives that will extend into old age and that many of these experiences will take place online. The swell in college enrollments of students older than the traditional college-going age that ends in the mid-20s is evidence that the term *student* knows no age boundaries. All people are facing a virtual tsunami of information that must be learned and used at home and at work. The best education for life in the 21st century must be built on the twin pillars of *learning how to learn* and how to think critically about the vast array of information that confronts everyone.

One theme that runs throughout this book highlights the diversity of students enrolled in higher education. Most postsecondary students and an increasing number of high school students take some coursework in psychology—perhaps hoping to learn more about themselves and to prepare for their future lives as workers, parents, and citizens in a world that is growing increasingly "flat" (Friedman, 2005) and complex. Psychology educators can confidently predict that many of their students will work at jobs that do not exist currently, but educators can only guess at what these jobs might be. It is also with considerable certainty that psychology educators can predict that their students will face new ethical challenges created by advances in technology, medicine, and the sciences. It is an international imperative that educators help all of today's students achieve their full potential because the world will need international talent, with high ethical standards, to solve old and new problems such as terrorism, pollution, hunger, loneliness, war, aging societies, and more.

HOW ARE PSYCHOLOGY EDUCATORS DOING?

Given the critical task of preparing college students for an uncertain future at a time of rapidly accelerating change, it is useful to examine how well psychology educators are achieving the goals of higher education. Institutional missions vary widely, as do the students being educated and the reasons they attend colleges and universities. Therefore, the answer to specific questions about curricula and modes of teaching needs to be contextualized, which is another theme that is repeated throughout this book. The mismatch between the way higher education is organized and its ability to meet the educational needs of students is discussed in several chapters, most notably in the call for a science-educator model of teaching in psychology and across all academic departments. Most faculty rewards, which include salary, promotion, tenure, and honorific titles, require "good enough teaching" plus excellence in research; few institutions consider research on teaching and learning in colleges on par with research in other "substantive" areas. Increasingly, the public is noticing the discrepancy between what is promised in the glossy brochures that tout quality teaching that are published by colleges and university admissions offices and the way this promise is played out on college campuses.

The National Center for Public Policy and Higher Education, a non-profit group concerned about quality education, gives letter grades to every state in the United States on various dimensions of education. They have issued grades every 2 years since 2000. In their December 2008 report, they found that "our higher-education performance is not commensurate with the current needs of our society and our economy" (Hunt, 2008, ¶ 13). The 2008 report recognized that although a college degree is a passport to a middle-class life, low college completion rates undercut the supply of college-educated workers. Persistent and substantial disparities by race in college attendance and a decline in the proportion of U.S. citizens completing college relative to other countries are serious problems for the individuals higher education has failed and for the future of the United States. It is a scathing report that psychology educators cannot afford to ignore.

Other national groups and blue-ribbon panels have arrived at similar dismal conclusions about the readiness of the workforce. The Conference Board is a global independent organization that works in the public interest. They found that too few college students excel at the basic skills needed for the 21st-century workforce—oral and written communication, work ethic, and critical thinking and problem solving (Partnership for 21st Century Skills, 2006). Although the Conference Board, which consists of employers, is a different sort of organization from the National Center for Public Policy and Higher Education, the Conference Board also gives higher education a poor report card. Many of their recommendations overlap with those found throughout this book—use real-world examples to advance learning and increase the use of technology as an aid to learning.

Throughout this book, my colleagues and I highlight many high-impact learning methods that cross educational settings and make for smoother transitions from high school and community colleges to baccalaureate programs and postgraduate education. The chapter authors call for a strong core of courses in the psychology major and in the general education courses that cut across the curriculum. We need advocates on every campus, in every corporate board room, in state legislatures, and at the national and international level to take our recommendations and indicators of quality programs seriously. We must attract, retain, and graduate a greater proportion of the population, with special emphasis on students from groups that are underrepresented in higher education. This call for action is not just a matter of social equality; it is necessary for this country and the future of this planet because the world cannot meet the growing technological and ethical demands of the coming decades without a better educated workforce and populace.

THE SITUATION IS CRITICAL

Newspaper headlines often tell of problems in higher education. California, which has the largest population and is among the most racially and ethnically diverse states, is facing a serious shortage of college-educated workers (Lifsher, 2008). Other states are expected to follow California's inability to find enough educated workers in the next 2 decades. Demographic predictions show that California will soon have no single racial or ethnic majority, and current data show that the gap between Whites and other racial and ethic groups employed in management and professional occupations in California is larger than in any other state (23% vs. a mean of 15%; Kelly, 2008). Large increases in racial and ethnic diversity have not led to equality. The inequality in educational attainment is another concern that is echoed repeatedly in several chapters in this book. All colleges and universities need culturally competent faculty, a curriculum that reflects multiple cultural realities, and an educational program that recognizes the learning needs and goals of individual students. Psychology educators can and must do a better job of educating all citizens for the 21st century. The thoughtful answers to critical questions about higher education and the quality principles for undergraduate education that are presented in this book provide a useful blueprint for enhancing higher education in the coming decades. My colleagues and I invite all concerned stakeholders to join with us to build a better future.

APPENDIX A:
STEERING COMMITTEE MEMBERS AND AMERICAN PSYCHOLOGICAL ASSOCIATION ADMINISTRATIVE STAFF

STEERING COMMITTEE MEMBERS

Diane F. Halpern, Claremont McKenna College, Conference Chair
Barry Anton, University of Puget Sound, APA Board of Directors Liaison
Bernard C. Beins, Ithaca College
Charles T. Blair-Broeker, Cedar Falls High School
Charles L. Brewer, Furman University, APA Board of Educational Affairs Liaison
William Buskist, Auburn University
Bettina J. Casad, California Polytechnic Institute, Pomona
Wallace E. Dixon Jr., East Tennessee State University
Yolanda Y. Harper, The University of Memphis
Mary E. Kite, Ball State University
Patricia Puccio, College of DuPage
Courtney A. Rocheleau, Appalachian State University

AMERICAN PSYCHOLOGICAL ASSOCIATION (APA) ADMINISTRATIVE STAFF

Cynthia Belar, APA Education Directorate
Robin Hailstorks, APA Education Directorate
Martha Boenau, APA Education Directorate
Chris Munsey, APA *Monitor on Psychology*

APPENDIX B:
PARTICIPANTS IN THE 2008 NATIONAL CONFERENCE ON UNDERGRADUATE EDUCATION IN PSYCHOLOGY

WORKING GROUP 1: WHY DO WE NEED TO RETHINK HOW WE EDUCATE STUDENTS IN PSYCHOLOGY?

Thomas V. McGovern, Arizona State University West, Working Group Chair

Wallace E. Dixon Jr., East Tennessee State University, Steering Committee Liaison

Laurie Corey, Westchester Community College

Jacquelyn Cranney, University of New South Wales

Jeffrey D. Holmes, Ithaca College

Janet E. Kuebli, Saint Louis University

Kristin A. Ritchey, Ball State University

Randolph A. Smith, Lamar University

Sheila J. Walker, Scripps College

WORKING GROUP 2: WHO IS TEACHING PSYCHOLOGY, AND WHAT IS THE QUALITY OF INSTRUCTION?

Daniel J. Bernstein, University of Kansas, Working Group Chair

Courtney A. Rocheleau, Appalachian State University, Steering Committee Liaison

William Addison, Eastern Illinois University

Cindy Altman, Duquesne University

Debra Hollister, Valencia Community College

Meera Komarraju, Southern Illinois University

Loreto Prieto, Iowa State University

Cecilia Shore, Miami University

WORKING GROUP 3: WHAT IS BEING TAUGHT AND LEARNED IN PSYCHOLOGY COURSES, INCLUDING THE IMPACT OF FRAGMENTATION OF PSYCHOLOGY TOWARD SPECIALIZED DISCIPLINARY SOCIETIES AND NEW INTERDISCIPLINARY SPECIALTIES (E.G., NEUROSCIENCE) ON THE PSYCHOLOGY MAJOR?

Dana S. Dunn, Moravian College, Working Group Chair

Charles L. Brewer, Furman University, Steering Committee Liaison
Patricia Puccio, College of DuPage, Steering Committee Liaison
Robin L. Cautin, Manhattanville College
Regan A. R. Gurung, University of Wisconsin—Green Bay
Kenneth D. Keith, University of San Diego
Loretta N. McGregor, Arkansas State University
Steve A. Nida, The Citadel
Mary Jean Voight, Boylan Catholic High School

WORKING GROUP 4: WHO ARE THE STUDENTS IN UNDERGRADUATE PSYCHOLOGY AND HOW DO WE CHALLENGE THE TRADITIONAL "ONE-SIZE-FITS-ALL" CURRICULAR APPROACH TO MEETING THE NEEDS OF A DIVERSE STUDENT POPULATION?

Linh Nguyen Littleford, Ball State University, Working Group Chair
William Buskist, Auburn University, Steering Committee Liaison
Susan M. Frantz, Highline Community College
Dennis B. Galvan, Gallaudet University
Robert W. Hendersen, Grand Valley State University
Maureen A. McCarthy, Kennesaw State University
Melanie C. Page, Oklahoma State University
Antonio E. Puente, University of North Carolina

WORKING GROUP 5: WHEN AND WHERE ARE STUDENTS TAKING PSYCHOLOGY COURSES?

Jeffrey Andre, James Madison University
Ann T. Ewing, Mesa Community College, Working Group Chair
Charles T. Blair-Broeker, Cedar Falls High School, Steering Committee Liaison
Jessica Henderson Daniel, Harvard Medical School
Amy C. Fineburg, Spain Park High School
Jennifer J. Higa, University of Hawaii—Honolulu Community College
Salvador Macias III, University of South Carolina Sumter
Kenneth A. Weaver, Emporia State University

WORKING GROUP 6: WHAT ARE THE MODES OF TEACHING FOR DIFFERENT CONTENT, CONTEXTS, AND STUDENTS?

Stephen L. Chew, Samford University, Working Group Chair
Mary E. Kite, Ball State University, Steering Committee Liaison
Robin M. Bartlett, Northern Kentucky University
James E. Dobbins, Wright State University School of Professional Psychology

Elizabeth Yost Hammer, Xavier University of Louisiana
Trudy Frey Loop, The Altamont School
Julie Guay McIntyre, The Sage Colleges
Karen C. Rose, Widener University

WORKING GROUP 7: HOW CAN WE PROMOTE LEARNING WITH NEW TECHNOLOGIES THAT INCLUDE INTERACTIVE LEARNING AGENTS, ONLINE PROGRAMS THAT TEACH COLLABORATIVE PEER EVALUATION, GAME-BASED MODELS OF LEARNING, AND VIRTUAL LEARNING ENVIRONMENTS AMONG OTHERS?

Keith Millis, Northern Illinois University, Working Group Chair
Yolanda Y. Harper, University of Memphis, Steering Committee Liaison
Suzanne Baker, James Madison University
Judith E. Owen Blakemore, Indiana University-Purdue University
Fred Connington, Liberty High School
Wei-Chen Hung, Northern Illinois University
Art Kohn, Portland Community College
Jeffrey Stowell, Eastern Illinois University

WORKING GROUP 8: HOW ARE WE USING KNOWLEDGE GAINED OVER THE LAST DECADE ABOUT EFFECTIVE TEACHING AND LEARNING?

Frank C. Worrell, University of California, Berkeley, Working Group
    Chair
Bettina J. Casad, California Polytechnic Institute, Pomona, Steering
    Committee Liaison
David B. Daniel, James Madison University
Mark McDaniel, Washington University
Wayne S. Messer, Berea College
Harold L. Miller Jr., Brigham Young University
Vincent Prohaska, Lehman College of the City University of New York
Martha S. Zlokovich, Psi Chi

WORKING GROUP 9: WHAT ARE THE DESIRED OUTCOMES OF AN UNDERGRADUATE EDUCATION IN PSYCHOLOGY?

R. Eric Landrum, Boise State University, Working Group Chair
Bernard C. Beins, Ithaca College, Steering Committee Liaison

Mukul Bhalla, Argosy University
Karen Brakke, Spelman College
Deborah S. Briihl, Valdosta State University
Rita M. Curl-Langager, Minot State University
Tom P. Pusateri, Kennesaw State University
Jaye Jang Van Kirk, San Diego Mesa College

CONFERENCE KEYNOTE SPEAKERS

James Bray, Baylor College of Medicine, APA President-Elect
Daniel Fallon, Carnegie Foundation
Thomas V. McGovern, Arizona State Univesity, West
David Myers, Hope College

APPENDIX C:
PHOTO OF PARTICIPANTS

Participants in the APA National Conference on Undergraduate Education in Psychology
University of Puget Sound, Washington

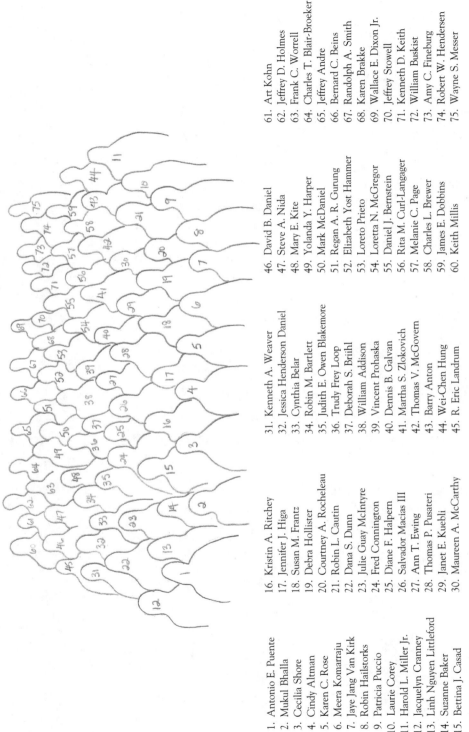

1. Antonio E. Puente
2. Mukul Bhalla
3. Cecilia Shore
4. Cindy Altman
5. Karen C. Rose
6. Meera Komarraju
7. Jaye Jang Van Kirk
8. Robin Hailstorks
9. Patricia Puccio
10. Laurie Corey
11. Harold L. Miller Jr.
12. Jacquelyn Cranney
13. Linh Nguyen Littleford
14. Suzanne Baker
15. Bettina J. Casad

16. Kristin A. Ritchey
17. Jennifer J. Higa
18. Susan M. Frantz
19. Debra Hollister
20. Courtney A. Rocheleau
21. Robin L. Cautin
22. Dana S. Dunn
23. Julie Guay McIntyre
24. Fred Connington
25. Diane F. Halpern
26. Salvador Macias III
27. Ann T. Ewing
28. Thomas P. Pusateri
29. Janet E. Kuebli
30. Maureen A. McCarthy

31. Kenneth A. Weaver
32. Jessica Henderson Daniel
33. Cynthia Belar
34. Robin M. Bartlett
35. Judith E. Owen Blakemore
36. Trudy Frey Loop
37. Deborah S. Briihl
38. William Addison
39. Vincent Prohaska
40. Dennis B. Galvan
41. Martha S. Zlokovich
42. Thomas V. McGovern
43. Barry Anton
44. Wei-Chen Hung
45. R. Eric Landrum

46. David B. Daniel
47. Steve A. Nida
48. Mary E. Kite
49. Yolanda Y. Harper
50. Mark McDaniel
51. Regan A. R. Gurung
52. Elizabeth Yost Hammer
53. Loreto Prieto
54. Loretta N. McGregor
55. Daniel J. Bernstein
56. Rita M. Curl-Langager
57. Melanie C. Page
58. Charles L. Brewer
59. James E. Dobbins
60. Keith Millis

61. Art Kohn
62. Jeffrey D. Holmes
63. Frank C. Worrell
64. Charles T. Blair-Broeker
65. Jeffrey Andre
66. Bernard C. Beins
67. Randolph A. Smith
68. Karen Brakke
69. Wallace E. Dixon Jr.
70. Jeffrey Stowell
71. Kenneth D. Keith
72. William Buskist
73. Amy C. Fineburg
74. Robert W. Hendersen
75. Wayne S. Messer

Not pictured: Martha Boenau, Stephen L. Chew

REFERENCES

Abes, E. S., Jones, S. R., & McEwen, M. K. (2007). Reconceptualizing the multiple dimensions of identities: The role of meaning making capacity in the construction of multiple identities. *Journal of College Student Development, 48,* 1–22.

Adams, M. (Ed.). (1992). *Promoting diversity in college classrooms: Innovative responses for the curriculum, faculty, and institutions.* San Francisco: Jossey-Bass.

Adelman, C. (2004). *The empirical curriculum: Changes in postsecondary course-taking, 1972–2000.* Washington, DC: U.S. Department of Education.

Allen, I. E., & Seaman, J. (2005). *Growing by degrees: Online education in the United States.* Needham, MA: The Sloan Consortium.

Allen, I. E., & Seaman, J. (2007). *Online nation: Five years of growth in online learning.* Needham, MA: The Sloan Consortium.

Alzubaidi, A. S., & Ghanem, A. (1997). Perspectives on psychology in Yemen. *International Journal of Psychology, 32,* 363–366.

American Association of Community Colleges. (2008a). *CC STATS home.* Retrieved March 31, 2009, from http://www.aacc.nche.edu/research/home.htm

American Association of Community Colleges. (2008b). *Students at community colleges.* Retrieved March 31, 2009, from http://www.aacc.nche.edu/research/home_students.htm

American Psychological Association. (2002a). Ethical principles of psychologists and code of conduct. *American Psychologist, 57,* 1060–1073.

American Psychological Association. (2002b). *Principles of good practices in distance education and their application to professional education and training in psychology.* Retrieved June 25, 2008, from http://www.apa.org/ed/graduate/distance_ed.pdf

American Psychological Association. (2003). Guidelines on multicultural education, training, research, practice, and organization change for psychologists. *American Psychologist, 58,* 377–402.

American Psychological Association. (2005). *National standards for high school psychology curricula.* Retrieved August 24, 2008, from http://www.apa.org/ed/natlstandards.html

American Psychological Association. (2007a). *APA guidelines for the undergraduate psychology major.* Retrieved November 11, 2008, from http://www.apa.org/ed/psymajor_guideline.pdf

American Psychological Association. (2007b). *APA membership data.* Retrieved June 26, 2008, from https://research.apa.org/members.html

American Psychological Association. (2008). *Teaching, learning, and assessing in a developmentally coherent curriculum.* Retrieval April 1, 2009, from http://www.apa.org/ed/resources.html

American Psychological Association, Center for Workforce Analysis and Research (2007). *2005 doctoral employment survey.* Retrieved June 26, 2008, from http://research.apa.org/des05.html#debt

American Psychological Association, Committee on Lesbian and Gay Concerns. (1993). *Graduate faculty in psychology interested in lesbian and gay issues, 1993*. Washington, DC: Author.

American Psychological Association, Committee on Women in Psychology. (1995). *Task force on the changing gender composition of psychology*. Retrieved June 30, 2008, from http://www.apa.org/pi/taskforce/homepage.html

American Psychological Association, Office of Ethnic Minority Affairs. (2008). *A portrait of success and challenge—progress report: 1997–2005*. Retrieved June 26, 2008, from http://www.apa.org/pi/oema/cemrrat_report.html

American Psychological Association, Task Force on Strengthening the Teaching and Learning of Undergraduate Psychological Sciences. (2008). *Teaching, learning, and assessing in a developmentally coherent curriculum*. Retrieved February 19, 2009, from http://www.apa.org/ed/pcue/bea_coherent.pdf

American Psychological Association, Task Force on Undergraduate Major Competencies. (2002a). *The assessment cyberguide for learning goals and outcomes*. Retrieved July 2, 2008, from http://www.apa.org/ed/guidehomepage.html

American Psychological Association, Task Force on Undergraduate Major Competencies. (2002b). *Undergraduate major learning goals and outcomes: A report*. Retrieved June 25, 2008, from http://www.apa.org/ed/pcue/taskforcereport.pdf

Andreoli-Mathie, V. A., & Ernst, R. (1999, September–October). The national forum on psychology partnerships: From vision to reality. *PTN: Psychology Teacher Network, 9*(4), pp. 1, 5, 8, 16.

Angelo, T. A., & Cross, K. P. (1993). *Classroom assessment techniques: A handbook for college teachers* (2nd ed.). San Francisco: Jossey-Bass.

Antonacci, D. M., & Modaress, N. (2008). Envisioning the educational possibilities of user-created virtual worlds. *AACE Journal, 16*, 115–126.

Appleby, D. C. (2000). Job skills valued by employers who interview psychology majors. *Eye on Psi Chi, 4*(3), 17.

Appleby, D. C. (2007). *The savvy psychology major* (4th ed.). Dubuque, IA: Kendall/Hunt.

Arreola, R. G. (2007). *Developing a comprehensive evaluation system*. Bolton, MA: Anker.

Association of American Colleges and Universities. (2002). *Greater expectations: A new vision for learning as a nation goes to college*. Retrieved February 12, 2008, from http://www.greaterexpectations.org/

Association of American Colleges and Universities. (2005). *Liberal education outcomes: A preliminary report on student achievement in college*. Retrieved February 23, 2009, from http://www.aacu.org/advocacy/pdfs/LEAP_Report_FINAL.pdf

Association of American Colleges and Universities. (2007). *College learning for the new global century: A report from The National Leadership Council for Liberal Education and America's Promise*. Retrieved April 28, 2008, from http://www.aacu.org/publications/

Association of American Colleges and Universities. (2008). *How should colleges assess and improve student learning? Employers' views on the accountability challenge:*

A *survey of employers conducted on behalf of the Association of American Colleges and Universities*. Washington, DC: Author. (ERIC Document Reproduction Service No. ED499718)

Association of American Colleges and Universities and the Council for Higher Education Accreditation. (2008). *New leadership for student learning and accountability: A statement of principles, commitments to action*. Retrieved February 23, 2009, from http://www.chea.org/pdf/2008.01.30_New_Leadership_Statement.pdf

Australian Psychology Accreditation Council. (2008). *Rules for accreditation and accreditation standards for psychology courses*. Retrieved August 17, 2008, from http://www.apac.psychology.org.au/

Bain, K. (2004). *What the best college teachers do*. Cambridge: Harvard University Press.

Bainbridge, W. S. (2007). The scientific research potential of virtual worlds. *Science, 317*, 472–476.

Barkley, E. F., Cross, K. P., & Major, C. H. (2004). *Collaborative learning: A handbook for college faculty*. San Francisco: Jossey-Bass.

Beckman, M. (1997). Learning in action. *College Teaching, 45*, 72–75.

Benassi, V. A., & Fernald, P. S. (1993). Preparing tomorrow's psychologists for careers in academe. *Teaching of Psychology, 20*, 149–155.

Benjamin, L. T., Jr. (1986). Why don't they understand us? A history of psychology's public image. *American Psychologist, 41*, 941–946.

Benjamin, L. T., Jr. (2001). American psychology's struggles with its curriculum: Should a thousand flowers bloom? *American Psychologist, 56*, 735–742.

Benjamin, L. T., Jr., & Baker, D. B. (2004). *From séance to science: A history of the profession of psychology in America*. Belmont, CA: Wadsworth.

Bernard, R. M., Abrami, P. C., Lou, Y., Borokhovski, E., Wade, A., Wozney, L., et al. (2004). How does distance education compare with classroom instruction? A meta-analysis of the empirical literature. *Review of Educational Research, 74*, 379–439.

Bernstein, D. J. (2008). Resource review: Peer review and evaluation of the intellectual work of teaching. *Change, 40*(2), 48–51.

Bernstein, D. J., & Huber, M. T. (2006). *What is good teaching? Raising the bar through Scholarship Assessed*. Washington, DC: International Society for the Scholarship of Teaching and Learning.

Biernat, M., Vescio, T. K., Theno, S. A., & Crandall, C. S. (1996). Values and prejudice: Understanding the impact of American values on outgroup attitudes. In C. Seligman, J. M. Olson, & M. P. Zanna (Eds.), *The psychology of values* (pp. 153–189). Mahwah, NJ: Erlbaum.

Bjork, R. A. (1994). Memory and metamemory considerations in the training of human beings. In J. Metcalfe & A. Shimamura (Eds.), *Metacognition: Knowing about knowing* (pp. 185–205). Cambridge: Massachusetts Institute of Technology Press.

Bjork, R. A., & Bjork, E. L. (2006). Optimizing treatment and instruction: Implications of a new theory of disuse. In L. G. Nilsson & N. Ohta (Eds.), *Memory and society: Psychological perspectives* (pp. 396–401). New York: Wiley.

Bligh, D. A. (2000). *What's the use of lectures?* San Francisco: Jossey-Bass.

Bloom, B. (1956). *Taxonomy of education objectives: The classification of educational goals.* Essex, England: Longman Group.

Bonk, C. (2004). *The perfect e-storm: Emerging technology, enormous learner demand, enhanced pedagogy, and erased budgets.* London: The Observatory on Borderless Higher Education.

Borden, V. M. H., & Rajecki, D. W. (2000). First-year employment outcomes of psychology baccalaureates: Relatedness, preparedness, and prospects. *Teaching of Psychology, 27,* 164–168.

Borden, V. M. H., & Zak Owens, J. L. (2001). *Measuring quality: Choosing among surveys and other assessments of college quality.* Washington, DC: American Council on Education and Association for Institutional Research. (ERIC Document Reproduction Service No. ED457767)

Bordon, M. H. (2004). Accommodating student swirl: When traditional students are no longer the tradition. *Change, 33*(2), 10–17.

Boyer, E. L. (1990). *Scholarship reconsidered: Priorities of the professoriate.* San Francisco: Carnegie Foundation for the Advancement of Teaching.

Bransford, J. D., Brown, A. L., & Cocking, R. R. (1999). *How people learn: Brain, mind, experience, and school.* Washington, DC: National Academy Press.

Brewer, C. L., Hopkins, J. R., Kimble, G. A., Matlin, M. W., McCann, L. I., McNeil, O. V., et al. (1993). Curriculum. In T. V. McGovern (Ed.), *Handbook for enhancing undergraduate education in psychology* (pp. 161–182). Washington, DC: American Psychological Association.

Bronfenbrenner, U. (1979). *The ecology of human development.* Cambridge: Harvard University Press.

Bronstein, P. A., & Quina, K. (1988). *Teaching a psychology of people: Resources for gender and sociocultural awareness.* Washington, DC: American Psychological Association.

Brothen, T., & Wambach, C. (2004). The value of time limits on Internet quizzes. *Teaching of Psychology, 31,* 62–64.

Brown, J. O. (2002). Know thyself: The impact of portfolio development on adult learning. *Adult Education Quarterly, 52,* 228–245.

Bubany, S. T., Krieshok, T. S., Black, M. D., & McKay, R. A. (2008). College students' perspectives on their career decision making. *Journal of Career Assessment, 16,* 177–197.

Bucher, R. D. (2004). *Diversity consciousness: Opening our minds to people, cultures, and opportunities* (2nd ed.). Englewood Cliffs, NJ: Prentice Hall.

Buskist, W. (2002). Effective teaching: Perspectives and insights from Division Two's 2- and 4-year awardees. *Teaching of Psychology, 29,* 188–193.

Buskist, W., Beins, B. C., & Hevern, V. W. (Eds.). (2004). *Preparing the new psychology professoriate: Helping graduate students become competent teachers.* Retrieved July 1, 2008, from Society for the Teaching of Psychology Web site: http://teachpsych.org/resources/e-books/pnpp/html/pnpp05.html

Buskist, W., Benson, T., & Sikorski, J. F. (2005). The call to teach. *Journal of Social and Clinical Psychology, 24,* 111–122.

Buskist, W., & Davis, S. F. (Eds.). (2006). *Handbook of the teaching of psychology.* Malden, MA: Blackwell Publishers.

Buxton, C. E., Cofer, C. N., Gustad, J. W., MacLeod, R. B., McKeachie, W. J., & Wolfle, D. (1952). *Improving undergraduate instruction in psychology.* New York: Macmillan.

Cacioppo, J. T. (2007, September). Psychology is a hub science. *Observer, 20*(8). Retrieved June 30, 2008, from http://www.psychologicalscience.org/observer/getArticle.cfm?id=2203

Caldwell, J. E. (2007). Clickers in the large classroom: Current research and best-practice tips. *CBE Life Sciences Education, 6,* 9–20.

Career Readiness Certificate Consortium. (2005). *The Career readiness certificate: About the CRC.* Retrieved July 11, 2008, from http://www.crcconsortium.org/about-crc.htm

Cauley, K., Canfield, A., Clasen, C. Hemphill, S., Dobbins, J., Jaballas, E., & Walbroehk, G. (2001). Service learning: Integrating student learning and community service [Special section]. *Education for Health, 14,* 173–181.

Cepeda, N. J., Pashler, H., Vul, E., Wixted, J. T., & Rohrer, D. (2006). Distributed practice in verbal recall tasks: A review and quantitative synthesis. *Psychological Bulletin, 132,* 354–380.

Chew, S. L. (2005). Seldom in doubt but often wrong: Addressing tenacious student misconceptions. In D. S. Dunn & S. L. Chew (Eds.), *Best practices in teaching general psychology* (pp. 211–223). Mahwah, NJ: Erlbaum.

Chickering, A. W., & Gamson, Z. F. (1987, Fall). Seven principles for good practice in undergraduate education. *Washington Center News.* (Reprinted from *AAHE Bulletin,* 1987, Fall, 3–7). Retrieved November 10, 2008, from http://learningcommons.evergreen.edu/pdf/fall1987.pdf

Chickering, A. W., & Reisser, L. (1993). *Education and identity* (2nd ed.). San Francisco: Jossey-Bass.

Chism, N. V. N., & Szabó, B. (1997). How faculty development programs evaluate their services. *The Journal of Staff, Program, & Organization Development, 15,* 55–62.

Choa, R., & Good, G. G. (2004). Nontraditional students' perspective on college education: A qualitative study. *Journal of College Counseling, 7,* 5–12.

Clarke, H., & Bishop, P. (2006). Faculty competency by design: A model for institutional transformation. In S. Chadwick-Blossey & D. Reimondo Robertson (Eds.), *To improve the academy* (Vol. 24). San Francisco: Jossey-Bass.

Cohen, P. A., & McKeachie, W. J. (1980). The role of colleagues in the evaluation of teaching. *Improving College and University Teaching, 28*, 147–154.

College Board. (2007a). *AP examination volume changes (1997–2007)*. Retrieved June 26, 2008, from http://apcentral.collegeboard.com/apc/public/repository/2007_Exam_Volume_Change.pdf

College Board. (2007b). *Psychology course description.* New York: Author.

College Board. (2007c). *Student grade distributions.* Retrieved June 26, 2008, from http://apcentral.collegeboard.com/apc/public/repository/2007_STUDENT_GRADE_DISTRIBUTIONS.pdf

College Board. (2008). *The 4th annual AP report to the nation.* Retrieved October 26, 2008, from http://professionals.collegeboard.com/profdownload/ap-report-to-the-nation-2008.pdf

Collins, A., Brown, J. S., & Holum, A. (1991). Cognitive apprenticeship: Making thinking visible. *American Educator, 15*(3), 6–11, 38–46.

Cranney, J., Provost, S., Katsikitis, M., Martin, F., White, F., & Cohen, L. (2008). *Designing a diverse, future-oriented vision for undergraduate psychology in Australia.* Retrieved March 26, 2009, from http://www.altc.edu.au/carrick/webdav/site/carricksite/users/siteadmin/public/fellowships_report_cranney_dec08.pdf

Cranney, J., & Turnbull, C. (2008). *Graduate attributes of the undergraduate Australian psychology program.* Retrieved August 17, 2008, from http://www.apac.psychology.org.au/Content.aspx?ID=108

Crawford, M. (1986). The accreditation process: Facing new challenges. In J. E. Callan, D. R. Peterson, & G. Stricker (Eds.), *Quality in professional psychology training: A national conference and self-study* (pp. 3–8). Washington, DC: American Psychological Association.

Dahlsgaard, K., Peterson, C., & Seligman, M. E. P. (2005). Shared virtue: The convergence of valued human strengths across culture and history. *Review of General Psychology, 9*, 203–213.

Daniel, D. B., & Broida, J. (2004). Using Web-based quizzing to improve exam performance: Lessons learned. *Teaching of Psychology, 31*, 207–208.

Daniel, D. B., & Poole, D. A. (2009). Learning for life: An ecological approach to pedagogical research. *Perspectives on Psychological Science, 4*, 91–96.

Davis, J. R. (1995). *Interdisciplinary courses and team teaching: New arrangements for learning.* Westport, CT: Greenwood Publishing Group.

Davis, S. F., & Buskist, W. (Eds.). (2002). *The teaching of psychology: Essays in honor of Wilbert J. McKeachie and Charles L. Brewer.* Mahwah, NJ: Erlbaum.

Dean, R. S., & Kulhavy, R. W. (1981). Influence of spatial organization in prose learning. *Journal of Educational Psychology, 73*, 57–64.

Deci, E. L., & Ryan, R. M. (1985). *Intrinsic motivation and self-determination in human behavior.* New York: Plenum Press.

Dees, D. M., Ingram, A., Kovalik, C., Allen-Huffman, M., McClelland, A., & Justice, L. (2007). A transactional model of college teaching. *International Journal of Teaching and Learning in Higher Education, 19*, 130–139.

Dewey, J. (1933). *How we think: A restatement of the relation of reflective thinking to the educative process.* Boston: Heath.

deWinstanley, P. A., & Bjork, R. A. (2002). Successful learning: Presenting information in ways that engage effective processing. In D. F. Halpern & M. D. Hakel (Eds.), *Applying the science of learning to university teaching and beyond, New directions for teaching and learning* (No. 89, pp. 19–31). San Francisco: Jossey-Bass.

Dey, E. L., & Associates. (2008). *Should colleges focus more on personal and social responsibility? Initial findings from campus surveys conducted for the Association of American Colleges and Universities as part of its initiative, Core Commitments: Educating Students for Personal and Social Responsibility.* Retrieved June 1, 2008, from http://www.aacu.org/core_commitments/documents/PSRII_Findings_April2008.pdf

Dickerson, B. J., Bell, K., Lasso, K., & Waits, T. (2002). Do undergraduate college students self-segregate? In R. M. Moore III (Ed.), *The quality and quantity of contact: African Americans and Whites on college campuses* (pp. 254–286). Lanham, MD: University Press of America.

Dickey, M. D. (2005). Three-dimensional virtual worlds and distance learning: Two case studies of active worlds as a medium for distance education. *British Journal of Educational Technology, 36,* 439–451.

Digest of Education Statistics. (2005a). *Chapter 3: Postsecondary education.* Retrieved July 6, 2008, from http://nces.ed.gov/programs/digest/d07/ch_3.asp

Digest of Education Statistics. (2005b). *Total first-time freshmen fall enrollment in degree-granting institutions, by attendance status, sex of student, and type and control of institution: 1955 through 2005* (Table 189). Retrieved June 26, 2008, from http://nces.ed.gov/programs/digest/d07/tables/dt07_189.asp

Dooley, L. M. (2005). Accreditation, or standards for academic programs? *Human Resource Development Quarterly, 16,* 299–300.

Duncan, D., & Mazur, E. (2005). *Clickers in the classroom: How to enhance science teaching using classroom response systems.* San Francisco: Pearson Education.

Dunlap, J. C., & Grabinger, S. (2003). Preparing students for lifelong learning: A review of instructional features and teaching methodologies. *Performance Improvement Quarterly, 16,* 6–25.

Dunn, D. S., McCarthy, M. A., Baker, S., Halonen, J. S., & Hill, G. W. (2007). Quality benchmarks in undergraduate psychology programs. *American Psychologist, 62,* 650–670.

Dunn, D. S., Mehrotra, C., & Halonen, J. S. (Eds.). (2004). *Measuring up: Educational assessment challenges and practices for psychology.* Washington, DC: American Psychological Association.

Dweck, C. S. (2002). Messages that motivate: How praise molds students' beliefs, motivation, and performance (in surprising ways). In J. Aronson (Ed.), *Improving academic achievement: Impact of psychological factors on education* (pp. 37–60). San Diego, CA: Academic Press.

Edgerton, R., O'Meara, K. A., & Rice, R. E. (2005). *Faculty priorities reconsidered: Rewarding multiple forms of scholarship*. San Francisco: Jossey-Bass.

Ernst, R., & Petrossian, P. (1996). Teachers of psychology in secondary schools (TOPSS): Aiming for excellence in high school psychology instruction. *American Psychologist, 51*, 256–258.

ETS. (2008). Addressing achievement gaps: The language acquisition and educational achievement of English-language learners. *Policy Notes, 16*(2), 1–16. Retrieved August 12, 2008, from http://www.ets.org/Media/Research/pdf/PIC-PNV16N2.pdf

European Commission. (2007). *The Bologna process: Towards the European higher education area*. Retrieved February 23, 2009, from http://ec.europa.eu/education/policies/educ/bologna/bologna_en.html

EuroPsy: The European Certificate in Psychology. (2006). Retrieved August 17, 2008, from http://www.efpa.be/doc/EuroPsyJune%202006.pdf

Fassinger, R. E. (2008, February). *Sexual orientation and gender identity*. Paper presented at the meeting of the American Psychological Association Council of Representatives, Washington, DC.

Forsyth, D. R. (2003). *The professor's guide to teaching: Psychological principles and practices*. Washington, DC: American Psychological Association.

Freeman, C. E. (2004). *Trends in educational equity of girls & women: 2004* (NCES Publication No. 2005-016). Retrieved June 24, 2008, from the National Center for Education Statistics Web site: http://nces.ed.gov/pubs2005/2005016.pdf

Friedman, T. L. (2005). *The world is flat*. New York: Farrar, Straus, & Giroux.

Gaff, J. G., Pruitt-Logan, A. S., & Weibl, R. A. (2000). *Building the faculty we need: Colleges and universities working together* (Report No. ED438764). Retrieved July 2, 2008, from http://www.eric.ed.gov/ERICWebPortal/custom/portlets/recordDetails/detailmini.jsp?_nfpb=true&_&ERICExtSearch_SearchValue_0=ED438764&ERICExtSearch_SearchType_0=no&accno=ED438764

Gardner, P. (2007). *Moving up or moving out of the company? Factors that influence the promoting or firing of new college hires*. Retrieved February 23, 2009, from the Michigan State University, Collegiate Employment Research Institute Web site: http://ceri.msu.edu/publications/pdf/brief1-07.pdf

Garrison, D. R., Anderson, T., & Archer, W. (2000). Critical inquiry in a text-based environment: Computer conferencing in higher education. *The Internet and Higher Education, 2*, 87–105.

Gibbs, G., & Coffey, M. (2004). The impact of training university teachers on their teaching skills, their approach to teaching and the approach to learning of their students. *Active Learning in Higher Education, 5*, 87–100.

Gibson, S. G., Harris, M. L., & Colaric, S. M. (2008). Technology acceptance in an academic context: Faculty acceptance of online education. *Journal of Education for Business, 83*, 355–359.

Glassick, C. E., Huber, M. T., & Maeroff, G. I. (1997). *Scholarship assessed: Evaluation of the professoriate*. San Francisco: Jossey-Bass.

Glenberg, A. M. (1979). Component-levels theory of the effects of spacing of repetitions on recall and recognition. *Memory & Cognition, 7,* 95–112.

Gloria, A. M., Rieckman, T. R., & Rush, J. D. (2000). Issues and recommendations for teaching an ethnic/culture-based course. *Teaching of Psychology, 27,* 102–107.

Graesser, A. C., Chipman, P., & King, B. G. (2007). Computer-mediated technologies. In J. M. Spector, M. D. Merrill, J. van Merrienboer, & M. P. Driscoll (Eds.), *Handbook of research on educational communications and technology* (pp. 629–678). New York: Routledge.

Graesser, A. C., Jeon, M., & Duffy, D. (2008). Agent technologies designed to facilitate interactive knowledge construction. *Discourse Processes, 45,* 298–322.

Greenwald, A. G., & Gillmore, G. M. (1997). Grading leniency is a removable contaminant of student ratings. *American Psychologist, 52,* 1209–1217.

Griggs, R. A., Jackson, S. L., & Napolitano, T. J. (1994). Brief introductory textbooks: An objective analysis. *Teaching of Psychology, 21,* 136–140.

Grossman, P. D. (2001). *Making accommodations: The legal world of students with disabilities.* Retrieved June 20, 2008, from http://www.aaup.org/AAUP/pubsres/academe/2001/ND/Feat/gross.htm

Gurung, R. A. R. (2003). Pedagogical aids and student performance. *Teaching of Psychology, 30,* 92–95.

Gurung, R. A. R. (2004). Pedagogical aids: Learning enhancers or dangerous detours? *Teaching of Psychology, 31,* 164–166.

Gurung, R. A. R., & Daniel, D. B. (2005). Evidence-based pedagogy: Do text-based pedagogical features enhance student learning? In D. S. Dunn & S. L. Chew (Eds.), *Best practices for teaching Introduction to Psychology* (pp. 41–55). Mahwah, NJ: Erlbaum.

Hall, A. (1982). The educational and work experiences of psychology graduates of the College of Wooster: 1966–1980. *American Psychologist, 37,* 450–451.

Hall, J. E., & Lunt, I. (2005). Global mobility for psychologists: The role of psychology organizations in the United States, Canada, Europe, and other regions. *American Psychologist, 60,* 712–726.

Halonen, J. S., Bosack, T., Clay, S., McCarthy, M., Dunn, D. S., Hill, G. W., IV, et al. (2003). A rubric for learning, teaching, and assessing scientific inquiry in psychology. *Teaching of Psychology, 30,* 196–208.

Halonen, J. S., Harris, C. M., Pastor, D. A., Abrahamson, C. E., & Huffman, C. J. (2005). Assessing general education outcomes in introductory psychology. In D. S. Dunn & S. L. Chew (Eds.), *Best practices for teaching introduction to psychology* (pp. 195–208). Mahwah, NJ: Erlbaum.

Halpern, D. F. (1998). Teaching critical thinking for transfer across domains: Dispositions, skills, structure training, and metacognitive monitoring. *American Psychologist, 53,* 449–455.

Halpern, D. F. (2000). *Sex differences in cognitive abilities* (3rd ed.). Mahwah, NJ: Erlbaum.

Halpern, D. F., & Hakel, M. D. (2003). Applying the science of learning to the university and beyond: Teaching for long-term retention and transfer. *Change, 35*(4), 36–41.

Hart Research Associates. (2004). *Summary of existing research on attitudes toward liberal education outcome for the Association of American Colleges and Universities.* Retrieved April 28, 2008, from http://www.aacu.org

Hart Research Associates. (2008). *How should colleges assess and improve student learning? Employers' views on the accountability challenge: A survey of employers conducted on behalf of the Association of American Colleges and Universities.* Retrieved April 28, 2008, from http://www.aacu.org

Hativa, N. (2000). *Teaching for effective learning in higher education.* Boston: Kluwer Academic.

Hayes, N. (1996). What makes a psychology graduate distinctive? *European Psychologist, 1*, 130–134.

Heffernan, K. (2001). *Fundamentals of service-learning course construction.* Providence, RI: Campus Compact.

Heppner, M. J. (1994). An empirical investigation of the effects of a teaching practicum on prospective faculty. *Journal of Counseling and Development, 72*, 500–507.

Herreid, C. F. (Ed.). (2007). *Start with a story.* Arlington, VA: National Science Teachers Association Press.

Hestenes, D., Wells, M., & Swackhamer, G. (1992). Force concept inventory. *The Physics Teacher, 30*, 141–158.

Higher Education Research Institute. (2008). *The spiritual life of college students: A national study of college students' search for purpose and meaning.* Retrieved June 26, 2008, from http://spirituality.ucla.edu/spirituality/reports/FINAL_REPORT.pdf

Hilbert, T. S., & Renkl, A. (2008). Concept mapping as a follow-up strategy to learning from texts: What characterizes good and poor mappers? *Instructional Science, 36*, 53–73.

Hinman, L. M. (2002) Academic integrity and the World Wide Web. *Computers and Society, 32*, 33–42.

Hmelo-Silver, C. E. (2004). Problem-based learning: What and how do students learn? *Educational Psychology Review, 16*, 235–266.

Hollmann, F. W., Mulder, T. J., & Kallan, J. E. (2000). *Methodology and assumptions for the population projections of the United States: 1999 to 2100* [Population Division Working Paper No. 38]. Washington, DC: U. S. Census Bureau. Retrieved February 24, 2009, from http://www.census.gov/population/www/documentation/twps0038.pdf

Howard, A., Pion, G. M., Gottfredson, G. D., Flattau, P. E., Oskamp, S., Pfallin, S. M., et al. (1986). The changing face of American psychology: A report from the Committee on Employment and Human Resources. *American Psychologist, 41*, 1311–1327.

Huber, M. T., & Hutchings, P. (2004). *Integrative learning: Mapping the terrain*. Washington, DC: Association of American Colleges and Universities and the Carnegie Foundation for the Advancement of Teaching.

Humphreys, D. (2000). National survey finds diversity requirements common around the country. *Diversity Digest, 5*, 1–2.

Humphreys, D., & Davenport, A. (2005). What really matters in college. *Liberal Education, 9*(3), 36–43.

Hunt, J. B., Jr. (2008). *Measuring up 2008: The national report card of higher education: Foreword*. Retrieved December 26, 2008, from http://measuringup2008.highereducation.org/commentary/hunt.php

Hurtado, S. (1992). The campus racial climate: Contexts of conflict. *The Journal of Higher Education, 63*, 539–569.

Hurtado, S. (2007). Linking diversity with the educational and civic missions of higher education. *The Review of Higher Education, 30*, 185–196.

Hurtado, S., Griffin, K. A., Arellano, L., & Cuellar, M. (2008, May). *Assessing the value of climate assessments: Progress and future directions*. Paper presented at the annual forum of the Association for Institutional Research, Seattle, WA.

Hutchings, P. (Ed.). (1998). *The course portfolio: How faculty can examine their teaching to advance practice and improve student learning*. Washington, DC: American Association for Higher Education.

Institute of International Education. (2007a). *International student enrollment and U.S. higher education, selected years 1950/60 –2006/07*. Retrieved June 26, 2008, from http://opendoors.iienetwork.org/?p=113122

Institute of International Education. (2007b). *International students by field of study*. Retrieved June 26, 2008, from http://opendoors.iienetwork.org/?p=113124

Institute of International Education. (2007c). *Summary of Open Doors report*. Retrieved June 26, 2008, from http://opendoors.iienetwork.org/?p=113249

Institute of International Education. (2007d). *Top 20 leading destinations of U.S. study abroad students*. Retrieved June 26, 2008, from http://opendoors.iienetwork.org/?p=113274

Jackson, L. C. (1999). Ethnocultural resistance to multicultural training: Students and faculty. *Cultural Diversity and Ethnic Minority Psychology, 5*, 27–36.

Jaeger, P. T., & Bowman, C. A. (2005). *Understanding disability: Inclusion, access, diversity, and civil rights*. Westport, CT: Praeger.

James, W. (1962). *Talks to teachers on psychology, and to students on some of life's ideals*. New York: Dover. (Original work published 1899)

Johnson, R. L., & Rudmann, J. L. (2004). Psychology at community colleges: A survey. *Teaching of Psychology, 31*, 183–185.

Jones, S. R., & McEwen, M. K. (2000). A conceptual model of multiple dimensions of identity. *Journal of College Student Development, 41*, 401–414.

Jung, I., Choi, S., Lim, C., & Leem, J. (2002). Effects of different types of interaction on learning achievement, satisfaction and participation in Web-based instruction. *Innovations in Education & Teaching International, 39*, 153–162.

Kan, Z. (2008, June). *Chinese psychologists share their personal experiences of developing psychological research on Chinese societies*. Paper presented at the Chinese Psychologist Conference, Beijing, China.

Karpicke, J. D., & Roediger, H. L., III. (2007). Expanding retrieval practice promotes short-term retention, but equally spaced retrieval enhances long-term retention. *Journal of Experimental Psychology: Learning, Memory, and Cognition, 33*, 704–719.

Karpicke, J. D., & Roediger, H. L., III. (2008). The critical importance of retrieval for learning. *Science, 319*, 966–968.

Keeley, J., Smith, D., & Buskist, W. (2006). The Teacher Behaviors Checklist: Factor analysis of its utility for evaluating teaching. *Teaching of Psychology, 33*, 84–91.

Keller, P. A., Craig, F. W., Launius, M. H., Loher, B. T., & Cooledge, N. J. (2004). Using student portfolios to assess program learning outcomes. In D. S. Dunn, C. M. Mehrotra, & J. S. Halonen (Eds.), *Measuring up: Education assessment challenges and practices for psychology* (pp. 187–207). Washington, DC: American Psychological Association.

Kelly, P. J. (2008). *Beyond social justice: The threat of inequality to workforce development in the western United States*. Boulder, CO: Western Interstate Commission for Higher Education.

Kerr, N. (1983). The dispensability of member effort and group motivation losses: Free-rider effects. *Journal of Personality and Social Psychology, 44*, 78–94.

Kite, M. E., Russo, N. F., Brehm, S. S., Fouad, N. A., Hall, C. I., Hyde, J. S., et al. (2001). Women psychologists in academe: Mixed progress, unwarranted complacency. *American Psychologist, 56*, 1080–1098.

Kleiner, B., & Lewis, L. (2005). *Dual enrollment of high school students at postsecondary institutions: 2002–2003* (NCES Publication No. 2005-008). Washington, DC: U.S. Department of Education.

Klinger, T. (1999). Applying sociocultural psychology to the service-learning experience: Service-learning as a pedagogical tool for developing critical thinking in college students. *Korean Journal of Thinking and Problem Solving, 9*, 25–37.

Koedinger, K. R., Anderson, J., Hadley, W., & Mark, M. A. (1997). Intelligent tutoring goes to school in the big city. *International Journal of Artificial Intelligence in Education, 8*, 30–43.

Komarraju, M. (2008). A social-cognitive approach to training teaching assistants. *Teaching of Psychology, 35*, 327–334.

Kuh, G. D., Kinzie, J., Buckley, J. A., Bridges, B. K., & Hayek, C. K. (2006). *What matters to student success: A review of the literature*. Commissioned report for the National Symposium on Postsecondary Student Success. National Postsecondary Education Cooperative. Retrieved June 12, 2007, from http://nces.ed.gov/IPEDS/research/pdf/Kuh_Team_Report.pdf

Kuh, G. D., Kinzie, J., Buckley, J. A., Bridges, B. K., & Hayek, C. K. (2007). *Piecing together the student success puzzle: Research, propositions, and recommendations:*

ASHE Higher Education Report, Volume 32, Number 5. San Francisco: Jossey-Bass.

Kulik, J. A., Brown, D. R., Vestewig, R. E., & Wright, J. (1973). *Undergraduate education in psychology.* Washington, DC: American Psychological Association.

Kuther, T. L., & Morgan, R. D. (2004). *Careers in psychology: Opportunities in a changing world.* Belmont, CA: Wadsworth.

Kyle, T. M., & Williams, S. (2000). *1998–1999 APA survey of undergraduate departments of psychology.* Retrieved August 21, 2008, from the American Psychological Association Web site: http://research.apa.org/9899undergradreport.pdf

LaFromboise, T., Coleman, H., & Gerton, J. (1993). Psychological aspects of bicultural competence: Evidence and theory. *Psychological Bulletin, 114,* 395–412.

Laird, T. F. N. (2005). College students' experiences with diversity and their effects on academic self-confidence, social agency, and disposition toward critical thinking. *Research in Higher Education, 46,* 365–387.

Landrum, R. E., & Harrold, R. (2003). What employers want from psychology graduates. *Teaching of Psychology, 30,* 131–133.

Landrum, R. E., Klein, A. L., Horan, M., & Wynn, D. (2008). *Applying to graduate school: Plans of senior-level psychology majors.* Unpublished manuscript.

Larkin, J. E., Pines, H. A., & Bechtel, K. M. (2002). Facilitating students' career development in psychology courses: A portfolio project. *Teaching of Psychology, 29,* 207–210.

Leeming, F. C. (2002). The exam-a-day procedure improves performance in psychology classes. *Teaching of Psychology, 29,* 210–212.

Lehman, D. R., Lempert, R. O., & Nisbett, R. E. (1988). The effects of graduate training on reasoning: Formal discipline and thinking about everyday-life events. *American Psychologist, 43,* 431–442.

Lerner, R. M. (2002). Adolescence: Development, diversity, context, and application. Upper Saddle River, NJ: Pearson Education, Inc.

Leslie, D. W., & Gappa, J. M. (2002). Part-time faculty: Competent and committed. In C. L. Outcalt (Ed.), *Community college faculty: Characteristics, practices, and challenges* (pp. 59–67). San Francisco: Jossey-Bass.

Lewis, K. G. (2003). *Training focused on postgraduate teaching assistants: The North American model.* Retrieved May 25, 2003, from the National Forum of Teaching and Learning Web site: http://www.ntlf.com/html/lib/bib/backup/lewis.htm

LGBT centers today: A snapshot. (2006, March 15). *Student Affairs Leader, 34,* 2.

Lifelong Learning at Work and at Home. (n.d.). *25 learning principles to guide pedagogy and the design of learning environments: Applying the science of learning: What we know about learning and how we can improve the teaching-learning interaction.* Retrieved June 26, 2008, from http://psyc.memphis.edu/learning

Lifsher, M. (2008, December 8). State may see shortage of educated workers, group says. *Los Angeles Times.* Retrieved December 9, 2008, from http://www.latimes.com/business/la-fi-workforce8-2008dec08,0,4427711.story

Lipp, O. V., Terry, D. J., Chalmers, D., Bath, D., Hannan, G., Martin, F., et al. (2006). *Learning outcomes and curriculum development in psychology.* Retrieved March 26, 2009, http://www.altc.edu.au/carrick/webdav/site/carricksite/users/siteadmin/public/grants_2005project_learningoutcomes_psychology_finalreport.pdf

Lloyd, M. A., & Brewer, C. L. (1992). National conferences on undergraduate psychology. In A. E. Puente, J. R. Matthews, & C. L. Brewer (Eds.), *Teaching psychology in America: A history* (pp. 263–284). Washington, DC: American Psychological Association.

Lorch, R. F., Jr., & Lorch, E. P. (1996). Effects of organizational signals on free recall of expository text. *Journal of Educational Psychology, 88,* 38–48.

Lou, Y., Bernard, R., & Abrami, P. C. (2006). Media and pedagogy in undergraduate distance education: A theory-based meta-analysis of empirical literature. *Educational Technology Research and Development, 54,* 1042–1629.

Lucas, S. G., & Bernstein, D. (2005). *Teaching psychology: A step-by-step guide.* Mahwah, NJ: Erlbaum.

Ludwig, T. E., Daniel, D. B., Froman, R., & Mathie, V. A. (2004, December). *Using multimedia in classroom presentations: Best principles.* Paper presented at the meeting of the Society for the Teaching of Psychology Pedagogical Innovations Task Force.

Lunt, I. (2002). A common framework for the training of psychologists in Europe. *European Psychologist, 7,* 180–191.

Lunt, I. (2005). The implications of the "Bologna Process" for the development of a European qualification. *European Psychologist, 10,* 86–92.

Lutsky, N., Torney-Purta, J., Velayo, R., Whittlesey, V., Woolf, L., & McCarthy, M. (2005). *American Psychological Association working group on internationalizing the undergraduate psychology curriculum: Report and recommended learning outcomes for internationalizing the undergraduate curriculum.* Retrieved May 26, 2008, from http://www.apa.org/ed/resources.html

Macias, S., & Macias, D. R. (2009). Is Psychology 101 more scientific than other science courses . . . yes! *PTN: Psychology Teacher Network, 18*(4), 14–15.

Magolda, M. B. (2001). *Making their own way: Narratives for transforming higher education to promote self development.* Sterling, VA: Stylus.

Maguire, L. L. (2005). Literature review—Faculty participation in online distance education: Barriers and motivators. *Online Journal of Distance Learning Administration, 8*(1). Retrieved August 17, 2008, from http://www.westga.edu/~distance/ojdla/spring81/maguire81.htm

Mahan, J. M. (1982). Community involvement components in culturally-oriented teacher preparation. *Education, 103*(2), 163–172.

Maki, P. L. (2001). From standardized tests to alternative methods: Some current resources on methods to assess learning in general education. *Change, 33*(2), 29–31.

Maki, P. L. (2004). *Assessing for learning: Building a sustainable commitment across the institution.* Sterling, VA: Stylus.

Maki, R. H. (1998). Test predictions over text material. In D. J. Hacker, J. Dunlosky, & A. C. Graesser (Eds.), *Metacognition in educational theory and practice* (pp. 117–144). Mahwah, NJ: Erlbaum.

Maki, R. H., & Maki, W. S. (2007). Online courses. In F. T. Durso, R. S. Nickerson, S. T. Dumais, S. Lewandowsky, & T. J. Perfect (Eds.), *Handbook of applied cognition* (2nd ed., pp. 527–552). Hoboken, NJ: Wiley.

Mathie, V. A., Beins, B., Benjamin, L. T., Jr., Ewing, M. W., Hall, C. C. I., Henderson, B., et al. (1993). Promoting active learning in psychology courses. In T. V. McGovern (Ed.), *Handbook for enhancing undergraduate education in psychology* (pp. 183–214). Washington, DC: American Psychological Association.

Matlin, M. W. (2002). Cognitive psychology and college-level pedagogy: Two siblings that rarely communicate. In D. F. Halpern & M. D. Hakel (Eds.), *Applying the science of learning to university teaching and beyond: New directions for teaching and learning* (No. 89, pp. 87–103). San Francisco: Jossey-Bass.

Matsumoto, D., & Juang, L. (2008). *Culture and psychology* (4th ed.). Belmont, CA: Thompson-Wadsworth.

Mautone, P. D., & Mayer, R. E. (2001). Signaling as a cognitive guide in multimedia learning. *Journal of Educational Psychology, 93*, 377–389.

Mayer, R. E. (2005). Cognitive theory of multimedia learning. In R. E. Mayer (Ed.), *The Cambridge handbook of multimedia learning* (pp. 31–48). New York: Cambridge University Press.

Mayhew, M. J., & Fernandez, S. D. (2007). Pedagogical practices that contribute to social justice outcomes. *The Review of Higher Education, 31*, 55–80.

McAlpine, L., & Weston, C. (2002). Reflection: Issues related to improving professors' teaching and students' learning. In P. Goodyear & N. Hativa (Eds.), *Teacher thinking, beliefs and knowledge in higher education* (pp. 59–78). Dordrecht, The Netherlands: Kluwer Academic.

McDaniel, M. A., Anderson, J. L., Derbish, M. H., & Morrisette, N. (2007). Testing the testing effect in the classroom. *European Journal of Cognitive Psychology, 19*, 494–513.

McDaniel, M. A., & Einstein, G. O. (2005). Material appropriate difficulty: A framework for determining when difficulty is desirable for improving learning. In A. F. Healy (Ed.), *Experimental cognitive psychology and its applications* (pp. 73–85). Washington, DC: American Psychological Association.

McDaniel, M. A., Howard, D. C., & Einstein, G. O. (in press). The read-recite-review study strategy: Effective and portable. *Psychological Science*.

McDaniel, M. A., McDermott, K. B., Agarwal, P. K., & Roediger, H. L., III. (2008, June). *Test-enhanced learning in the classroom: The Columbia Middle School project, Year 2*. Poster session presented at the meeting of the Institute of Education Sciences, Washington, DC.

McDevitt, T. M., & Ormrod, J. E. (2008). Fostering conceptual change about child development in prospective teachers and other college students. *Child Development Perspectives, 2*(2), 85–91.

McGovern, T. V. (1992). Evolution of undergraduate curricula in psychology, 1892–1992. In A. E. Peunte, J. R. Matthews, & C. L. Brewer (Eds.), *Teaching psychology in America: A history* (pp. 13–38). Washington, DC: American Psychological Association.

McGovern, T. V. (Ed.). (1993). *Handbook for enhancing undergraduate education in psychology*. Washington, DC: American Psychological Association.

McGovern, T. V. (2004). Liberal arts, diverse lives, and assessing psychology. In D. S. Dunn, C. M. Mehrotra, & J. S. Halonen (Eds.), *Measuring up: Assessment challenges and practices for psychology* (pp. 259–275). Washington, DC: American Psychological Association.

McGovern, T. V., & Brewer, C. L. (2003). Undergraduate education. In D. K. Freedheim (Ed.), *Handbook of psychology: History of psychology* (Vol. 1, pp. 465–481). New York: Wiley.

McGovern, T. V., & Brewer, C. L. (2005). Paradigms, narratives, and pluralism in undergraduate psychology. In R. J. Sternberg (Ed.), *Unity in psychology: Possibility or pipedream?* (pp. 125–143). Washington, DC: American Psychological Association.

McGovern, T. V., Furumoto, L., Halpern, D. F., Kimble, G. A., & McKeachie, W. J. (1991). Liberal education, study in depth, and the arts and sciences major—Psychology. *American Psychologist, 46,* 598–605.

McKeachie, W. J., & Milholland, J. E. (1961). *Undergraduate curricula in psychology.* Chicago: Scott, Foresman.

McKeachie, W. J., & Svinicki, M. (2006). *McKeachie's teaching tips: Strategies, research, and theory for college and university teachers* (12th ed.). Boston: Houghton Mifflin.

McKeegan, P. (1998). Using undergraduate teaching assistants in a research methodology course. *Teaching of Psychology, 25,* 11–14.

McSwain, C., & Davis, R. (2007). *College access for the working poor: Overcoming burdens to succeed in higher education.* Retrieved June 26, 2008, from the Institute of Higher Education Policy Web site: http://www.cpec.ca.gov/CompleteReports/ExternalDocuments/College_Access_for_the_Working_ Poor_2007_Report.pdf

Messer, W., Griggs, R., & Jackson, S. (1999). A national survey of undergraduate psychology degree options and major requirements. *Teaching of Psychology, 26,* 164–170.

Metcalfe, J., Kornell, N., & Son, L. K. (2007). A cognitive-science based programme to enhance study efficacy in a high and low risk setting. *European Journal of Cognitive Psychology, 19,* 743–768.

Meyers, S. A., & Prieto, L. R. (2000). Training in the teaching of psychology: What is done and examining the differences. *Teaching of Psychology, 27,* 258–261.

Milem, J. F. (2003). The educational benefits of diversity: Evidence from multiple sectors. In M. Chang, D. Witt, J. Jones, & K. Hakuta (Eds.), *Compelling interest: Examining the evidence on racial dynamics in higher education* (pp. 126–169). Palo Alto, CA: Stanford University Press.

Milem, J. F., Chang, M. J., & Antonio, A. L. (2005). *Making diversity work on campus: A research-based perspective.* Retrieved June 12, 2008, from the Association of American Colleges and Universities Web site: http://www.aacu.org/inclusive_excellence/documents/Milem_et_al.pdf

Millis, B., & Cottell, P. (1998). *Cooperative learning for higher education faculty.* Phoenix, AZ: Oryx Press.

Montalvo, F. T., & Torres, M. C. G. (2004). Self-regulated learning: Current and future directions. *Electronic Journal of Research in Educational Psychology, 2,* 1–34.

Moore, J. W., Hauck, W. E., & Furman, J. (1975). Verbal learning and self- and super-imposed organization. *The Journal of Experimental Education, 44,* 4–7.

Morgan, B. L., & Johnson, E. J. (1997). Using a senior seminar for assessing the major. *Teaching of Psychology, 24,* 156–159.

Mowrer, R. R., Love, S. S., & Orem, D. B. (2004). Desirable teaching qualities transcend the nature of the student. *Teaching of Psychology, 31,* 106–108.

Mueller, A., Perlman, B., McCann, L. I., & McFadden, S. H. (1997). A faculty perspective on teaching assistant training. *Teaching of Psychology, 24,* 167–171.

National Association for the Education of Young Children. (1993). *A conceptual framework for early childhood professional development.* Retrieved August 24, 2008, from http://www.naeyc.org/about/positions/pdf/psconf98.pdf

National Center for Education Statistics. (2003). *The condition of education* (NCES Publication No. 2003-067). Retrieved June 26, 2008, from http://nces.ed.gov/programs/coe/2003/pdf/34_2003.pdf

National Center for Education Statistics. (2004). *The top 30 postsecondary courses completed by bachelor's degree recipients who graduated from high school in 1972, 1982, and 1992* (Table 30-1). Retrieved July 8, 2008, from http://nces.ed.gov/programs/coe/2004/section5/table.asp?tableID=109

National Center for Education Statistics. (2005). *Number and percentage of children ages 5–17 who spoke a language other than English at home and who spoke English with difficulty: Selected years, 1979–2005* (Table 6-1). Retrieved July 7, 2008, from http://nces.ed.gov/programs/coe/2007/section1/table.asp?tableID=668

National Center for Education Statistics. (2006). *Projections of education statistics to 2015.* Retrieved July 8, 2008, from http://nces.ed.gov/programs/projections/projections2015/sec2c.asp

National Center for Education Statistics. (2007a). *Bachelor's degrees conferred by degree-granting institutions, by discipline division: Selected years, 1970–71 through 2005–06* (Table 261). Retrieved June 26, 2008, from http://nces.ed.gov/programs/digest/d07/tables/dt07_261.asp

National Center for Education Statistics. (2007b). *Degrees in psychology conferred by degree-granting institutions, by level of degree and sex of student: Selected years, 1949–50 through 2005–06* (Table 303). Retrieved June 26, 2008, from http://nces.ed.gov/programs/digest/d07/tables/dt07_303.asp

National Center for Education Statistics. (2008). *Integrated postsecondary education data system (IPEDS) fall enrollment survey: Digest of Education Statistics: 2007*. Retrieved May 26, 2008, from http://nces.ed.gov/ Programs/digest/d07/ch_3.asp

National Institutes of Health. (2006). *Better living through behavioral and social sciences* [Fact sheet]. Washington, DC: Author.

Nesbit, J. C., & Adesope, O. O. (2006). Learning with concept and knowledge maps: A meta-analysis. *Review of Educational Research, 76*, 413–448.

Neulight, N., Kafai, Y. B., Kao, L., Foley, B., & Galas, C. (2007). Children's participation in a virtual epidemic in the science classroom: Making connections to natural infectious diseases. *Journal of Science Education and Technology, 16*, 47–58.

New Media Consortium and the Educause Learning Initiative. (2008). *The horizon report*. Retrieved February 18, 2008, from http://www.nmc.org/pdf/2008-Horizon-Report.pdf

Niemivirta, M. (1998). Individual differences in motivational and cognitive factors affecting self-regulating learning: A pattern-oriented approach. In P. Nenniger, R. S. Jager, & M. Wosnitza (Eds.), *Advances in motivation* (pp. 32–42). Landau, Germany: Verlag Empirische Padagogik.

Novak, J. D. (1990). Concept maps and Vee diagrams: Two metacognitive tools to facilitate meaningful learning. *Instructional Science, 19*, 29–52.

O'Neil, J. (1992). Putting performance assessment to the test. *Educational Leadership, 49*(8), 14–19.

Osborne, R. E., & Renick, O. (2006). Service learning. In W. Buskist & S. F. Davis (Eds.), *Handbook of the teaching of psychology* (pp. 137–141). Malden, MA: Blackwell Publishers.

Osborne, R. E., & Wagor, W. F. (2004). Course assessment: Developing and assessing assessable objectives by using an integrative assessment model. In D. S. Dunn, C. M. Mehrotra, & J. S. Halonen (Eds.), *Measuring up: Educational assessment challenges and practices for psychology* (pp. 125–140). Washington, DC: American Psychological Association.

Ozorak, E. W. (2004). Integrating service-learning into psychology courses. In B. Perlman, L. I. McCann, & S. H. McFadden (Eds.), *Lessons learned: Practical advice for the teaching of psychology* (Vol. 2, pp. 137–146). Washington, DC: American Psychological Society.

Packard, E. (2007, March). Regional associations initiate increased collaboration. *Monitor on Psychology, 38*, 10.

Paivio, A. (1986). *Mental representations*. New York: Oxford University Press.

Palincsar, A. S., & Brown, A. L. (1984). Reciprocal teaching of comprehension-fostering and comprehension-monitoring activities. *Cognitive and Instruction, 1*, 117–175.

Palladino Schultheiss, D. E. (2008). *Psychology as a major: Is it right for me and what can I do with my degree?* Washington, DC: American Psychological Association.

Parette, H. P., Wojcik, B. W., Peterson-Karlan, G., & Hourcade, J. J. (2005). Assistive technology for students with mild disabilities: What's cool and what's not. *Education and Training in Developmental Disabilities, 40*, 320–331.

Partnership for 21st Century Skills. (2006). *Are they really ready to work? Employers' perspective on the basic knowledge and applied skills of new entrants to the 21st century U.S. workforce.* Retrieved December 9, 2008, from http://www.21stcenturyskills.org/documents/FINAL_REPORT_PDF09-29-06.pdf

Pascarella, E., & Terenzini, P. (2005). *How college affects students: Vol. 2. A third decade of research.* San Francisco: Jossey-Bass.

Pashler, H., Bain, P., Bottge, B., Graesser, A., Koedinger, K., McDaniel, M., et al. (2007). *Organizing instruction and study to improve student learning.* Retrieved on June 26, 2008, from the National Center for Education Research Web site: http://ncer.ed.gov

Peirce, C. S. (1972). The fixation of belief. In E. C. Moore (Ed.), *Charles S. Peirce: The essential writings* (pp. 120–136). New York: Harper & Row.

Peiro, J. M., & Lunt, I. (2002). The context for a European framework for psychologists' training. *European Psychologist, 7,* 169–179.

Perlman, B., & McCann, L. I. (1999a). The most frequently listed courses in the undergraduate curriculum. *Teaching of Psychology, 26,* 177–182.

Perlman, B., & McCann, L. I. (1999b). The structure of the psychology undergraduate curriculum. *Teaching of Psychology, 26,* 171–176.

Perry, W. G. (1999). *Forms of ethical and intellectual development in the college years: A scheme.* San Francisco: Jossey-Bass. (Original work published 1970)

Peter, K., & Forrest Cataldi, E. (2005). *The road less traveled? Students who enroll in multiple institutions* (NCES Publication No. 2005-157). Retrieved October 21, 2005, from http://nces.ed.gov/pubs2005/2005157.pdf

Peter, K., & Horn, L. (2005). *Gender differences in participation and completion of undergraduate education and how they have changed over time* (NCES Publication No. 2005-169). Retrieved June 26, 2008, from http://nces.ed.gov/pubs2005/2005169.pdf

Peterson, C., & Seligman, M. E. P. (2004). *Character strengths and virtues: A handbook and classification.* Washington, DC: American Psychological Association.

Peterson, L. (1995). *Starting out, starting over: Finding the work that's waiting for you.* Palo Alto, CA: Davies-Black.

Peterson, M. (2006). Learner interaction management in an avatar and chat-based virtual world. *Computer Assisted Language Learning, 19,* 79–103.

Phillippe, K. (Ed.). (2000). *National profile of community colleges: Trends and statistics* (3rd ed.). Washington, DC: American Association of Community Colleges.

Pintrich, R. R., & DeGroot, E. V. (1990). Motivational and self-regulated learning components of classroom academic performance. *Journal of Educational Psychology, 82,* 33–40.

Piotrowski, C., & Vodanovich, S. J. (2004). Is Web-based instruction popular in psychology? A national survey. *Computers in Human Behavior, 20,* 727–732.

Pope, K., & Vetter, V. (1992). Ethical dilemmas encountered by members of the American Psychological Association. *American Psychologist, 47,* 397–411.

Pope-Davis, D. B., Brueax, C., & Lie, W. (1997). A multicultural immersion experience: Filling a void in multicultural training. In D. B. Pope-Davis & H. K. L. Coleman (Eds.), *Multicultural counseling competencies: Assessment, education and training, and supervision* (pp. 227–241). Thousand Oaks, CA: Sage.

Prensky, M. (2000). *Digital game-based learning.* New York: McGraw-Hill.

Psychology is the fourth most popular undergraduate major (2008, June). *Monitor on Psychology, 39,* 11.

Puente, A. E., Blanch, E., Candland, D. K., Denmar, F. L., Laman, C., Lutsky, N., et al. (1993). Toward a psychology of variance: Increasing the presence and understanding of ethnic minorities in psychology. In T. V. McGovern (Ed.), *Handbook for enhancing undergraduate education in psychology* (pp. 71–92). Washington, DC: American Psychological Association.

Puente, A. E., Matthews, J. R., & Brewer, C. L. (Eds.). (1992). *Teaching psychology in America: A history.* Washington, DC: American Psychological Association.

Quality Assurance Agency for Higher Education. (2007). *Psychology.* Retrieved March 29, 2009, from http://qaa.ac.uk/academicinfrastructure/ benchmark/statements/ Psychology07.pdf

Rajecki, D. W., Johnson, K. E., Poynter-Jeschke, M., Appleby, D. C., Williams, C. C., Daniels, et al. (2005). A brief career intervention: Psychology students' changed views of life beyond a baccalaureate. *Journal of the Scholarship of Teaching and Learning, 5,* 19–34.

Rankin, S. R., & Reason, R. D. (2005). Differing perceptions: How students of color and White students perceive campus climate for underrepresented groups. *Journal of College Student Development, 46,* 43–61.

Reynolds, J. H., & Glaser, R. (1964). Effects of repetition and spaced review upon retention of a complex learning task. *Journal of Educational Psychology, 55,* 297–308.

Richland, L. E., Linn, M. C., & Bjork, R. A. (2007). Instruction. In F. T. Durso (Ed.), *Handbook of applied cognition* (2nd ed., pp. 555–583). New York: Wiley.

Richlin, L. (2001). Scholarly teaching and the scholarship of teaching. *New Directions in Teaching and Learning, 86,* 57–68.

Richlin, L. (2006). *Blueprint for learning: Constructing college courses to facilitate, assess, and document learning.* Sterling, VA: Stylus.

Roediger, H. L., & Karpicke, J. D. (2006). Test-enhanced learning: Taking memory tests improves long-term retention. *Psychological Science, 17,* 249–255.

Roediger, H. L., & Karpicke, J. D. (2006). The power of testing memory: Basic research and implications for educational practice. *Perspectives on Psychological Science, 1,* 181–210.

Roschelle, A. R., Turpin, J., & Elias, R. (2000). Who learns from service learning? *American Behavioral Scientist, 43,* 839–847.

Ross, M. E., Green, S. B., Salisbury-Glennon, J. D., & Tollefson, N. (2006). College students' study strategies as a function of testing: An investigation into metacognitive self-regulation. *Innovative Higher Education, 30,* 361–375.

Rourke, L., Anderson, T., Garrison, D. R., & Archer, W. (1999). Assessing social presence in asynchronous text-based computer conferencing. *The Journal of Distance Education, 14*(2). Retrieved June 26, 2008, from http://www.jofde.ca/index.php/jde/article/viewArticle/153/341

Saenze, V. B., & Barrera, D. S. (2007). *Findings from the 2005 college student survey (CSS): National aggregates.* Retrieved June 24, 2008, from http://www.gseis.ucla.edu/heri/PDFs/2005_CSS_REPORT_FINAL.pdf

Santrock, J. W. (2008). *Children.* New York: McGraw Hill.

Saville, B. K. (2004). From apprentice to professional: Community college teacher training. In W. Buskist, B. C. Beins, & V. W. Hevern (Eds.), *Preparing the new psychology professoriate: Helping graduate students become competent teachers* (pp. 31–36). Retrieved July 1, 2008, from the Society for the Teaching of Psychology Web site: http://teachpsych.org/resources/e-books/pnpp/html/pnpp05.html

Scheirer, C. J., & Rogers, A. M. (1985). *The undergraduate psychology curriculum: 1984.* Washington, DC: American Psychological Association.

Schneider, C. G. (2003). *Practicing liberal education: Formative themes in the re-invention of liberal learning.* Retrieved April 28, 2008, from the Association of American Colleges and Universities Web site: http://www.aacu.org/publications/practicing_liberal_education.cfm

Schneider, C. G., & Schoenberg, R. (1998). *The academy in transition: Contemporary understandings of liberal education.* Washington, DC: Association of American Colleges and Universities.

Schon, D. A. (1983). *The reflective practitioner: How professionals think in action.* New York: Basic Books.

Schunk, D. H., & Zimmerman, B. J. (1998). *Self-regulated learning: From teaching to self-reflective practice.* New York: Guilford Press.

Schwartz, D. L., & Bransford, J. D. (1998). A time for telling. *Cognition and Instruction, 16,* 475–522.

Schwartz, D. L., Bransford, J. D., & Sears, D. A. (2005). Efficiency and innovation in transfer. In J. Mestre (Ed.), *Transfer of learning from a modern multidisciplinary perspective* (pp. 1–52). Greenwich, CT: Information Age Publishing.

Seijts, G., Taylor, L., & Latham, G. (1998). Enhancing teaching performance through goal setting, implementation and seeking feedback. *International Journal for Academic Development, 3,* 156–168.

Seldin, P. (1997). *The teaching portfolio: A practical guide to improved performance and promotion/tenure decisions* (2nd ed.). Bolton, MA: Anker.

Shank, P. (2007). *The online learning idea book: 95 proven ways to enhance technology-based and blended learning.* New York: Wiley.

Shorter Oxford English Dictionary. (5th ed., Vol. 1). (2002). Oxford, England: Oxford University Press.

Shulman, L. E. (2004). *Teaching as community property: Essays on higher education.* San Francisco: Jossey-Bass.

Silverman, R., & Welty, W. (1990). Teaching with cases. *Journal on Excellence in College Teaching, 1*, 88–97.

Sitzman, T., Kraiger, K., Stewart, D., & Wisher, R. (2006). The comparative effectiveness of Web-based and classroom instruction: A meta-analysis. *Personnel Psychology, 59*, 623–664.

Smith, D. (2002, March). The community college connection. *Monitor on Psychology, 33*. Retrieved August 24, 2008, from http://www.apa.org/monitor/mar02/community.html

Smith, R. A., & Fineburg, A. C. (2005). Standards and outcomes: Encouraging best practices in teaching introductory psychology. In D. S. Dunn & S. L. Chew (Eds.), *Best practices for teaching introduction to psychology* (pp. 179–194). Mahwah, NJ: Erlbaum.

Snyder, T. D., Dillow, S. A., & Hoffman, C. M. (2008). *Digest of education statistics: 2007* (NCES Publication No. 2008-022). Washington, DC: National Center for Education Statistics. Retrieved March 27, 2009, from http://nces.ed.gov/pubsearch/pubsinfo.asp?pubid=2008022

Solomon, P. R., Kavanaugh, R. D., Goethals, G. R., & Crider, A. (1982). Overcoming fragmentation in the undergraduate psychology curriculum. *Teaching of Psychology, 9*, 201–205.

Sorcinelli, M. D., Austin, A. E., Eddy, P. L., & Beach, A. L. (2006). *Creating the future of faculty development: Learning from the past, understanding the present.* Bolton, MA: Anker.

Spellings, M., & Monroe, S. (2007). *Students with disabilities preparing for postsecondary education: Know your rights and responsibilities.* Retrieved June 20, 2008, from http://www.ed.gov/about.offices/list/ocr/transition.html

Stanovich, K. E. (2007). *How to think straight about psychology* (8th ed.). Boston: Allyn & Bacon.

Steinkuehler, C. A., & Williams, D. (2006). Where everybody knows your (screen) name: Online games as "third places." *Journal of Computer-Mediated Communication, 11*, 885–909.

Sternberg, R. J. (2004). The CAPS Model: Assessing psychology performance using the theory of successful intelligence. In D. S. Dunn, C. M. Mehrotra, & J. S. Halonen (Eds.), *Measuring up: Educational assessment challenges and practices for psychology* (pp. 111–124). Washington, DC: American Psychological Association.

Steuer, F., & Ham, K. (2008). Psychology textbooks: Examining their accuracy. *Teaching of Psychology, 35*, 160–168. doi:10.1080/00986280802189197

Stoloff, M., McCarthy, M. A., Keller, L., Lynch, J., Makara, K., Simmons, S., et al. *The undergraduate psychology major curriculum: An examination of structure and sequence.* Teaching of Psychology.

Stoloff, M., Sanders, N., & McCarthy, M. (n.d.). *Profiles of undergraduate programs in psychology.* Retrieved August 24, 2008, from the American Psychological Association Web site: http://www.apa.org/ed/pcue/profiles_intro.html

Stowell, J. R., & Nelson, J. M. (2007). Benefits of electronic audience response systems on student participation, learning, and emotion. *Teaching of Psychology*, *34*, 253–258.

Sue, D., Sue, D. W., & Sue, S. (2006). *Understanding abnormal behavior* (8th ed.). Boston: Houghton Mifflin.

Sullivan, B. F., & Thomas, S. L. (2007). Documenting student learning outcomes through a research-intensive senior capstone experience: Bringing the data together to demonstrate progress. *North American Journal of Psychology*, *9*, 321–330.

Tang, M., Fouad, N. A., & Smith, P. L. (1999). Asian Americans' career choices: A path model to examine factors influencing their career choices. *Journal of Vocational Behavior*, *54*, 142–157.

Thomas, A. K., & McDaniel, M. A. (2007). The negative cascade of incongruent generative study-test processing in memory and metacomprehension. *Memory & Cognition*, *35*, 668–678.

Thomas, S. (2006). Pervasive learning games: Explorations of hybrid educational gamescapes. *Simulation & Gaming*, *37*, 41–55.

Tillema, H. H. (2001). Portfolios as developmental assessment tools. *International Journal of Training and Development*, *5*, 126–135.

Tomcho, T. J., Foels, R., Rice, D., Johnson, J., Moses, T. P., Warner, R. A., et al. (2008). Review of *TOP* teaching strategies: Links to students' scientific inquiry skills development. *Teaching of Psychology*, *35*, 147–159.

Tomei, L. (2004). The impact of online teaching on faculty load: Computing the ideal class size for online courses. *Journal of Instructional Technology and Distance Learning*, *1*, 39–50.

Trimble, J. E., Stevenson, M. R., & Worrell, J. P. (2003). *Toward an inclusive psychology: Infusing the introductory psychology textbook with diversity content*. Washington, DC: American Psychological Association.

Tufte, E. R. (2004). *The cognitive style of Powerpoint*. Cheshire, CT: Graphics Press.

U. S. Census Bureau. (2008, August 14). *An older and more diverse nation by midcentury*. Retrieved October 30, 2008, from http://www.census.gov/Press-Release/www/releases/archives/population/012496.html

U.S. Department of Education. (2006). *A test of leadership: Charting the future of U.S. higher education*. Washington, DC: Author. (ERIC Document Reproduction Service No. ED493504)

U.S. Department of Education. (2007). *Earned degrees conferred*. Retrieved August 24, 2008, from http://nces.ed.gov/programs/digest/d07/tables/dt07_303.asp

U.S. Department of Labor. (2008, April). College enrollment and work activity of 2007 high school graduates. *Bureau of Labor Statistics News*. Retrieved August 29, 2008, from http://www.bls.gov/news.release/pdf/hsgec.pdf

Valerius, L., & Hamilton, M. L. (2001). The community classroom: Serving to learn and learning to serve. *College Student Journal*, *35*, 339–344.

van Merriënboer, J. J. G., & Sweller, J. (2005). Cognitive load theory and complex learning: Recent developments and future directions. *Educational Psychology Review, 17*, 147–177.

VanderStoep, S. W., Fagerlin, A., & Feenstra, J. S. (2000). What do students remember from introductory psychology? *Teaching of Psychology, 27*, 89–92.

VanLehn, K., Graesser, A. C., Jackson, G. T., Jordan, P., Olney, A., & Rose, C. P. (2007). When are tutorial dialogues more effective than reading? *Cognitive Science, 31*, 3–52.

Villalpando, O. (2002). The impact of diversity and multiculturalism on all students: Findings from a national study. *NASPA Journal, 40*, 124–144.

Waits, T., Setzer, J. C., & Lewis, L. (2005). *Dual credit and exam-based courses in U.S. public schools: 2002-03* (NCES Publication No. 2005-009). Washington, DC: U.S. Department of Education, National Center for Education Statistics.

Wallin, D. L. (2007). Part-time faculty and professional development: Notes from the field. *New Directions for Community Colleges, 140*, 67–73.

Weaver, K. A. (2005). 1992 through 2001: An incredible ten years for high school psychology. *Journal of Social and Clinical Psychology, 24*, 97–110.

What is the diploma programme? (n.d.). Retrieved August 25, 2008, from the International Baccalaureate Web site: http://www.ibo.org/diploma/.

Whitten, L. A. (1993). Infusing Black psychology into the introductory psychology course. *Teaching of Psychology, 20*, 13–21.

Wiggins, G., & McTighe, J. (1998). *Understanding by design*. Alexandria, VA: Association for Supervision and Curriculum Development.

Williams, D. A., Berger, J. B., & McClendon, S. A. (2005). Toward a model of inclusive excellence and change in post-secondary institutions. Retrieved June 12, 2008, from the Association of American Colleges and Universities Web site: http://www.aacu.org/inclusive_excellence/documents/Williams_et_al.pdf

Williams, K., Harkins, S., & Latane, B. (1981). Identifiability as a deterrent to social loafing: Two cheering experiments. *Journal of Personality and Social Psychology, 40*, 303–311.

Wirt, J., Choy, S., Rooney, P., Provasnik, S., Sen, A., & Tobin, R. (2004). *The condition of education 2004* (NCES Publication No. 2004-077). Retrieved June 26, 2008, from http://nces.ed.gov/programs/coe/2004/pdf/18_2004.pdf

Wolters, C., Pintrich, P. R., & Karabenick, S. A. (2005). Measuring academic self-regulated learning. In K. A. Moore & L. Lippman (Eds.), *Conceptualizing and measuring indicators of positive development: What do children need to flourish?* New York: Kluwer Academic/Plenum Publishers.

Yee, N. (2006). The labor of fun: how video games blur the boundaries of work and play. *Games Culture, 1*(1), 68–71.

Yee, N., Bailenson, J. N., Urbanek, M., Chang, F., & Merget, D. (2007). The unbearable likeness of being digital: The persistence of nonverbal social norms in online virtual environments. *CyberPsychology & Behavior, 10*, 115–121.

Yilmaz, L., Ören, T., & Aghaee, N. (2006). Intelligent agents, simulation, and gaming. *Simulation & Gaming, 37*, 339–349.

Zechmeister, E. B., & Reich, J. N. (1994). Teaching undergraduates about teaching undergraduates: A capstone course. *Teaching of Psychology, 21*, 24–28.

Zhang, Y. (2007). *Transforming emotions with Chinese medicine: An ethnographic account from contemporary China.* Albany: State University of New York Press.

Zhao, Y., Lei, J., & Yan, B. (2005). What makes the difference? A practical analysis of research effectiveness of distance education. *Teachers College Record, 107,* 1836–1884.

Zhu, E. (2006). Interaction and cognitive engagement: An analysis of four asynchronous online discussions. *Instructional Science, 34,* 451–480.

Zimbardo, P. G. (2004). Does psychology make a significant difference in our lives? *American Psychologist, 59,* 339–351.

INDEX

Disabilities
  awareness of and delivery of instruction,
    71–72
Discussion boards
  for teaching critical thinking, 103
Distance learning, 114. *See also* Online
    courses
  assessment of, 119
  course management system and, 118
  faculty for, 118
  interactions in, 117, 118
  outcomes of, 119
  research on effectiveness of, 118–119
  teaching and, 119–120
Diversity, 63–64
  achievement through technology and,
    124
  all forms of, 156
  as central topic, 167
  curricular, 69–72
    benefits of, 69
  in curricular review, 61
  demographic, 78
  demographic changes in U.S., 156
  domains in
    access and equity, 65–67
    campus climate, 72–76
    curricular, 69–72
    learning and development, 67–69
  ethnic
    high school students and, 157
    of psychology graduate students,
      156–157
  evaluation of, 65
  of faculty, 33
  faculty infusion in curriculum, 166
  in formal curriculum, 69–70
    diversity-focused model, 70
    diversity-infused approach, 70
    interdisciplinary courses, 70–71
  inclusive teaching methods for, 44
  in informal curriculum, 71
  instructor preparation for, 35
  international, student sensitivity to, 153
  psychological literacy and, 11
  racial, at college level, 177
  skills for, 156
  as social outcome of undergraduate psy-
    chology, 155–157
  sociocultural, awareness of, 107–108,
    153
  student, 176

student development and, 68–69
  of student development trajectories, 67–
    68
  as student learning experience, 164
  in undergraduate curriculum, 55, 57
Diversity instruction
  delivery and acceptance of, 71
Dooley, L. M., *149*
Dunn, D. S.
  on quality benchmarks for undergradu-
    ate curriculum, 53, 55, 60
Dynamic process model of teaching and
    learning
  contribution to scholarship of teaching
    and learning, 134
  critical reflection in, 131, 134
  effective learning in, 131, 134
  effective teaching in, 134
  learner perspective on, 131
  promising principles in, 131, 132–133
  teacher–learner interaction in, 134
  translation of principles into practice in,
    131
    content characteristics in, 135
    context characteristics in, 135
    student characteristics in, 135
    teacher characteristics in, 134–135
  translation of promising principles into
    practice, 132–133, 134–135

Economic policy
  education for impact on, 158
  psychology and, 158
Effective teaching
  evaluation of practice to build empiri-
    cal literature, 139–140
  as life-long process, 139
  self-assessment of, 139
Effective teaching and learning
  recommendations for
    for educational institutions and profes-
      sional organizations, 143
    for policy makers and grant-making in-
      stitutions, 143
    for teachers and learners, 142–143
Elementary school
  psychological science in, 90
Employers
  on preparation of college graduates,
    151–152
  reasons for firing new hires, 151
Ethical behavior

APA *Guidelines for Undergraduate Psychology Major*, 101
  critical thinking skills in psychology, 102–104
  personal development, 109–111
  sociocultural and international awareness, 107–109
  values in psychology, 104–107
Learning outcomes
  AAC&U, external validity of, 22
  assessment and evaluation of, 61
  assessment of, 15, 169–170
  in Australia, 9–10, 18
  in Bologna Process, 16–17
  in distance learning, 119
  in Europe, 9–10, 16–17
  in evaluation of instruction, 42
  as indicator of excellent teaching, 41–42
  interactions for, 30
  of introductory psychology course
    for nonmajors, 153–154
  for major and minor concentration
    psychology departments and, 169
  for majors, 9
  measurable
    in UK statement and APA materials, 17
  psychological literacy as, 10
  of psychology education
    from educator perspective, 151
    from employer perspective, 151–152
    from student perspective, 151
  technology and, 127
  in undergraduate education, 15, 18, 54, 146–149
  of undergraduate psychology programs
    recommendations for, 159–150
  for undergraduates
    for nonmajors, 153–154
    personal skills, 152–153
    professional skills, 150–152
  for undergraduates in society, 154–155
Learning strategies, student, 98
Lecture
  for teaching critical thinking, 102
Liberal learning
  formative themes in, 21, 22
Lifelong learning, 176
  necessity of, 176
  psychologically literate citizen and, 21
  psychological literacy and, 12–13

Linguistic diversity
  of undergraduates, 66
Lunt, I., *17*

Master's degree
  European Federation of Psychologists'
    Associations, 16–17
Media
  depictions of psychological science, 173
  misinformation in, 87
  relationships with, 91–92
Mental health care
  psychology's impact on, 158
Metacognition
  for effective learning, 133, 141, 143
Metacognitive learning, 133, 138
Middle school
  psychological science in, 90
Misinformation
  ethics and correction of, 87–88

National Conference on Undergraduate Education
  slogan for, 4–5
National Institutes of Health Fact Sheet
  psychologists and behavioral health issues, *158*
Nationality
  of undergraduates, 66

Online courses. *See also* Distance learning
  assessment of, 119
  challenges for instructors, 119
  recommendations
    APA development and support for, 127
    quality standards for, 127–128
  for teaching critical thinking, 102–103
  teaching of, 119–120
Online testing
  for summative assessment, 117
Outlining
  for effective teaching and learning, 132

Pedagogy
  for diversity, 15
  evidence-based, 30
  variables in, 114
Personal development
  as learning goal, 102–104
  through portfolios, 109–110
  through student presentations, 110–111

for military personnel, 85
in precollege programs, 82–83
in professional development, 86
in programs in other disciplines, 85–86
recommendations concerning, 88–93
    acknowledgement of contributions
        from, 89–90
    establish as science requirement, 90–
        91
    expand and improve Web resources,
        91
    identify and expand in elementary
        and middle school curricula, 90
    improvement of Web resources, 91–
        93
    raising of public awareness, 93
    vs. psychology, 88–89
Psychologist, public misperception of, 86–87
Psychology
    attributes of, 150
    as bridge between social and physical
        sciences, 162
    in core curriculum of other departments,
        163
    in general education programs, 163
    impact of
        on economic and public policy, 158
        on health care, 158–159
    renaming as psychological science, 88–
        89
Psychology courses
    application of learned knowledge, skills,
        values in, 150
    developmental sequencing of, 169
    domain-specific content in, 150
    in professional programs, 13
Psychology degree
    strengths and limitations of, 77
Psychology education
    growth in, 4
Psychology major
    APA Guidelines for, 147
        content domains in, 54–55
        curricular, 53, 54
        learning goals, 101
        sociocultural and international
            awareness, *107*
    basic domains of, 168
    Brewer Report framework for, 48
    in 4-year programs, 84
    introductory course for, 59
    learning outcomes in, 54

research methods and statistics for, 60,
    61
Psychology minor
    introductory psychology course for, 60
Psychology Partnerships Project
    materials produced by, 14–15
Public misperception
    of psychological science, 91
    of psychologist, 86–87
    teacher's responsibility to correct, 86
Public policy
    education for impact on, 158
    in mental health, 158
    psychologically literate citizens and, 173
    psychology and, 158

Quality assurance
    accreditation and, 160
Quality benchmarks
    for psychological literacy and psycho-
        logically literate citizens, 14
    for undergraduate curriculum, 53–54, 55
Quality of instruction
    knowledge, methods, assessment tech-
        niques in, 37–38
Quality principle(s)
    for academic administrators
        encouragement of lifelong learning,
            171
        encouragement of scholarship of
            teaching and learning, 170–171
        support of faculty experimentation,
            171
    faculty strive to become scientist–edu-
        cators, 164–167
    for majors and nonmajors, 162
    for policy makers and general public
        understanding of necessity of psy-
            chological literacy, 172–173
    psychology departments and programs
        create coherent curriculum, 167–170
    student responsibility for monitoring
        and enhancing their own learning,
        163–164
    support for laboratories and laboratory-
        based classes, 171

Race
    in campus climate research, 73
    of faculty members, 33
Reflection
    student, 131, 134

teacher, 139
in teaching, 98
types of, 100
Religion
in student development, 68
Religious diversity
of undergraduates, 65
Research
on campus climate, 73
on distance learning, 118–119
field, and problem solving, 19–20
on psychologically literate citizen, 23–24
in teaching, 111–112
on teaching, 111–112, 143
on teaching and learning, 177
vs. applied psychology, 50–51
on Web, 92–93
Research methods and statistics
for psychology majors and minors, 60, 61
Responsibilities
of students, 163–164

Scholarship of teaching and learning (SOTL)
teacher contribution to, 134
Scientific methodology
in high school courses, 90–91
in undergraduate courses, 91
in undergraduate curriculum, 55, 56, 57, 61
Scientific thinking
psychological literacy and, 13
Scientist–educator
comparison with scientist–practitioner, 30
quality of instruction and, 37. *See also* Quality of instruction
defining, 38–40
evaluating, 40–42
Scientist–educator model
components of, from entry to advanced levels, 38–40
current teacher and, 32–33
evaluation in, 31, 43
evidence-based inquiry in, 30, 31
evidence-based practice in, 30
interactions in, 31
learning goals in, 30–31
quality teaching in
incentives and rewards for, 42–43
recommendations for, 43–45

Self-regulated learning, 143
Service learning
for promotion of sociocultural awareness, 107–108
Sexual identity
of faculty members, 33
of undergraduates, 65–66
Simulations
interactive, 123
Skills. *See also* Critical thinking skills
basic, 166
core, in undergraduate education, 146–147
in curriculum, 169
for ethical decision-making, 157
personal, 152–153
professional, 150–152
of psychologically literate citizen, 14
workforce, 152, 177
Social outcomes
for undergraduate psychology student
accountability, 155
embracing diversity, 155–157
ethical practice, 157–158
impact on economic and public policy, 158
impact on health care, 159–158
internationalization, 159
Social responsibility
of psychologically literate citizens, 10
Society
ecological development model of, students and, 154
Sociocultural awareness
service learning for, 107–108
Socioeconomic backgrounds
of undergraduates, 66
Spacing
for effective teaching and learning, 133, 137
Specialization
benefits of, 49
and decline in basic content domains, 50
and decline in general perspective on psychology as discipline, 49–50
and decline in required core courses, 50
fragmentation of discipline and, 49
proliferation of, 49
Spellings Commission, U.S. Department of Education
on learning outcomes, 146, 147

number and variety of, 95–96
selection and implementation of, 95
Teaching models
contextual (TACOMA), 96–101
dynamic process, 129, 130
scientist–educator, 29–45
Teaching strategies
goal-based selection of, 101–111
student–teacher interaction in, 111
in TACOMA model, 98, 99
Technological competence
faculty development of and fostering in
students, 167
Technology
acceptable use policy for, 126
adoption of
impetus for, 125
by instructors and students, 125–
126
leadership model in, 125
ethical issues in, 126
impact on teaching and learning, 115
new and developing, 123–124
new and emerging, 120
for collaborative learning, 121
course-in-a-box, 120
intelligent tutors, 122
learning environments, 121–122
virtual worlds, 121–122
psychological content and form of, 52–
53
recommendations
for ethics, 128
for faculty support and development,
127
for online courses and programs,
127–128
for technology and learning outcomes, 127
in traditional classroom
course management systems, 117
online testing, 117
presentation software, 116
student response systems, 116–117
variables in, 114
Testing as learning tool, 133, 138
examples of, 140–141
Text-embedded signaling, 138
Traditional classroom
distance learning and, 117–120
Transfer-appropriate processing, 133, 137–
138

Ubiquitous learning, 123
Undergraduate curriculum
APA *Guidelines for the Undergraduate*
Psychology Major, 53, 54–55
contextual factors in, 49–51
accountability movement, 52–53
consumer-driven culture and, 51–52
decline in traditional subfields for
PhD, 51
increase in applied psychology, 50–
51
specialization with resulting fragmentation, 49–50
swirling, 51–52
technological revolution, 52–53
transfer students, 52
core
defined, 48
need for, 53
core model for
diversity and ethics in, 55, 57
domains in, 56, 58
relationships among areas of, 56
scientific methods in, 55, 56, 57, 61
curricular reform, 53
diversity in, 69–71
framework for psychology major, 48
introductory course content, 59–60
reform of, 48–53
Undergraduate education
accountability and, 146
APA conferences, 13
Bologna Process and, 147
core knowledge and skills in, 146–147
international standards for, 147
St. Mary's conference and, 14–15
Undergraduate major
learning goals for, 101
Undergraduate psychology
in Australia, 18
consensus in, 15
at juncture of humanities and sciences,
25
outcomes in, 15, 18, 54
for postbaccalaureate global alternatives, 19
UK principles for, 17
Undergraduate students
desired outcomes for, 149–154
Understanding
deep exploratory processing for, 132,
137

ABOUT THE EDITOR

Diane F. Halpern, PhD, is a professor of psychology at Claremont McKenna College. She has won many awards for her teaching and research, including the Outstanding Professor Award from the Western Psychological Association, the American Psychological Foundation Award for Distinguished Teaching, the Distinguished Career Award for Contributions to Education given by the American Psychological Association, and the California State University's State-Wide Outstanding Professor Award. Dr. Halpern was president of the American Psychological Association in 2004 and is a past president of the Society for Teaching of Psychology. Her recent books include *Thought and Knowledge: An Introduction to Critical Thinking*; *Sex Differences in Cognitive Abilities*; and *Women at the Top: Powerful Leaders Tell Us How to Combine Work and Family*. She joined Mike Gazzaniga and Todd Heatherton as the third author of the third edition of *Psychological Science*, an introductory psychology textbook.